Assembly Places and Practices in Medieval Europe

For John Blair

Assembly Places and Practices in Medieval Europe

Aliki Pantos and Sarah Semple

EDITORS

FOUR COURTS PRESS

This book was set in 10.5 on 12.5 point Ehrhardt by
Mark Heslington Ltd, Scarborough, North Yorkshire for
FOUR COURTS PRESS LTD
7 Malpas Street, Dublin 8, Ireland
Email: info@four-courts-press.ie
and in North America for
FOUR COURTS PRESS
c/o ISBS, 920 N.E. 58th Avenue, Suite 300, Portland, OR, 97213.

A catalogue record for this title
is available from the British Library.

ISBN 1–85182–665–3

Printed in England
by MPG Books Ltd, Bodmin, Cornwall.

Contents

PART III: ISLE OF MAN, SCANDINAVIA AND CONTINENTAL EUROPE

List of Illustrations

Acknowledgments

First and foremost thank you to all those who have contributed to this volume and to the conference which preceded it, including Patrick Wormald who kindly agreed to act as chair at comparatively short notice. The enthusiasm of the participants has played an important part in the completion of this project. We are especially grateful to Elizabeth FitzPatrick, who was instrumental in helping to organize the conference, and who has continued to be a source of support and good advice throughout the preparation of the volume.

Our thanks also go to St Hugh's College, Oxford; Queen's College, Oxford; the Institute of Archaeology, Oxford; and the National University of Ireland, Galway, for providing financial support for the conference itself, and to the Institute of Archaeology for providing a venue. Further funding for publication was generously made available by the Marc Fitch Fund, the Arnold Fund at the Modern History Faculty, Oxford and by Trinity College, Carmarthen.

Introduction

ALIKI PANTOS & SARAH SEMPLE

About minor matters the chiefs deliberate, about the more important the whole tribe. Yet even when the final decision rests with the people, the affair is always thoroughly discussed by the chiefs. They assemble, except in the case of a sudden emergency, on certain fixed days, either at new or at full moon; for this they consider the most auspicious season for the transaction of business ... When the multitude think proper, they sit down armed. Silence is proclaimed by the priests, who have on these occasions the right of keeping order. Then the king or the chief, according to age, birth, distinction in war, or eloquence, is heard, more because he has influence to persuade than because he has power to command. If his sentiments displease them, they reject them with murmurs; if they are satisfied, they brandish their spears. The most complimentary form of assent is to express approbation with their spears.[1]

Tacitus, *Germania* Ch. 11.

The passage quoted above is perhaps the most famous description of an early popular assembly ever written. It was composed at the end of the first century AD by the Roman historian Tacitus and purports to describe the behaviour of the Continental Germanic tribes. Most modern scholars would no longer accept Tacitus's depiction of early Germanic society as accurate; it is widely accepted that the Germania is as much a comment on the Rome of Tactitus's own time as a work of history. Traditionally, however, the image it portrays has been an influential one, as important for philosophers and politicians as for historians.

The idea of the 'folk-moot' appears as a recurrent and significant motif in European political and popular thought almost from the Reformation to the twentieth century, and this philosophical or ideological background has necessarily coloured historical and archaeological approaches to the subject. Its influence is particularly visible in England where the concept of the 'primitive popular assembly' first came to historical and political prominence in the lead

---

1 *The Agricola and Germania*, trans. A.J. Church and W.J. Brodribb, 1877, 87–110.

up to the Civil War. The Reformation period had already witnessed a substantial increase in scholarly interest in pre-Conquest history, as supporters of Henry VIII's break with the papacy turned to the Anglo-Saxon age for evidence of the ancient independence of the English Church.[2] Archbishop Parker and his contemporaries put forward the argument that the Norman Conquest marked the beginning of a period of inexorable decline in the Church in England, and that by breaking with Rome it was merely returning to older, purer religious practices.[3] By the late sixteenth and early seventeenth century this idea was increasingly being extended to the political sphere. Proponents of what is known as 'the theory of the Norman Yoke' claimed that the Norman Conquest had corrupted not only the Church, but a primitive constitution based on 'free institutions' and ancient laws which the English people had been striving to reinstate ever since.[4]

Although interpretations varied, the idea that popular assembly was central to this ancient constitution was commonplace and was seized upon by the Parliamentary opposition. In the Anglo-Saxon *witan* and shire courts, as well as in the writings of Tacitus, they found 'historical' support for their claims to parliamentary privilege and their opposition to royal power. Thus papers read before the Society of Antiquaries in the early years of the reign of James I claimed that the Anglo-Saxons had held popularly-elected parliaments, and Parliament issued editions of earlier works such as the *Modus Tenendi Parliamentum* and the *Mirror of justice*, which purported to record how these were held.[5] In 1647 Nathaniel Bacon published a history of the development of Parliament from Saxon times which explicitly suggested that the power of the monarch was secondary to that of Parliament. In a passage clearly influenced by the extract from Tacitus quoted above, Bacon stated that the office of king had probably originated as 'a Commander in the field, an Officer pro tempore, and no necessary member in the constitution of their state'. Thus, he claimed, 'a Saxon king was no other than a primum mobile set in regular motion by Lawes established by *the whole body of the Kingdom*' (my italics).[6]

The idea of the ancient assembly remained politically influential after the end of the first English Civil War, as radicals groups like the Levellers pressed for further constitutional reform. The Levellers rejected the idea that the common law had in large part preserved ancient liberties since pre-Norman times, and demanded large-scale reform. But they nevertheless clung to the idea of the primitive assembly, combining it with religious and philosophical theories on 'natural rights' to argue that complete democracy was the natural form of government, since all men were equal under God. For them, the early assemblies described by Tacitus, and the representative government they still

2 MacDougall 1982, 31ff.   3 Horsman 1976, 387.   4 Hill 1958, 52.   5 Hill 1958, 54–6.
6 MacDougall 1982, 61.

believed the Anglo-Saxons to have practised, were evidence of this.[7] The regicide Thomas Scot even claimed Anglo-Saxon precedent at his trial, attempting to justify the fact that Charles I had been executed on the authority of a single chamber on the grounds that 'there was nothing but a House of Commons' in Saxon times.[8]

Inevitably, support for such views waned alongside radicalism in the second half of the seventeenth century and more conservative interpretations of the role and origins of Parliament came back into vogue. Indeed, during the Restoration 'Anglo-Saxonism' in general was politically far less popular, although scholarly work on the period advanced considerably.[9] However, the Glorious Revolution of 1688–9 soon brought the assembly to prominence again. The succession of the Germanic, Protestant William of Orange to the English throne once more made it popular to see English government as having 'Gothic' roots. Moreover, Parliament's success in curtailing the power of the monarchy and confirming its own importance was explicitly presented as the reinstatement of ancient rights and liberties which had been in existence from the Saxon period.[10]

Late eighteenth-century radicals, pressing for still further parliamentary reform, also returned to themes similar to those used in the previous century. For instance, the influential *Historical essay on the English constitution* (1771) claimed that it was possible, through 'historical' research, to rediscover the essentials of the Saxon constitution which had been swept away by the Norman Conquest. It described Anglo-Saxon government as based on an elected principle in which all were considered equal, and saw the state as consisting of a federation of local communities, formed from the bottom up. Each level of this hierarchy – tithing, shire, witan – was said to have had its own assembly, culminating finally in an annual national parliament established by Alfred the Great.[11]

For both conservatives and radicals, then, by the mid-eighteenth century the ancient Germanic roots of the English and their constitution were an accepted fact, and a central part of this conviction was the belief that the modern English Parliament was the direct descendant of the Anglo-Saxon *witan* and even the folk-moots of Tacitus.

Elsewhere in Europe attitudes to early assembly developed along similar lines. As a result of the humanist movement interest in the Germanic past had been strong in the numerous German states of the Holy Roman Empire since the fifteenth century. As in England, in the century which followed, the Reformation encouraged interest in the subject as its supporters sought to legitimize their overthrow of the Roman Church by comparing it with the

7 Hill 1958, 68ff. 8 Ibid., 64. 9 MacDougall 1982, 65–70. 10 Wright 1997, 126. 11 Newman 1987, 184–9; Hill 1958, 85ff; Briggs *c.*1985, 215–20.

defeat of the corrupt Roman Empire by the Germanic tribes.[12] Tacitus's *Germania*, which was discovered at about this time, soon became an important source, being widely used to demonstrate the noble character of the early Germans and the essential freedom of their society. In association with this, some also drew attention to the supposed racial and linguistic purity of the German people as described by Tacitus[13] and efforts were made to trace most of the nations of Europe back to Germanic roots.[14] The idea of a primitive Germanic constitution embodying free assembly quickly became a political tool on the Continent, just as in England. In his *Franco-Gallia* of 1573, for instance, the French Protestant François Hotman stressed the Germanic origins of the early Franks in order to claim that they had originally had free representative institutions of the sort described by Tacitus. He used this argument to advocate an elective monarchy for France on the basis of historical precedent.[15]

In the eighteenth century similar ideas played an important part in the lead up to French Revolution. Defenders of the *these nobiliaire* against the absolutist monarchy argued for an immemorial constitution which went back to the free assembly-holding Franks, from whom they (the nobility) were directly descended. They were influenced in their arguments by English interpretations of the events of the previous century. The Compte de Boulainvilliers, for instance, wrote:

> We must conclude that the safety of a people can be secured only by those states that are governed on the model supplied by the ancient destroyers of the Roman Empire, of which there remains more than a trace only in England.[16]

Montesquieu, likewise, held up the English system of political government as the ideal, tracing 'this beautiful system' to the woods of Germany described by Tacitus.[17] Others, despite holding different views as to the most desirable form government, nevertheless also looked to Tacitus for support. Mably, for instance, rejected the idea that the Franks and Gauls had never become integrated; his view was that the French nobility came into being only after the reign of Charlemagne and hence had no exclusive claim to government. But he still considered that the original form of government in France was that described in the *Germania*, and accordingly he advocated a mixed government in which all three estates took part.[18]

---

12 Hill 1958, 58.   13 See *Germania*, bk 1.   14 MacDougall 1982, 42–4; Polikov 1974, 77–90.
15 Hill 1958, 58.   16 Boulainvilliers, *Histoire de l'ancien gouvernement de la France* (Amsterdam, 1727), ii, 186: quoted in translation in Wright 1997, 129.   17 Montesquieu, *De l'Esprit des lois*, trans. Nugent 1751, i, 175, 177.   18 Wright 1997, 143–8.

In the New World, likewise, the idea of the ancient assembly played its part in politics. Many Americans accepted that the Anglo-Saxons had a democratic, free system of government and saw the 'Free and Independent States' as seeking to regain this Golden Age. Thomas Jefferson in particular was an avid student of Old English and advocated its widespread teaching in schools on the grounds that students 'will imbibe with the language their free principles of government'.[19]

From the sixteenth to late eighteenth centuries, then, the ancient popular assembly had a fundamental role, as part of a wider movement of 'Germanism' or 'Anglo-Saxonism', in political events in Europe and further afield. There was a widespread perception, largely based on the writings of Tacitus, that 'primitive' assemblies were both representative and fundamental to Germanic society, and these ideas were used to support a variety of political and social arguments.

In the late eighteenth and nineteenth centuries, the early Germans and their institutions continued to be a topic of interest. With the advent of Darwinism and advances in the new sciences of ethnology and philology, however, the idea of racial, as well as political, origins gradually began to gain importance. Whereas previously the primitive assembly had largely been used to argue for constitutional reform on the basis of historical precedent, it now started to be seen partly as the badge of a superior 'Germanic' race.[20]

For many in England the expansion of the British Empire could be seen as reflecting the superior nature of the 'Anglo-Saxon' character. Mid-late nineteenth-century British antiquarians and historians emphasized both the role of institutional history and the pre-eminence of the Germanic race, which many saw as intimately connected. Robert Knox in his *Races of men* (1850), for instance, claimed that the Germanic (or in his terms Scandinavian) race would soon become pre-eminent since it was

> the only race which truly comprehends the meaning of the word 'liberty' … their laws, manners, institutions, they brought with them from the woods of Germany, and they have transferred them to the woods of America.[21]

By no means all scholars were so outspoken. Yet a strong element of 'Germanism' is identifiable in the work of even the most celebrated nineteenth-century Anglo-Saxonists and constitutional historians, particularly with regard to popular assembly. Kemble, for instance, who was strongly influenced by the work of German scholars such as Jacob Grimm, laid great

19 Hauer 1983, 880. 20 Horsman 1976, 387. 21 Horsman 1976, 406

emphasis on the Germanic origins of the English and their political system. In *The Saxons in England* (1849) he wrote regarding the *witan*:

> We need not lament that the present forms and powers of our parliament
> are not those which existed a thousand years ago, as long as we recognize
> in them only the matured development of an old and useful principle.
> We shall not appeal to Anglosaxon custom to justify the various points of
> the Charter; but we may still be proud to find in their practice a germ of
> institutions which we have, through all vicissitudes, been taught to
> cherish as the most valuable safeguards of our peace as well as our
> freedom. Truly there are few nations whose parliamentary history has so
> ample a foundation as our own.[22]

Stubbs likewise considered the roots of English liberty to lie in the assemblies described by Tacitus. For him, whilst these were not democratic, they were participatory and their descendents were the shire and hundred courts of Anglo-Saxon England, which, by surviving the Conquest, provided the basis for the establishment of Parliament.[23] On this subject J.R. Green stated in 1874:

> It is with a reverence such as is stirred by the sight of the head-waters of
> some mighty river that one looks back to these tiny moots, where the men
> of the village met to order the life and the village industry as their
> descendants, the men of later England, meet in Parliament at
> Westminster, to frame laws and do justice for the great empire which has
> sprung from this little body of farmer-commonwealths in Sleswick.[24]

Associated with the approach of these scholars was a continued perception that language and race were connected and that societies which shared a language also had a shared cultural heritage. Both Kemble and later Freeman applied the model of the new science of philology to institutional history, aiming to demonstrate how English common law could be traced back to its 'primitive' Teutonic roots in the same way that languages could be shown to have developed. Gomme at least thought this could also be done through institutions. His *Primitive folk moots* (1880) was based on the premise that

> in the open-air meeting we have hit upon an element of primitive polit-
> ical life, which may perhaps carry the study of Comparative Juris-
> prudence beyond its hitherto restricted boundary of Aryan history.[25]

22 Kemble 1849, i, 240. 23 Campbell 1995, 78. 24 Green 1892, i, 7. 25 Gomme 1880, 13.

It was, of course, in the next century in Germany that the idea of the innate superiority of the ancient Germanic tribes was to have its most important manifestation. This is not the place to consider the development of Nazism and the National Socialist ideology in detail. However, it is interesting to note that the concept of the ancient assembly once again played a part in this political movement. The late-eighteenth and nineteenth centuries in Germany were a period of prolonged territorial, political and economic instability. This brought about an increased concern with national identity and encouraged the growth of a nationalism which focused increasingly on the idea of the *Völk*. The *Völkisch* movement ultimately had its roots in the political theories of the Enlightenment. Philosophers such as Rousseau had stressed the concept of 'general will' and popular sovereignty.[26] These ideas, combined with a long-standing tradition of the essential freedom of early German society as manifested in the *folk-moots* of Tacitus, gave rise to a belief in an early Germanic Golden Age in which the importance of the *Völk* had been paramount.

By the nineteenth century, however, *Völkisch* ideology was becoming increasingly bound up with a variety of Romantic, mystical, mythological and occultist ideas, including a belief in supposedly ancient 'Aryan' myths and the superiority of the Germanic race. In part a reaction against increasing industrialisation, the *Völkisch* nationalists sought to return to their ancient Germanic roots. They attempted to revive folk-songs and ancient 'Germanic' customs and symbols. They stressed the importance of nature and landscape and held open-air folk-festivals, for instance to celebrate the summer solstice.[27]

Within this context, the assembly once again came to prominence as a symbol of Germanic society. When a national festival was held at Hambach on the Rhine in 1832, it was organized to coincide with the time of year when the ancient Germanic thing had been held.[28] In the early twentieth century this idea was taken further by Ernst Wachler who in 1907 founded the Mountain Theatre in the Harz Mountains. The first theatre of its kind, it was envisaged as a modernized version of the Germanic thing in which specially written plays reflecting *Völkisch* philosophy would be staged. During the 1930s more than forty similar *thingplätze* were constructed by the National Socialists, and many more were planned. These huge open-air amphitheatres were intended to host large popular spectacles and communal 'Germanic' celebrations. They were situated in the countryside – often in the midst of woods or close to sites of known or perceived pagan significance – and were intended to embody the ancient mystical significance of such places. Although their use in no way mirrored the judicial functions of the historical thing, the purpose of these

26 Mosse 1964, 1–2.   27 Ibid., 67–87.   28 Mosse 1964, 83–4.

stadia was clearly to provide an link with the Germanic past and the assemblies described by Tacitus, thereby fostering a sense of 'Aryan' history.[29]

From the Reformation to the Third Reich, then, the idea of the popular assembly has played a part in a broad range of European historical, political and philosophical thought. The ends to which the concept was applied varied considerably, but certain significant elements remained constant throughout, chief among which were ideas that popular assemblies for judicial/governmental purposes were a specifically Germanic phenomenon and that, at some level, they represented unbroken continuity with the earliest times.

For modern scholars such simplistic views are no longer tenable. For instance, over the last fifty years substantial progress has been made in understanding the legal/judicial role of the moot in late Anglo-Saxon society. The shire and hundredal assemblies of the late tenth and eleventh centuries are now considered to have had very little in common with the institutions described by Tacitus, being instead part of a sophisticated and well regulated royal administrative system.[30] However, while considerable attention has been paid, at least in England, to the legislative and governmental role of the moot, comparatively little attention has been paid to the sites at which assemblies took place, and the thing-place as a class of archaeological site is still poorly understood. Moreover, it can be argued that such work as has been done often reflects old-fashioned approaches to such locations. There is a tendency, for instance, for studies still to concern themselves primarily with the prehistoric pagan origins of assembly-places, rather than seeking to understand them in their contemporary early medieval context.[31] On other occasions recent research continues to build upon nineteenth- and early-twentieth century findings, the validity of which can be questioned.[32]

Whilst no one would now seek to identify the Scandinavian thing or the Anglo-Saxon *witan* as a reflection of a widespread, racial, 'Germanic' culture, it is true that evidence for popular assemblies can be found, not only in Anglo-Saxon England and Scandinavia, but in broadly contemporary societies throughout Northern Europe. Furthermore, in many cases these assemblies share distinctive features: for example the reuse of ancient monuments as meeting-places. The widespread occurrence of this phenomenon, in cultures of a similar date that are known to have interacted with one another, is clearly interesting. This, combined with recent trends in archaeological and historical research – particularly landscape archaeology/phenomenology, the reuse and folklore of ancient monuments, and the evolution of early political/territorial

---

29 Mosse 1964, 80–1; Taylor 1974, 210–18. **30** See for example Loyn 1974; Wormald 1986; 1999a; 1999b; Keynes 1990; 1991. **31** See Pantos, below, 155–6. **32** Ibid.; Pantos 2002, 10–26 ; cf. Friðriksson 1999, 105–45.

units – has led scholars from a variety of different countries and academic backgrounds to turn to the topic once again.[33]

The present volume results from a two-day conference held at the Institute of Archaeology in Oxford in March 2000 organized by Aliki Pantos, Elizabeth FitzPatrick and Sarah Semple. This brought together a group of scholars working on aspects of assembly in medieval Europe to present the results of their work and discuss their findings. Drawing on sources as diverse as place-names, early law-codes, landscape study and geophysical analysis, speakers addressed topics ranging from the state of current research to the potential early development of assembly-sites and their role in the political organization of early territorial units. The event provided a forum for a truly interdisciplinary exchange of ideas and allowed similarities and differences of evidence and/or interpretation to be discussed with the aim of identify promising avenues for future research.

The papers presented here are divided into three groups on the basis of their geographical focus: Ireland, Scotland and Wales; England; and Scandinavia, the Isle of Man and Continental Europe. This range reflects the interests of those who gave papers at the conference and also includes two additional contributions, solicited after the event from Thomas Charles-Edwards and Howard Williams. A range of topics are considered within this volume, however, morphology, form and landscape location predominate reflecting an increasing interest within medieval studies in contextualizing resources for the study of landscape.[34]

Readers will note a geographical bias. With the exception of Paul Barnwell's paper on the early Frankish *mallus*, the European mainland is not discussed. The work presented here shows that within the regions considered a number of shared themes appear in the evidence for assembly. Key elements include the use of pre-existing monuments as assembly-places; the conjunction of royal or political assembly-places with cult sites; and strong indications that in both Scandinavia and England, as in Ireland and Scotland, assembly-places may have comprised extensive areas with multiple foci. It remains to be seen how such characteristics compare with administrative arrangements elsewhere in Europe.

In Part 1 Richard Warner discusses the ideological significance of Irish inauguration mounds as a royal seats, suggesting with reference to mythological traditions as well as interpretation of archaeological sites, that the concept had its roots in Iron Age beliefs concerning pre-existing Neolithic monuments. He then considers the continuation of this tradition into the early medieval period, and the development of associated sites. This topic is taken up in

---

33 See for example Barnwell and Mostert 2003.   34 Lucy and Reynolds 2002, 4–5.

greater detail in Elizabeth FitzPatrick's discussion of the landscape contexts of
medieval royal inauguration sites in Ireland and the beliefs surrounding them.
In particular, she underlines the importance of traditional dynastic associations in the choice of such sites, and discusses the likelihood that these
traditions were not only reinterpreted, but intentionally created. FitzPatrick's
paper also considers in detail the differing terms for 'mound' found in place-
names associated with these sites. This discussion directly parallels Thomas
Charles-Edwards's examination of three Welsh legal terms for 'court' – *llys*,
gorsedd, dadl. He charts the probable evolution of these terms, giving a fasci-
nating insight into aspects of the procedure of medieval Welsh judicial
assemblies, as well as the type of location selected. The fourth paper in this
group is concerned with early assembly-sites in Scotland, in particular Scone
the traditional inauguration site of the Scottish kings. In contrast to the
commonly held view, Steve Driscoll argues that the morphology of the site
indicates it did not develop from Pictish roots, but instead reflects the appearance of new Gaelic political forces in the late ninth century.

In comparison with Ireland, archaeological considerations of early meeting-
places in England are at an early stage, since in the past the topic has been
almost entirely the province of place-name scholars. In Part 2, Aliki Pantos
shows how a cross-disciplinary approach can provide new and valuable insights
into late Anglo-Saxon administrative arrangements. At the opposite end of the
chronological scale, Howard Williams and Sarah Semple turn to archaeological
sources to suggest possible precursors to the moots evidenced in late Anglo-
Saxon law-codes. It will become apparent from this section that the nature of
assembly in England between the seventh and ninth centuries remains a difficult topic. Andrew Reynolds's work on the highly-defined topography of the
late Anglo-Saxon administrative system, which demonstrates the dispersed
arrangement of meeting-place, execution site and minster by the tenth
century, stands in marked contrast to the kind of multi-functional
burial/cult/assembly-site envisaged by Williams and Semple.[35] There is a
need for more detailed study of when and how the separation between
assembly and cult emerged in England. Recent evidence for the establishment
of execution sites as early as the seventh century at liminal locations such as
prehistoric monuments and administrative boundaries suggests that the
dispersal of functions may originate at this early stage, although the motivations for this spatial re-organization remain to be seen.[36]

In Scandinavia, on the other hand, Stefan Brink's work has demonstrated a
unity of political and cult functions at assembly-places, even at a relatively late
date. In the first paper of Part 3 Brink discusses the evidence for six Swedish
thing-sites, demonstrating that it is possible to identify a distinctive set of

35 Reynolds 1999, 96–110. 36 Pitts et al. 2002, 131–46.

physical criteria representative of a meeting-place. In addition, Brink notes that in many instances place-names with royal or sacred associations can be found nearby. Tim Darvill considers a Scandinavian meeting-place in the British Isles – Tynwald Hill, Isle of Man – the only monument of its kind still to be used for assembly in modern times. His hitherto unpublished findings from an archaeological survey of the site suggest the complex may have its origins in prehistoric times, potentially indicating similar processes of continuity or reuse found at sites discussed elsewhere in this volume. The concluding paper in Part 3 shifts the focus of the discussion, not only from archaeological to documentary sources, but also from Scandinavia and the British Isles to Continental Europe, and from places of assembly to the practices enacted at them. Nevertheless, Paul Barnwell's discussion of the early Frankish *mallus* demonstrates a number of striking parallels with the evidence from other areas, in spite of the fact that available sources are of a very different character.

The strength of this volume, as of the conference which preceded it, lies in the fact that it brings together the work of scholars from different disciplines, working on different regions. It thus enables the evidence from a range of medieval societies and cultures to be compared and contrasted, and highlights significant similarities. In taking a predominantly landscape based approach with a strong emphasis on archaeological evidence, these papers represent a new departure for the study of assembly-places. Furthermore, the papers presented here successfully integrate the archaeological evidence with that drawn from literary, documentary and onomastic sources, demonstrating the significance of interdisciplinary study for understanding administrative frameworks in the medieval period. For these reasons we hope that this volume will not only provide an enjoyable introduction to assembly studies, but that the papers presented here might inspire others to undertake further work on the topic and finally, that dialogue between scholars working on the origins and ideology of assembly will be further encouraged.

Oxford 2004

REFERENCES

Barnwell, P.S. and Mostert, M. (eds), 2003: *Political assemblies in the earlier Middle Ages*, Studies in the Early Middle Ages, 7. Turnhout, Belgium.
Briggs, A., *c.*1985: 'Saxons, Normans and Victorians' in *The collected essays of Asa Briggs*. Chicago. 215–35.
Campbell, J., 1995: 'William Stubbs (1825–1901)', in H. Damico and J.B. Zavadil (eds), *Medieval scholarship: biographical studies on the formation of a discipline*, vol. 1. New York. 77–87.

Church, A.J. and Brodribb, W.J. (trans.), 1877: *The Agricola and Germania*, London.

Friðriksson, A., 1994: *Sagas and popular antiquarianism in Icelandic archaeology*, Worldwide Archaeology Series, 10. Aldershot.

Gomme, G.L., 1880: *Primitive folk-moots*. London.

Green, J.R., 1892: *A short history of the English people* (illustrated edn.). London.

Hauer, S.R., 1983: 'Thomas Jefferson and the Anglo-Saxon language', *Proceedings of the Modern Language Association* 98, 879–98.

Hill, C., 1958: *Puritanism and revolution: studies in the interpretation of the English revolution of the 17th century*. London.

Horsman, R., 1976: 'Origins of racial Anglo-Saxonism in Great Britain before 1850', *Journal of the History of Ideas* 37, 387–410.

Kemble, J.M., 1847: *The Saxons in England*. London.

Keynes, S., 1990: 'Royal government and the written word in Late Anglo-Saxon England', in R. McKitterick (ed.), *The uses of literacy in early medieval Europe*. Cambridge. 226–57.

Keynes, S., 1991: 'Crime and punishment in the reign of Æthelred the Unready', in I. Wood and N. Lund (eds), *People and places in Northern Europe 500–1600*. Woodbridge. 67–81.

Loyn, H.R., 1974: 'The hundred in England in the tenth and eleventh centuries', in H. Hearder and H.R. Loyn (eds), *British government and administration*. Cardiff. 1–15.

Lucy, S. and Reynolds, A.J., 2002: 'Burial in early medieval England and Wales: past, present and future', in Lucy, S. and Reynolds, A.J. (eds), *Burial in early medieval England and Wales*. London.

MacDougall, H.A., 1982: *Racial myth in English history: Trojans, Teutons, and Anglo Saxons*. Montreal.

Mosse, G.L., 1964: *The crisis of German ideology*. New York.

Newman, G., 1987: *The rise of English nationalism: a cultural history, 1740–1830*. New York.

Nugent, T. (trans.), 1751: *The spirit of laws by Baron de Montesquieu* (New edn. with introduction by Franz Neumann, New York, c.1949).

Pantos, A., 2002: 'Assembly-places in the Anglo-Saxon period: aspects of form and location'. Unpublished DPhil thesis, University of Oxford.

Pitts, M., Bayliss, A., McKinley, J., Boylston, A., Budd, P., Evans, J., Chenery, C., Reynolds, A.J. and Semple, S., 2002: 'An Anglo-Saxon decapitation and burial at Stonehenge', *Wiltshire Archaeological and Natural History Magazine* 95, 131–46.

Polikov, L. (trans. E. Howard), 1974: *The Aryan myth: a history of racist and nationalist ideas in Europe*. New York.

Reynolds, A.J., 1999: *Later Anglo-Saxon England: life and landscape*. Stroud.

Taylor, R.R., 1974: *The word in stone: the role of architecture in the National Socialist ideology*. Berkeley.

Wormald, P., 1986: 'Charters, law and the settlement of disputes in Anglo-Saxon England', in W. Davies and P. Fouracre (eds), *The settlement of disputes in early medieval Europe*. Cambridge. 149–68.

Wormald, P., 1999a: 'Lordship and justice in the early English kingdom: Oswaldslow revisited', in P. Wormald, *Legal culture in the early medieval West: law as text, image and experience*. London. 114–36.

Wormald, P., 1999b: *The making of English law: King Alfred to the twelfth century.* Oxford.

Wright, J.K., 1997: *A classical republican in eighteenth-century France: the political thought of Mably.* Stanford.

PART I

Ireland, Scotland and Wales

Notes on the inception and early development of the royal mound in Ireland

RICHARD WARNER

This essay assesses the literary and archaeological evidence for early Irish royal ('inauguration') mounds. It is suggested that they were an Iron Age invention (perhaps stimulated by traditions associated with Neolithic passage-tombs) whose purpose was to allow the 'king' to draw power and authority from the tribal divinities. The development and spread of the royal mound in the early medieval period is charted.

THE IRON AGE

Ireland has a rich tradition of ancient tales that were committed to writing after the eighth century AD, but whose details appear to describe a far older, pagan, society.[1] Much has been written about the reliability of those tales as sources for information on pre-literate times and, on the whole, most scholars today are far less ready than their predecessors to regard them as being 'windows on the Iron Age'. Nevertheless, it is generally accepted that they preserve traditions, particularly of a mythological nature, that go back many centuries before the beginning of the historic period (in about the seventh century AD) and stem from, even if they do not literally describe, a late prehistoric milieu. It must be said that a few writers, among whom I count myself, hold the opinion that there are some historical 'truths' within these traditions which are, though difficult, not impossible to extract.[2]

The ancient tales repeatedly focus upon a small number of places which were *believed* in the medieval period to have been centres of 'regional' kingship

---

1 In this essay I use the terms 'ancient' to describe the early medieval texts that appear to refer to prehistoric times and 'contemporary' to describe those texts referring to their own time.
2 The reader is directed to Jackson 1964; Aitchison 1987; McCone 1990; Mallory 1993; Warner 1990 and 1995, and further references therein, for examples of the different positions that can be taken on this matter.

in the preceding pagan Iron Age or earlier.[3] These places were (see fig. 1.1) *Temair* (sacred capital of the central province of *Mide*), which is the cluster of earthworks on the hill of Tara, Co. Meath;[4] *Emain* (sacred capital of the northern province of *Ulaid*), which is the cluster of earthworks at Navan, Co. Armagh;[5] *Ailend* (sacred capital of the south-eastern province of *Laigin*), which is now represented by the great earthwork enclosure at Knockaulin, Co. Kildare;[6] and *Cruachu* (sacred capital of the western province of *Connachta*), which is some part of the extended cluster of earthworks around Rathcroghan, Co. Roscommon.[7] The ancient sacred capital of the south-western province of *Mumu* is unrecorded. The high ritual status implied in the medieval texts for these sacred places in prehistoric times has been confirmed by excavation and other archaeological research. Furthermore, contemporary textual evidence shows that these places continued to have regional royal and ritual status through the first millennium AD and well into the second, and that there was then a belief that this status had a very ancient basis.[8]

NEOLITHIC ORIGINS?

At three of the four sacred royal places identified above (Tara, Knockaulin and Navan) the largest visible monument is an oval or circular, internally-ditched enclosure,[9] of several hectares in extent and with a very substantial surrounding ditch and bank. There is a similarity of form (and it is no more than that) between these enclosures and the Late Neolithic internally-ditched enclosures of Britain and Ireland often referred to as 'henges'. Furthermore, three of our royal places (Tara, Navan and Rathcroghan) have prominent mounds, one of which (the *Duma na nGiall* or 'Mound of the Hostages'[10] in the Tara enclosure) is a Late Neolithic passage tomb, re-used in the Early Bronze Age for further burials.[11] Mounds are a common feature of the Late Neolithic and Early Bronze Age. Such observations have led to the proposi-tions that either the royal enclosures were Neolithic and had been brought into service again in the Iron Age, or that there was a continuity of ritual and belief over 3000 years. Against the first proposition we need only record that the construction of the internally-ditched enclosures at Navan and Tara has now

---

3 General discussions in Wailes 1982; Raftery 1994, ch. 4; Aitchison 1994, ch. 2.   4 Newman 1997; Bhreathnach 1995.   5 Lynn 1997; Warner 1994.   6 Wailes 1990.   7 Herity 1983; 1984; Waddell 1983; 1988.   8 Byrne 1973 passim; this is the most useful source for all matters relating to Irish kingship.   9 The term 'hengiform', widely used for enclosures of Neolithic date in Britain, carries too strong a chronological implication to be useful as a general term in Ireland. 10 I should clarify the use of Irish names for the visible monuments at Tara. They all occur in medieval texts, in two of which their physical relationships are described, and they are medieval identifications.   11 Newman 1997, 71–5.

been firmly dated by excavation to the Iron Age[12] and the Knockaulin enclosure is likely to be of the same date.[13] As regards the second proposition, neither internally-ditched enclosures nor burial mounds can be shown to span the intervening period, so we are unable to demonstrate that continuity of ritual can explain the physical forms of the Irish Iron Age ritual sites. I am inclined to the opinion that Irish Iron Age ritual and belief reinterpreted and perhaps appropriated ancient monuments with no understanding of the original rituals or belief-systems associated with those places.[14]

If continuity of monument *form* or of *ritual* are unsupportable, is there evidence for continuity of *sanctity* of place?[15] In the Iron Age the entrance of the great mound of Newgrange, a Late Neolithic passage-tomb in the complex of earthworks at the 'Bend of the Boyne', became the focus of Iron Age ritual depositions[16] the nature of which show that the tomb was regarded as a very important *genus loci* by Romano-British intruders, as well as by natives. Furthermore, a passage-tomb at Tara – the *Duma na nGiall* ('Mound of the Hostages') – was, again in the Iron Age, incorporated within the large internally-ditched enclosure already referred to, where it forms a prominent feature. A recognition of these mounds as sacred seems certain, but this was, in my opinion, due to their meaning to Iron Age and early medieval people rather than to any continuation of sanctity from the Neolithic period.[17]

THE IRON AGE MOUND

At Tara (fig. 1.1) the largest monument of the complex is the internally-ditched enclosure called *Ráth na Ríg* ('Fort of the kings'). This enclosure contains several smaller earthworks, including two significant, extant mounds.[18] Off-centre is the Neolithic *Duma na nGiall*. Nearer the centre of the enclosure is the *Forad*, a larger mound surrounded by two ditches with external banks,[19] which looks very like an Iron Age ring-barrow[20] other examples of which can be found elsewhere within the Tara complex. While we might suppose that the enclosure, which is of Iron Age date, was so placed as to incorporate the earlier passage-tomb, the larger size of the *Forad*, its probable ritual nature and its centrality within, and apparent cultural contemporaneity with, the enclosure would indicate that it was the focal feature of the enclosure and therefore of Tara.

12 Roche 1999; Mallory 2000. 13 Wailes 1990. 14 This seems to be roughly the view of Gibson 2000. 15 As suggested by Raftery 1972, 41. 16 Carson and O'Kelly 1977. 17 The destruction of other prehistoric mounds in the Iron Age (see for instance Raftery 1994, 41) seems to support this opinion. 18 Newman 1997, 68–90; at least one other is no longer visible. 19 Newman 1997, 77–83. In many papers on Tara this site and the *Tech Cormaic* have their names transposed. 20 Raftery 1981.

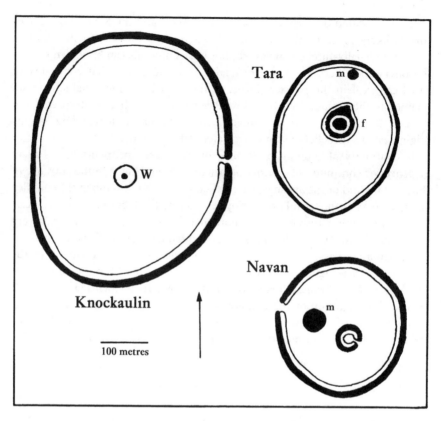

Figure 1.1 The three Iron Age sacred enclosures of Tara (m = 'Mound of the hostages', f = '*Forad*'), Navan (m = mound) and Knockaulin (w = wooden 'mauve' structure). Solid is bank or mound, unfilled in ditch.

We have to move to Navan, Co. Armagh, to get a clear perspective on the nature and interpretation of these ritual elements – the mound and the internally-ditched enclosure. Here, the almost circular, five-hectare enclosure has a very deep internal ditch and a massive bank. Just off-centre within the enclosure are a large mound and a low ring-barrow (fig. 1.1). Excavations showed that the mound had been raised over earlier structures – a Late Bronze Age ring-ditch and a series of Iron Age buildings.[21] Continuity is certain with the latter but not with the ring-ditch, which had almost filled. In 95 BC a circular wooden structure was erected consisting of four concentric circles of posts around a massive central oak post. Outside the whole and concentric with the outer ring of posts was a continuous plank wall whose diameter was about forty

21 Lynn 1997.

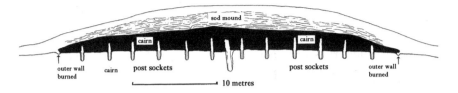

Figure 1.2 Cross-section of mound at Navan (from Lynn 1992).

metres (fig. 1.2). Almost immediately after its erection, and while it still stood, this structure was carefully filled with limestone blocks to a height of almost three metres, and then set on fire. The resultant charcoal-filled cairn was then covered with sods to produce a mound with a height of over five metres. The encircling enclosure-ditch produced, at its bottom, burnt timbers also of 95 BC which the excavator reasonably suggested came from the burnt structure under the mound.[22] We have firm evidence, then, that the Navan mound and the internally-ditched enclosure were constructed at about the same time – 95 BC – and, we might infer, for a single purpose.

CALLING THE GODS

It is not clear whether the concentric rings of the forty-metre wooden structure supported a roof or were free-standing – both alternatives are in accord with the evidence. It is, however, certain that the structure had a ritual purpose, for it contained not a shred of occupational material. As for its significance, I am content to see it as a huge 'house' constructed for, and then sacrificed to, a local god. Heinrich Wagner percipiently observed, before any of the archaeological evidence was forthcoming, that 'the Celts considered their political and religious centres such as *Temair*, *Cruachu* and *Emain* as replicas of the palaces of the gods of the other world'.[23] The conclusion that the Navan wooden structure represents the otherworld is inescapable. What then of the mound that incorporates it? Chris Lynn has constructed a detailed Dumézilian explanation of the whole structure.[24] It seeks to explain the elements in terms of Indo-European belief-systems and social structure, with illustrations from the ancient Irish tales. He suggests that, among other things, the wooden structure represented an otherworld hostel (*bruiden*) 'presided over by the lord of the other world' and that the stones of the cairn represented the dead Ulster

22 Mallory 2000.   23 Wagner 1977, 13.   24 Lynn 1992; 1994; 1996.

warriors 'with the implication that their strength, now transferred to the other world, might in future be available in times of crisis'. Furthermore he thinks that the Navan mound should be seen 'as a central place sacred to the local [god(s)]'.[25] I am very content to borrow these parts of his model without necessarily accepting his whole thesis. The mound at Navan, by enclosing the 'house' of the god, and thereby the entrance to the otherworld, provided a platform on which a priest/king[26] could 'communicate' with that otherworld visibly before his people. Doherty has written 'The king ... seated upon his *forad*, was the intermediary between his people and the other world'.[27] The mound also provided a high-point upon which the rituals could be seen by watchers on the bank of the surrounding enclosure.

THE MOUND AND THE IRISH OTHERWORLD

The inhabitants of the otherworld – the 'people of the *síd*' – were represented in the medieval tales as living in a parallel, but superior, world. They were believed to live in, or to be accessible through, *síd*-mounds which were often prehistoric tombs. The word *síd* (anglicized 'shee') is used in the medieval literature for the otherworld, and for the mound through which it was reached. The word seems, however, to be cognate with Latin *sedum* 'seat'.[28] The explanation, surely, is straightforward – the mound (or perhaps a chair upon it) was the *síd* – 'seat/place of sitting' – upon which the king communicated with the otherworld. By extension the word *síd* came to mean the otherworld itself. *Suide* ('sit') is part of the word *forad* (literally 'over-seat'), which is the medieval name of the mound that I have suggested was the focal point of the Tara enclosure. A cognate word appears in Welsh *gorsedd* – usually translated as 'throne-mound'. On a *gorsedd*, according to an early Welsh tale, Pwyll prince of Dyfed had a vision involving the goddess Rhiannon (see below). If I am right in my suggestion that the mound at Navan was the platform on which the Iron Age priest/king drew power from his gods (and from the dead warriors of his *tuath*?) for the good of his people, we have an explanation of the inversion of the bank-and-ditch of the surrounding enclosure. The medieval tales represented the *síd*-folk as powerful, dangerous and fickle warriors, whose uncontrolled entry into the real world was unwelcome and could be disastrous. The king, by inviting the otherworld to empower him, opened a route between that world and the real world. The internal ditch of the enclosure prevented

---

25 Lynn 1992, 56.   26 I use the term priest/king to emphasize the fact that the early Irish king appears to have had a strongly religious role, modified by the coming of Christianity. For all aspects of early kingship see Byrne 1973, ch. 1.   27 Doherty 1985, 52.   28 *Síd* is discussed by Ó Cathasaigh 1979 and Sims-Williams 1990.

the egress of the otherworld warriors from the sacred area surrounding the mound into the real world – it was a hillfort in reverse.[29]

I have, I hope, presented a reasonable explanation of the meaning and function of the Iron Age sacred enclosures with their mounds. One of the functions that required otherworld communication was undoubtedly the inauguration, or rather confirmation of the king, which involved a *feis* – a symbolic 'mating' with the 'tribal' land personified by a goddess. In this respect it is interesting that in the Tara enclosure stands a phallic pillar-stone – traditionally called the *Bod Fhergusa* ('Fergus's phallus').[30] I would suggest also that decisions that required great thought or 'vision' would also have required the use of the royal mound. In the ancient tales Navan figures as *Emain*, the most important, and probably the first, of the late prehistoric regal/ritual sites.[31] The name *Emain* is also used of the otherworld. It might be, then, that the Navan mound, perfectly designed for its full sacred function, was the *fons et origo* of all other royal mounds. We do not know if the Tara mound (the *Forad*) has a wooden structure at its centre. The mound usually taken to be the focus of Rathcroghan seems, on seismic evidence to have some sort of deep internal structure and a surrounding ditch or palisade.[32] Of particular interest is Knockaulin, the huge internally-ditched enclosure that was the late prehistoric ritual centre for Leinster (fig. 1.1). There is no mound in the enclosure but near its centre excavation revealed a circular multi-ringed structure of forty metres diameter very reminiscent of the Navan wooden structure.[33] The excavator has interpreted this as a sort of ring-platform containing at its centre a five-metre high conical, wooden tower. At the centre of Knockaulin, then, was a wooden rather than an earthen 'mound'. As to its date – it was constructed sometime during the Iron Age, before the late-first century AD. Therefore, what I have argued for the mound-and-enclosure for Navan should equally apply also to the other three sacred places.

INTO THE EARLY MEDIEVAL PERIOD

There is not the slightest doubt that socially and materially the changes that resulted from the influences from the Roman Empire and sub-Roman Britain and Europe, and from the introduction of Christianity, were profound and that, in the centuries around the fifth, the pagan Iron Age changed into the very different early medieval period. But there are reasons to believe that certain practices, particularly those associated with the rituals of kingship, survived and that these are discernible from archaeological evidence. I give one

---

29 This is more fully discussed in Warner 2000b.   **30** Newman 1997, 86.   **31** Binchy 1958, 135.   **32** Fenwick et al. 1999.   **33** Wailes 1990, 14 – 'mauve' phase. See also Lynn 1991.

clear example. The medieval ancient tales describe the house of one of the 'mythical' kings of *Emain* (Navan) in terms that are virtually indistinguishable from the Navan excavated wooden structure – huge diameter; circular; concentric post-rings.[34] The textual descriptions of the 'mythical' royal houses at *Cruachu* and at *Temair* (Rathcroghan and Tara) are very similar. One would be tempted to propose a survival of detailed descriptive information, were it not that actual royal houses were built in a like manner to the Navan structure, and of the same size, until the twelfth century AD.[35] We must accept that early medieval descriptions of contemporary royal houses have been added (with some formulaic exaggeration) to the base stories. This is clear evidence of continuity of form-and-function. Elizabeth FitzPatrick, in this volume, describes the association of mounds with inauguration and other royal ritual in the *late* medieval period. If we are to demonstrate that, as seems not unlikely, these textually well-attested sites are part of a continuum from the Iron Age, it behoves us to find acceptable evidence for continuity across the *early* medieval period.

Curiously our two best literary examples of royal mounds are either in, or purport to be in, southern Britain rather than Ireland. The first is an Irish medieval story relating the activities of a real seventh-century Ulster king – Congal Cláen – which, although it relates the doings of a historical person is written in a style very reminiscent of the 'ancient' tales.[36] It tells how Congal went to southern Britain to gather an army to assist him in his forthcoming battle with the 'high-king' Domnall mac Áedo. Congal held his conference (described both as a *dál* and as an *óenach*) with the British king on a 'mound (*telach*) which was near the king's fort (*dún*)'. The king with whom Congal conferred had the Irish name Eochaid Aingceis, and although there was substantial Irish settlement in southern Britain, which had begun in the fourth century,[37] and the Dyfed kings at least were of Irish descent, I am inclined to believe that this description is of an early medieval royal site in Ireland. Our other relevant reference is from a British source – the story of Pwyll which is quoted below. The 'throne-mound' on which Pwyll had his vision was *adjacent to his residence* of *Arberth*, an early medieval capital of Dyfed. In both these cases the royal mound is described as being adjacent to the royal residence.

---

34 In, for instance, the story *Tochmarc Emire*, conveniently translated in Cross and Slover 1936, 153. 35 Warner 1986b. 36 O'Donovan (ed.) 1842, the relevant passage is on p. 66. 37 Thomas 1994, especially ch. 6.

THE ROYAL MOUND AT CLOGHER

The dynasts from the midlands who ousted the Ulaid kings from Navan made one of their capitals at Clogher, in Co. Tyrone (*Clochar macc nDaimíni*). This place, which has been excavated but awaits full publication,[38] is one of only a few excavated early medieval sites of whose royal status there can be no doubt. The Clogher resident was king of a large *tuath* (*Uí Chremthainn*) and often over-king of a collection of *tuatha* (*Airgialla*). The central earthwork at Clogher (fig. 1.3, 1.4) is a very strongly defended univallate ringfort of some sixty metres internal diameter, constructed in the later sixth century. It is typical of a high-status settlement in the early medieval period, and the material recovered from the excavation confirms the historically derived information that this was a royal site.[39] Just outside the ringfort, separated from it by its deep ditch, is a triangular mound. The counter-scarp bank of the ringfort goes around part of the mound but the mound is not itself ditched.

Figure 1.3 The mound at Clogher in use for a lecture by the author.

The flat top of the mound is slightly higher than the interior of the ringfort (fig. 1.4), and excavation showed that the top of the mound was the original ground surface – the mound had been constructed by removing the hill-top around it, the spoil having been deposited on the side of the hill covering the ditch and bank of an earlier hillfort. Clearly the mound was not a re-utilized earlier feature and equally clearly a large amount of labour had been inten-

---

38 A fairly detailed discussion of its historical context will be found in Warner 2000a.   39 See Warner 1988.

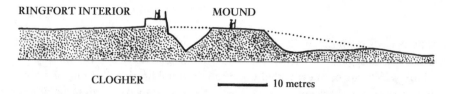

Figure 1.4 Profile of ringfort and mound at Clogher, reconstructed as in the early medieval period. Dotted line is original ground surface.

tionally expended in producing it. Only a limited area of the top of the mound was excavated, revealing a small circular gully with a central pit – I take this to indicate a tiny wooden building. No occupation debris was found here.

I have no hesitation in interpreting the Clogher mound as the royal mound, on which the ritual activities of royalty occurred. That an act of communion with the 'tribal' gods continued to underlie the process there can be no doubt, even though the Clogher kings were Christian from the late-sixth century. The mound is *outside* the ringfort, separated from it by a deep ditch, and it is at least possible that this separation reflected the perceived dangers inherent in the communication process, as described above.

MORE EARLY MEDIEVAL ROYAL MOUNDS

On recognising the significance of the Clogher mound I proposed that early medieval royal sites[40] would be expected to be closely associated with a mound. I was surprised that the first positive response to this proposal was not from my Irish colleagues but from Cornwall. I was told of a Cornish 'round' (a small fortification not unlike an Irish ringfort) that had a mound adjacent to it (fig. 1.5). The important feature of this site – at Gooderne – was that unlike the majority of Cornish 'rounds' that are of Iron Age date, this place has traditions attached to it that suggested that it was the fort of an early medieval ruler (a local *regulus* or petty-king much like the Irish kings).[41]

Luckily, pairings of residence (especially ring-fort) and royal mound are turning up often enough in Ireland to suggest that this might indeed be an expectation for Irish royal sites. We can start with Tara, whose status as a place of 'royal' ritual continued into the early medieval period. Inside the internally-

---

40 By 'royal sites' I mean sites that fulfilled the function of capital of the *tuath*, not simply settlements inhabited on occasion by kings. The proposition appears in Warner 1988, 57.
41 Preston-Jones and Rose 1986, 136.

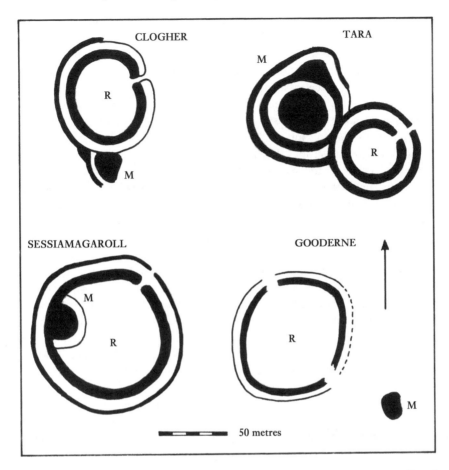

Figure 1.5 Four early medieval royal sites of Clogher, Tara, Sessiamagaroll and Gooderne (R = defended settlement/ringfort, M = mound). Solid is bank or mound, unfilled is ditch.

ditched, sacred enclosure, and abutting the *Forad* (which I have suggested above was the focal mound) is a small ringfort (the *Tech Cormaic*[42]) which should be dated on its form to the early medieval period (fig. 1.5). I suggest that this was the residence of the 'high-king' when he was present at Tara for ritual reasons[43] after the sixth century, and that it was placed adjacent to the *Forad* to afford the necessary close relationship with this earlier ritual/royal mound. At Tullaghoge, Co. Tyrone (*Telach Óc*), place of inauguration of late

---

42 Newman 1997, 83.   43 And his steward (*rechtaire*) when he was not. In 1988 (Warner 1988, 57) I suggested that the multivallate earthwork known as *Rath na Senad* was the royal residence and a mound between its banks was the inauguration mound. I now retract this suggestion.

medieval northern Uí Néill kings, there is no extant mound but seventeenth-century illustrations of the inauguration show that the stone throne on which the event took place was adjacent to the royal ringfort.[44] Some of the royal fort-mound pairings take the form of mound-outside-fort, as at Clogher and Tara, and in not a few cases these have been mistaken for Anglo-Norman motte-and-bailey sites (Clogher has even been so described). Indeed in some cases it is arguable that the associated pair were actually modified to serve that function by the Anglo-Norman lords who supplanted the Irish kings.[45]

At some other royal sites the kings have thrown superstitious caution to the wind and 'brought' the mound inside the fortified area of the settlement. When, in the fourth century AD the Ulaid were ousted from Navan they eventually set up the new capital of their reduced territory at *Dún Lethglaise* (Downpatrick, Co. Down).[46] On a spur of land once almost surrounded by tidal marsh is a large oval enclosure with a massive externally-ditched defensive earthwork of unknown date. Inside, and near the edge of the enclosure, is a large conical mound, either unfinished or severely damaged, with a surrounding ditch. The mound is usually assumed to be a Norman motte, although 'the whole makes no sense as a motte and bailey'.[47] It is not at all improbable that this mound was the new royal mound for the Ulaid kings. At Sessiamagaroll, Co. Tyrone is a strong, large univallate ringfort with a ditched mound within it, adjoining the bank (fig. 1.5).[48] There are good onomastic and historical reasons for regarding the site as the capital of a twelfth-century *tuath* (*Uí Echach*).

I must make the point that the early medieval royal mounds seem to be *at* the royal residence, requiring that in most cases the mound will be a *de novo* construction rather than a re-used ancient mound. Newgrange, the passage-tomb visited in the Iron Age for the purpose of appeasing the local gods, was called *Síd an Broga* (the 'otherworld-mound of the *Brúg*') in the medieval literature. It was thought to be the residence of Ireland's most important gods – the *Dagda, Manannán, Mac Ind Óc*.[49] Yet despite this quite obvious importance of the greatest Neolithic tomb in Ireland, there seems to be no textual evidence that Newgrange was a place of ritual for the ancient king/priests or of inauguration for the early medieval kings of the area.[50] It is also clear that while the use of a mound has bridged the interface from Iron Age to the

---

44 Hayes-McCoy 1970.   45 A probable example is Duneight in Co. Down, a capital of the *Dál Fiatach* in the eleventh century: Waterman 1963.   46 Warner 1998.   47 McNeill 1997, 12. 48 Patterson and Davies 1938. These authors believed, in a variation of the error referred to earlier, that this was a native attempt to turn a ringfort into a copy of an Anglo-Norman motte. 49 O'Kelly 1967, 60–2.   50 It is usually assumed that it was as a royal *habitation* that the nearby mound (passage-tomb) of Knowth was associated by name with the *Brega* kings: Byrne 1968. However, an alternative explanation of the association may be that it briefly served as their place of inauguration.

medieval period it is not now accompanied by the encircling internally-ditched enclosure found at each of the Iron Age ritual sites. Indeed at Tara the fort has been placed inside the older sacred enclosure. We must assume that fear of the otherworld was now reduced.

RITUAL AND ASSEMBLY

In the medieval period there seems to have been a locational distinction between the activities associated with the most basic rituals of kingship (including inauguration) and those associated with popular assembly – at which the king would also play a role. Thus, for example, Tara, the place associated with the pagan rites of the midland Uí Néill kings and of the 'high king' is several kilometres from Teltown (*Tailtiu*), where their *óenach* (the fair or assembly) was held.[51] Similarly the capital of the king of the Northern *tuath* of *Uí Chremthainn* – Clogher in Co. Tyrone – was distinct from their place of assembly at Findermore (*Findubair*), some four kilometres west. The named medieval *óenaig* are not featured in the core set of ancient tales and, although some were located at places with visible monuments, and traditions of great antiquity,[52] it is probable that they were all medieval foundations by means of which the ceremonies and events with which the common people (and the Church) were involved could be removed from the king's pagan 'mating' rite. If so we may perhaps assume that in the previous Iron Age the regional assemblies took place at, and probably outside, the sacred, royal sites. This would, perhaps, explain the large number of stray Iron Age and very early medieval artefacts from the vicinity of Navan.[53] *Óenach nEmna* (the assembly of Navan) – 'the most important assembly of its kind ... before the opening of the historical period'[54] – was replaced in the medieval period by the more distant *Óenach Macha*.[55]

OTHER CONSIDERATIONS

It will have been noticed that I have identified only four mounds that I have described as royal and that date to the Iron Age, but I have implied a proliferation of such sites for the medieval period. There are two explanations for this apparent imbalance. In the first place I have been quite careful, for both periods, only to describe as 'royal' those sites for which there is medieval textual evidence of such a status. For the Iron Age mounds I have used only

51 Binchy 1958; Swift 2000.   52 Swift 2000, 115; in general MacNeill 1962; Ettlinger 1954.
53 Warner 1986a.   54 Binchy 1958, 126.   55 Warner 1991, 47.

the ancient references to provincial centres – their status assured. Although other dwellings of 'kings' are mentioned in these ancient tales the references all seem anachronistic and unreliable. The contemporary textual information is more detailed and more reliable. Secondly, we know that kingdoms proliferated in the early medieval period – there were over a hundred at any time – and each king required the panoply of kingship. There were likely to have been far fewer kingdoms (if we can use such a term) in the Iron Age (Ptolemy, in the second century, names only sixteen).

A number of Irish hillforts[56] contain a prominent, often central, mound.[57] Few hillforts have been dated, but the limited evidence suggests that most belong to the Late Bronze Age.[58] None of the mounds within them have been excavated, although some appear to be Neolithic or Early Bronze Age. Few of these mound-containing hillforts, if any, have any part to play either in the ancient tales or are textually attested to have had a role in the politics of medieval Ireland. Among the exceptions, neither reliable, are two in Co. Donegal.[59] Glasbolie, a small hillfort with an off-centre mound, is traditionally associated with the medieval kings of *Tir Conaill*. Greenan hillfort, popularly supposed to have been *Ailech*, the capital of the early medieval *Cenél Eógain* kings, once had a small mound between its ramparts. There are also some large embanked enclosures that cannot be called hillforts but appear to have been intentionally constructed to be concentric to a large mound. That at Cornashee in Co. Fermanagh is traditionally held to have been the inauguration mound of the late medieval Maguire chieftains, but is archaeologically undated.[60]

What was the royal/ritual mound called in early medieval times? The medieval literature refers to a *Duma na nGiall* ('Mound of the Hostages') at both Tara and Navan. Tara also had a mound called *Forad* and this is traditionally identified with the mound at the centre of the enclosure that I have suggested was the royal/ritual mound. There are references in the ancient stories to a *Forodmag* ('plain of the *forad*') at Navan.[61] In one story the mythical king Conchobar sat with his nobles on the *forodmag* outside the *ríg-ráth* ('royal earthwork'). My interpretation of this reference is that the medieval writer knew nothing of the topography of Navan itself but was describing a contemporary situation whereby, as we have seen above and as he would have been well aware, a usual position for the royal mound was just outside the royal fort. I am inclined to think that *forad* was the proper term for the mound on which the early medieval royal rituals were held. There are numerous medieval texts that use the word *forad* in contemporary contexts that imply that it was a mound

---

56 A hillfort is a large defensive enclosure surrounding the top of a hill, and has one or more banks, each with an *external* ditch, or one or more stone walls.   57 Most are in the univallate hillforts: Raftery 1972, 43.   58 Raftery 1994, 58.   59 Lacy 1983, 111–15.   60 Lowry-Corry 1940, 180.   61 For the ancient topography of Navan see Mallory 1987.

which served as the seat, or platform, on which a king, or a dignitary such as a bishop, would preside over, or observe proceedings. In this wider usage of later times *foraid* would be found at *óenaig* (assembly-places) and in monasteries.[62]

I believe I have demonstrated both the likely origin of the royal/ritual mound, the *forad*, in the Iron Age and its continuation through the early medieval period. I have no doubt that this topic will receive more attention in the future and that more examples will be found. Perhaps the opportunity will arise to excavate one of the early medieval royal mounds thoroughly. I will close with the full text of the passage from the story Pwyll, Prince of Dyfed, from the *Mabinogion*, which seems to summarize many of the points that I have made (it is of some interest that the mythical Pwyll was both lord of Dyfed and lord of *Annwfn*, the otherworld).

> And once upon a time he [Pwyll] was at *Arberth*, a chief court of his, with a feast prepared for him, and great hosts of men along with him. And after the first sitting Pwyll arose to take a walk, and made for the top of a mound which was above the court and was called *Gorsedd Arberth*. 'Lord,' said one of the court, 'it is the peculiarity of the mound that whatever high-born man sits upon it will not go thence without one of two things: wounds or blows, or else his seeing a wonder.' '... as to the wonder, I should be glad to see that. I will go,' said he, 'to the mound, to sit'.[63]

REFERENCES

Aitchison, N., 1987: 'The Ulster Cycle: heroic image and historical reality', *Journal of Medieval History* **13**, 87–116.

Aitchison, N., 1994: *Armagh and the royal centres in early medieval Ireland: monuments, cosmology and the past*. Woodbridge.

Bhreathnach, E., 1995: *Tara: a select bibliography*, Discovery Programme Reports **3**. Dublin.

Binchy, D., 1958: 'The fair of Tailtiu and the feast of Tara', *Ériu* **18**, 113–38.

Byrne, F., 1968: 'Historical note on Cnogba (Knowth)', *Proceedings of the Royal Irish Academy* **66C**, 383–400.

Byrne, F., 1973: *Irish kings and high-kings*. London.

Carson, R. and O'Kelly, C., 1977: 'A catalogue of the Roman coins from Newgrange, Co. Meath, and notes on the coins and related finds', *Proceedings of the Royal Irish Academy* **77C**, 35–55.

Cross, P. and Slover, C., 1936: *Ancient Irish tales*. New York.

---

62 Doherty 1985, 51–2. **63** Jones and Jones 1949, 9. The pagination is that of the 1974 edition.

Doherty, C., 1985: 'The monastic town in early medieval Ireland', in H. Clarke and A. Simms (eds), *The comparative history of urban origins in non-Roman Europe*, B.A.R. International Series **255**. Oxford. 45–75.

Ettlinger, E., 1954: 'The association of burials with popular assemblies, fairs and races in ancient Ireland', *Études Celtiques* **6**, 30–61.

Fenwick, J. et al., 1999: 'The magnetic presence of Queen Medb', *Archaeology Ireland* **13**.1, 8–11.

Gibson, A., 2000: 'Circles and henges: reincarnations of past traditions?', *Archaeology Ireland* **14**.1, 11–14.

Hayes-McCoy, G., 1970: 'The making of an O'Neill: a view of the ceremony at Tullaghoge, Co. Tyrone', *Ulster Journal of Archaeology* **33**, 89–94.

Herity, M., 1983: 'A survey of the royal site of Cruachain in Connaught. I: introduction, the monuments and topography', *Journal of the Royal Society of Antiquaries of Ireland* **113**, 121–42.

Herity, M., 1984: 'A survey of the royal site of Cruachain in Connaught. II: prehistoric monuments', *Journal of the Royal Society of Antiquaries of Ireland* **114**, 125–38.

Jackson, K., 1964: *The oldest Irish tradition: a window on the Iron Age*. Cambridge.

Jones, G. and Jones, T., 1949: *The Mabinogion*. London.

Lacy, B. 1983: *Archaeological survey of County Donegal*. Donegal.

Lowry-Corry, D., 1940: entry in D. Chart (ed.), *Preliminary survey of the ancient monuments of Northern Ireland*. Belfast.

Lynn, C., 1991: 'Knockaulin (Dún Ailinne) and Navan: some architectural comparisons', *Emania* **8**, 51–6.

Lynn, C., 1992: 'The Iron Age mound in Navan Fort: a physical realisation of Celtic religious beliefs?', *Emania* **10**, 33–57.

Lynn, C., 1994: 'Hostels, heroes and tales: further thoughts on the Navan Mound', *Emania* **12**, 5–20.

Lynn, C., 1996: 'That mound again: the Navan excavations revisited', *Emania* **15**, 5–10.

Lynn, C. (ed.), 1997: *Excavations at Navan Fort 1961–71*. Belfast.

MacNeill, M., 1962: *The festival of Lughnasa*. Oxford.

Mallory, J., 1987: 'The literary topography of Emain Macha', *Emania* **2**, 12–18.

Mallory, J., 1993: 'The archaeology of the Irish dreamtime', *Proceedings of the Harvard Celtic Colloquium* **13**, 1–24.

Mallory, J., 2000: 'Excavations of the Navan ditch', *Emania* **18**, 21–35.

McCone, K., 1990: *Pagan past and Christian present*. Maynooth.

McNeill, T., 1997: *Castles in Ireland*. London.

Newman, C., 1997: *Tara: an archaeological survey*, Discovery Programme Monograph **2**. Dublin.

Ó Cathasaigh, T, 1979: 'The semantics of *Síd*', *Éigse* **17**, 137–55.

O'Donovan, J. (ed.), 1842: *The banquet of Dun na nGedh and the battle of Magh Rath*. Dublin.

O'Kelly, C., 1967: *Guide to Newgrange*. Wexford.

Patterson, T. and Davies, O., 1938: 'Sessiamagaroll Fort', *Ulster Journal of Archaeology* **1**, 42–3.

Preston-Jones, A. and Rose, P., 1986: 'Medieval Cornwall', *Cornish Archaeology* **25**, 135–85.

Raftery, B., 1972: 'Irish hill-forts', in C. Thomas (ed.), *The Iron Age in the Irish Sea province*, Council for British Archaeology Research Report 9. London. 37–58.

Raftery, B., 1981: 'Iron Age burials in Ireland', in D. Ó Corráin (ed.), *Irish Antiquity.* Cork. 173–204.

Raftery, B., 1994: *Pagan Celtic Ireland.* London.

Roche, H., 1999: 'Late Iron Age activity at Tara, Co. Meath', *Ríocht na Midhe* 10, 18–30.

Sims-Williams, P., 1990: 'Some Celtic otherworld terms', in A. Matonis and D. Melia (eds), *Celtic language, Celtic culture: a festschrift for Eric P. Hamp.* Van Nuys. 57–81.

Swift, C., 2000: 'Óenach Tailten, the Blackwater Valley and the Uí Néill Kings of Tara', in A. Smith (ed.), *Seanchas: studies in early and medieval Irish archaeology, history and literature.* Dublin. 109–20.

Thomas, C., 1994: *And shall these mute stones speak?* Cardiff.

Waddell, J., 1983: 'Rathcroghan – a royal site in Connacht', *Journal of Irish Archaeology* 1, 21–46.

Waddell, J., 1988: 'Rathcroghan in Connacht', *Emania* 5, 5–18 and 6, 42.

Wagner, H., 1974: 'Der königliche Palast in keltischer Tradition', *Zeitschrift für Celtische Philologie* 33, 6–14.

Wagner, H., 1977: 'The archaic Dind Ríg poem and related problems', *Ériu* 28, 1–16.

Wailes, B., 1982: 'The Irish 'royal sites' in history and archaeology', *Cambridge Medieval Celtic Studies* 3, 1–29.

Wailes, B., 1990: 'Dún Ailinne: an interim report', *Emania* 7, 10–21.

Warner, R., 1986a: 'Preliminary schedule of sites and stray finds in the Navan complex', *Emania* 1, 5–9.

Warner, R., 1986b: 'The early Christian ringfort at Lissue', *Lisburn Historical Society Journal* 6, 28–36.

Warner, R., 1988: 'The archaeology of early historic Irish kingship', in S. Driscoll and M. Nieke (eds), *Power and politics in early medieval Britain and Ireland.* Edinburgh. 47–68.

Warner, R., 1990: 'The prehistoric Irish annals: fable or history', *Archaeology Ireland* 4.1, 30–3.

Warner, R., 1991: 'The Drumconwell Ogham and its implications', *Emania* 8, 42–50.

Warner, R., 1994: 'The Navan archaeological complex', in J. Mallory and G. Stockman (eds), *Ulidia.* Belfast. 165–70.

Warner, R., 1995: 'Tuathal Techtmhar: a myth or ancient literary evidence for a Roman invasion?', *Emania* 13, 23–32.

Warner, R., 1998: 'Downpatrick, Armagh and Clogher', *Lecale Miscellany* 16, 21–7.

Warner, R., 2000a: 'Clogher: an archaeological window on early medieval Tyrone and mid Ulster', in C. Dillon and H. Jefferies (eds), *Tyrone: history and society.* Dublin. 39–54.

Warner, R., 2000b: 'Keeping out the otherworld: the internal ditch at Navan and other Iron Age "hengiform" enclosures', *Emania* 18, 39–44.

Waterman, D., 1963: 'Excavations at Duneight, Co. Down', *Ulster Journal of Archaeology* 26, 55–78.

Royal inauguration mounds in medieval Ireland: antique landscape and tradition

ELIZABETH FITZPATRICK

The practice of staging royal ceremonial and judicial and popular assemblies on natural hills and earthen mounds, whether sepulchral in origin or purpose-built for assembly, is a notable feature of several northern and western European societies. Among the more conspicuous of these open-air sites are the platformed-topped howes of Ottar and Thor at Old Uppsala in Sweden, the tiered mound of Tynwald Hill on the Isle of Man, the Moot Hill of Scone in eastern Scotland, and the Welsh Gorsedd Arberth celebrated in the *Four Branches of the Mabinogi*. It is to Ireland that the focus of this particular study is directed where a better understanding of late prehistoric,[1] early[2] and later medieval[3] royal concourse and its landscape setting has begun to unfold.

In Ireland a total of seventeen mounds, variously attested or alleged as medieval royal inauguration and assembly places have been recorded so far (fig. 2.1). Some of these are extant on the landscape, while others have been destroyed and are only known from antiquarian accounts. The combined evidence, and the conclusions drawn from it, are further compromised by the fact that the locations of a few of these mounds have not been securely identified. In some instances too, the former presence of a mound is merely implied by a sympathetic place-name.

The nomenclature relating to assembly mounds or hills in the Irish landscape is broad. The most precise word used of an assembly stage is Old Irish *forad*, which translates as a mound or platform, generally earthen, used as a seat or stand for spectators and also as an observation post. It varied both in shape and size, from the smallest intended for just one person, to the much larger capable of accommodating a number of persons.[4] Apart from the more renowned *Forad na Ríg* at Tara in Co. Meath, early medieval Irish texts cite *foraid* at other prehistoric and early medieval royal centres. Among these are

---

1 Wailes 1982, 1–23; Waddell 1983, 21–46; Bhreathnach 1995, 68–76; Lynn 1997; Newman 1997. **2** Warner 1988, 4768; Swift 1996, 1–21; Swift 2000, 109–20. **3** FitzPatrick 1998, 351–8; FitzPatrick 2001a, 357–74. **4** *DIL*, 327.

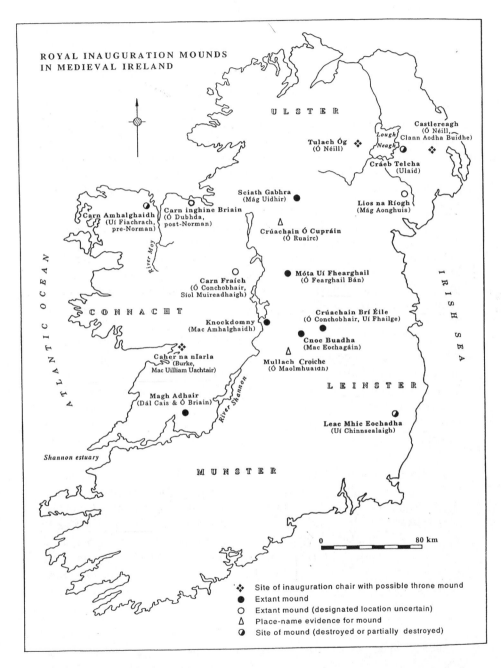

Figure 2.1 Mounds used for royal inauguration ceremonies in medieval Ireland (drawing by A. Gallagher)

Forad Mag Emna (Co. Armagh)[5] and the *foraid* of Uisnech (Co. Westmeath) and Tailten (Co. Meath).[6] The word *forad* seems to be a utilitarian term only, referring specifically to the function rather than the morphology of the mound or platform. Other than the fact that it is usually earthen, the *forad* is not typified. Swift, in her study of *Óenach Tailten* notes that the word *duma*, which is sometimes used of assembly mounds, particularly in the context of *óenach* or tribal assembly-sites, is not specific to any particular type of mound either. It is, as she points out, variously used of 'burial mounds, mounds for public ceremonies, fairy or *síde*-mounds, mounds for hunting huts ...'[7]

The best documentary evidence for inauguration mounds in Ireland occurs in native chronicles, prose and genealogical tracts and bardic poetry from the twelfth but more particularly the fourteenth century onwards. It is to be noted that none of the mounds cited in these texts are referred to as *forad/foradh*. Instead they tend to be specified in terms of their morphology or topography, as *cnoc* (hill, mound)[8] and *tulach* (hill, hillock, royal hill, hill of assembly);[9] *carn* (a heap, pile or cairn),[10] and *cruach/cruachain* (heap, conical pile, small rick, or hill).[11] The word *tulach*, variously anglicized as 'tully' and 'tulla', occurs in the place-name of one of the more renowned inauguration sites – that of the Uí Néill at Tulach Óg, east of Lough Neagh, near Cookstown in present-day Co. Tyrone – rendered as 'the hill of the assembly of warriors'.[12] This site was used for Uí Néill inaugurations at least as early as the mid-eleventh century[13] through to 1595.[14] The modern Irish *tulach* simply means a low hill, hillock or mound, but the Old Irish *tulach/tilach* implies a 'hill of assembly' and is often found in legal phrases. It may even relate to the Hittite *tuliia*, which translates as 'assembly of the council' or 'court-day'.[15] The *tulach* site, however, does not have a specific physical manifestation; it cannot be associated with a particular monument type. For the archaeologist, it points only to a low hill with assembly connotations.

On the other hand, Old Irish *carn*, which occurs as the root-word in the place-names of a number of inauguration mounds, appears to have a reasonably homogenous morphological identity. In modern archaeological nomenclature Old Irish *carn* has become synonymous with cairn – a term strictly applied to a large or small heap of stones erected to cover a burial, or to mark a boundary. But this narrow rendition of *carn*, which itself can mean a pile or heap of any material, precludes a true appreciation of the form *carn* monuments may take on the landscape. If the field identification of inauguration sites such as Carn Amhalghaidh, Carn inghine Briain and Carn Fraích, is

5 O'Rahilly 1961, 27, 28, 39. 6 *DIL*, 327; The *Annals of Ulster* for the year 831 also refer to the *foraid* – mounds of *óenach* Tailten. 7 Swift 2000, 115. 8 *DIL*, 125. 9 Ibid., 616. 10 Ibid., 101. 11 Ibid., 161. 12 Ó Doibhlin 1971, 3. 13 Hogan 1940, 422–3, 427; *AU*, 425 and 493. 14 *Cal. S. P. Ire.*, 1595, 386. 15 Wagner 1970, 46.

correct, they are all modest, compact mounds of earth or a combination of earth and stone, two of which are enclosed by a fosse and outer bank.

The Old Irish *cruachan*, anglicized 'croghan, croaghan, and croaghaun', is more elusive. Like *tulach* it can simply mean a hill, but where used of inauguration sites it again seems to intimate the presence of a mound. In the first two decades of the twentieth century, the Irish antiquaries H.T. Knox[16] and G.H. Orpen[17] had begun to discern some small but fundamental patterns regarding *cruachain* sites. They both noticed that the word *cruachan* turned up either as an element of the name of some inauguration monuments or as the name of the townland in which they were situated. There are several examples of this strong and hardly coincidental association. The most obvious is Crúachu or Ráth Crúachain, the royal heartland of Connacht, the approximate centre of which was the great mound of Rathcroghan. In the north midlands, the inauguration site of the later medieval Uí Ruairc chiefs of west Bréifne was Crúachain Ó Cupráin, a place which is generally identified with the townlands of Croaghan and Shancroaghan north-west of Killeshandra in Co. Cavan. This site receives its earliest mention as a meeting place in the *Annals of Loch Cé* for the year 1256.[18] In the central midlands the conspicuous hill of Crúachain Brí Éile in Ó Conchobhair's territory of Uí Fhailge may have been the inauguration place of the chiefs of that sept. A flat-topped mound (poetically recorded as Leacht Congal)[19] crowns the summit of the hill at 769 feet above sea level. In the southeast of Ireland, Leac Mhic Eochadha, the Uí Chinnsealaigh king-making place was identified by Orpen with a mound locally called 'Croaghan', near Croghan Kinsella, on the Carlow-Wexford border.[20] Still more inauguration sites are found in townlands carrying the place-name *cruachan*. Carn Amhalghaidh, an Uí Dhubhda inauguration site, lies in the townland of Croghan near Killala, Co. Mayo, and the Méig Uidhir inauguration mound of Sciath Gabhra in Cornashee, Co. Fermanagh (fig. 2.2) is adjoined on its north side by the townland of Croaghan.

While the anatomy of the inauguration mound used in medieval Gaelic Ireland remains to be explained through scientific excavation, there are a number of themes that emerge from an exploration of the landscape context, surface morphology and historical circumstances of some of them. One of those themes is the appropriation of prehistoric ceremonial landscapes by early medieval tribal groups and later medieval dynasties for assembly and inauguration purposes. In some instances specific monuments within earlier 'ritual' landscapes appear to have been adopted without alteration for use as assembly stages. It can also be argued that existing mounds may have been modified for

16 Knox 1911, 93–9. **17** Orpen 1911, 270–1. **18** *ALC*, i, 416–17. **19** Comerford 1883, 320–1. **20** Orpen 1911, 270–1.

Figure 2.2 Sciath Gabhra, the inauguration mound of the medieval Méig Uidhir chiefs of Fermanagh.

that purpose, while still others are possibly medieval additions to existing complexes.

THE APPROPRIATION OF ANTIQUITY

A number of medieval inauguration mounds are placed within complexes of monuments with prehistoric sepulchral/ceremonial attributes some of which, however, also demonstrate what is either a continuity of use or renewed occupation in the early medieval period. The use of terms like royal, ritual and ceremonial to describe the landscape settings of these monuments can create the skewed impression of parcels of country within kingdoms and lordships which were sacred and untouched except at times of royal ceremonial. But, on the contrary the argument can be made that these were very much 'living' landscapes mindfully carried through time and incorporated into secular and ecclesiastical life in different periods.

Carn Fraích and its immediate landscape, the inauguration place of the medieval Uí Chonchobhair chiefs of Síol Muireadhaigh is one such site. The legendary warrior Fraích, son of Fidach Foltruad, after whom the *carn* or mound was named, appears as the central character in the Old Irish prose tale *Táin Bó Fraích*.[21] He also features in an incident in the epic *Táin Bó Cúailnge* as contained in *Lebor na hUidre*. In *Táin Bó Cúailnge*, Fraích is slain at a ford, which thereafter is called Áth Fraích, and his body is carried back 'into the fairy mound, which was called Síd Fraích ever afterwards'.[22] O'Rahilly has explained that the prototype of the Fraích prose tale contained in *Lebor na hUidre* could be as early as the ninth century.[23] If this is so, by implication it provides the earliest reference to Síd Fraích otherwise known as Carn Fraích.

The identification of Carn Fraích with a small, flat-topped mound of earth and stone in the townland of Carns, less than two miles southwest of Tulsk in Co. Roscommon, was first made by the Irish antiquary John O'Donovan in 1837 (fig. 2.3). But his identification has not yet been proven beyond doubt. In his Ordnance Survey letters, O'Donovan, referring to the mound at Carns, wrote 'I can confidently say that I discovered Carnfree'.[24] Later, in a footnote to his edition of *AFM*, he suggested that a reference in the *Rennes Dindshenchas* to the location of Carn Fraích, confirmed his claim.[25] The only direct reference to the location of Carn Fraích occurs in one of three Carn Fraích extracts from the *Book of Lecan* incorporated into the *Rennes Dindshenchas*. According to the first of those accounts, following the death of the legendary warrior Fraích he was carried up to the 'Hill of the Assembly' (*Cnoc na Dála*) which is described as lying to the southeast of Crúachan (*ria Cruachnaib sairrdeas*), and 'there he was buried, and from him the cairn is named'.[26] If the compilers of the *Rennes Dindshenchas* were correct in their geography – and there is no reason to assume that this information is unreliable – the small but prominently appointed mound in the townland of Carns, which O'Donovan identified as Carn Fraích, fits their description.

The place-name Cnoc na Dála is also encountered in the *Rennes Dindshenchas*, and in the twelfth-century metrical *Dindshenchas*. While it would seem reasonable to assume that it refers to the conspicuous ridge, south of the village of Tulsk, at the summit of which Carn Fraích is situated, in the metrical *Dindshenchas* the explanation for the relationship of Carn Fraích to the hill introduces considerable ambiguity. The question is asked 'what was the former name of the pointed cairn?' and it is told that 'Cnoc na Dála was its name aforetime, in the days of Medb great and glorious'.[27] The old Irish *cnoc* carries a range of meanings including hill, mound and cairn,[28] which leaves the probability that Cnoc na Dála was, as the metrical *Dindshenchas* tells us, no more than an earlier name for the mound itself and not one applied to the entire ridge on which the mound sits. The versifier of the *Dindshenchas* variously describes Carn Fraích as the strong cairn (*cairn cruaid*), the round

21 Meid 1974, 9.   22 O'Rahilly 1976, 149.   23 Ibid.   24 O'Donovan 1837, 27–8.   25 *AFM*, iii, 221 (fn. a).   26 Stokes 1895, 137.   27 Gwynn 1913, iii, 356–7.   28 *DIL*, 125.

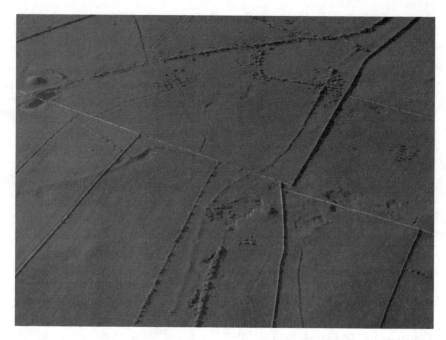

Figure 2.3 Aerial view of portion of the landscape of Carn Fraích, showing the alleged Carn Fraích just right of centre and Dumha Selga in left background. A series of field systems can be seen extending over much of the ridge and two ring-barrows are clearly visible in the immediate vicinity of Dumha Selga (photograph courtesy of G. Bracken).

cairn (*carn cruind*) and the peaceful elf-mound (*sith sidamail*). In accounting for its lore, he goes further and tells us that 'many names belonged to the Hill in succession'.[29] This ambiguity is also present in the Lismore fragments of *Acallam na Senórach* where, in an encounter between St Patrick and Caeilte, Patrick and his company assemble at Carn Fraích. Patrick speaks there with Caeilte about the existence of God – 'Then the whole company rose and moved on to the cairn of Fraech son of Feradach [*recte* Fidach], and Patrick went up upon the eminence'[30] (*Ocus éirghetar in slógh rompu do charn Fhraeich meic Fhiodhaig ocus táinic Pátraic suas isin cnuc*).[31] In this, there is no reference as such to Cnoc na Dála, but Carn Fraích is referred to both as a cairn or mound and an eminence (*cnuc*). Cnoc na Dála is also mentioned, if very briefly, as a synonym for Carn Fraích in the early fifteenth-century MS Laud 610 text of *Acallam na Senórach*, which again suggests that they are one and the same.[32] It may be concluded then that Cnoc na Dála is simply an alias for Carn Fraích.

29 Gwynn 1913, iii, 356–7. **30** O'Grady 1892, ii, 136. **31** Ibid., i, 125. **32** Stokes and Windisch 1900, 212 (from MS Laud 610, 145a1 – The White Earl's Book, written for James, 4th

Carn Fraích, as identified by O'Donovan, is situated at the highest point of a broad limestone ridge with thin soil cover, which extends over a mile in an east-west direction, incorporating the greater part of the townlands of Carns, Lismurtagh and Carrowgarve. The small circular and grass-covered stony mound, which is *c*.2m high and *c*.11m in diameter at base, is built upon limestone rock outcrop and retained by a single course of large contiguous stones around its base. The results of a geophysical survey conducted in 1995 suggest that it is composed primarily of loose stone and earth.[33] However, it did not prove possible to detect internal details like a cavity that might otherwise have indicated a burial chamber. The small summit of the mound is slightly dished and hummocky, no more than 5m in diameter (fig. 2.4). In the nineteenth century there was apparently a smaller cairn of stones positioned on the summit, but its origin is attributed to the Ordnance Survey of the time.[34] Some extra details of the guardianship of the mound and the choreography of the inauguration ceremony are contained in the Ó Conchobhair inauguration tract, the prototype of which it has been argued may have been compiled as early as the twelfth or thirteenth century.[35] It explains that during the inauguration ceremony, the inaugurator Ó Maolchonaire alone was allowed to stand on the mound with the king-elect.[36] Notwithstanding the protocol of the occasion, the small diameter of the summit of the mound that O'Donovan identified as Carn Fraích would have accommodated more than two people with difficulty. The tract goes on to explain that on the occasion of an inauguration Ó Connachtáin was charged with the duty of keeping 'the gate of the mound' and he was also responsible for making sure that the mound was maintained and ready to receive a royal candidate whenever necessary.[37] The reference to 'the gate of the mound (*ag doiseórracht an chairn*)' is interesting. Although there is no trace of a bank or fosse enclosing the mound identified by O'Donovan as Carn Fraích, the mound portrayed in the tract may have been set within some sort of enclosure – perhaps a wattle fence – with a gate entrance.

The use of inauguration 'furniture' either in the form of a stone chair or a footprint stone is not attested in any of the native sources that refer to Carn Fraích. According to an account written by a local antiquary in 1922, a stone supposedly marked with the 'tracks of two human feet' was removed from the mound for safe keeping during quarrying operations in its vicinity *c*.1840, but it was damaged while being removed.[38] The small heavily fissured stone in question now lies at the entrance to Clonalis House, Castlerea, Co.

earl of Ormond 1404–52). The line reads *tangadur rompo co Cnocc na dála bodes, risa raiter Carnn Fraich meic Fidaig.* **33** Fenwick and Delaney 1995, 6. Waddell, Barton and Fenwick (forthcoming). **34** Knox 1915, 3. **35** Simms 1980, 143. **36** Dillon 1961, 197. **37** Ibid., 197. **38** Jones 1922–3, 46.

Roscommon. What could be reservedly described as a single shod footprint with an oddly pointed heel occurs at the narrower end of the stone near its fractured side.

An impressive complex of prehistoric monuments extends over the area of the ridge on which the alleged Carn Fraích stands, among them the so-called Dumha Selga – a round-topped mound surrounded by a broad fosse (see fig. 2.3). In the immediate area of Dumha Selga there are three ring-barrows and the remains of an extensive field system. A larger ring-barrow and a smaller circular burial mound are positioned immediately south of the road that runs in an east-west direction north of Carn Fraích, and yet another ring-barrow lies in the townland of Carrowgarve. Directly east of Carn Fraích there are two pillar stones, one of which is prostrate, and the other, called Cloch Fhada na gCarn, is contained within a small embanked enclosure. These prehistoric monuments may well reflect at least two millennia of burial and other ritual activity on this high ground.

Among the more impressive monuments on the ridge are the conjoined circular earthworks, north-west of Carn Fraích, which straddle the boundary between the townlands of Lismurtagh and Carrowgarve. The southern earthwork comprises a decapitated mound, with a concave summit, which is enclosed by a fosse and outer bank, while its northern counterpart is a simple enclosure with a surrounding bank and external fosse. Geophysical survey of this monument suggests that the northern earthwork is a ringfort (with a possible house site in the interior) which deliberately subsumed part of the mound of earlier date lying on its south side.[39] It should be noted that this enclosed barrow is an equally good candidate for Carn Fraích. Could the ringfort later attached to the north side of the barrow have been added to provide additional assembly space? Or, could it in fact have been the residence of the keeper of the mound, as in the case of Ó Néill's steward, Ó hÁgáin, who resided in an enclosure on the summit of Tulach Óg – the inauguration site of the Uí Néill of Tír Eoghain? What O'Donovan's Carn Fraích has in its favour, however, is the splendid views in all directions that it commands at 119.5m above sea level – a prerequisite of Irish royal inauguration sites. In contrast, the ring-barrow in Lismurtagh/Carrowgarve at the lower elevation of 117.2m above sea level offers a more restricted prospect.

At the far east end of the ridge there are the remains of a deserted later medieval settlement or *seanbhaile* (homestead), and a medieval church surrounded by an impressive circular enclosure. This appears to be the *vallum* of an early church site – possibly the Patrician site that Tírechán refers to as

39 Fenwick and Delaney, 6; Waddell, Barton and Fenwick (forthcoming).

Selca, the place 'where there were the halls of the sons of Brión, together with a great number of holy bishops'.[40]

When was the landscape of the Fraích saga and the reputed burial place of the slain warrior appropriated by the Uí Chonchobhair dynasts of Síol Muireadhaigh for their inauguration ceremonies? The earliest intimation that Carn Fraích was used for this purpose occurs in the late twelfth-century poem 'Tainic an Croibhdherg go Crúachain', composed by Giolla Brighde Albanach in praise of Cathal Croibhdherg who became king of Connacht in 1189. The poet refers to the enkinging of Cathal in the lines 'The Redhand of Croghan has come as Berchan foretold, certain our knowledge, he has assumed his kingdom by Carn Fraeich, he has first stilled the storm'.[41] Another poem, 'Congaibh róm t'aghaidh, a Aodh', celebrating the succession of Cathal's son Aodh to the kingship in 1224 also sets the ceremony at Carn Fraích – '[The men of] Connacht come to Carn Fraoich to enking your soft fair hair'.[42] The native annals record four Uí Chonchobhair inaugurations at Carn Fraích between 1225 and 1407. The first of these concerns the election of Toirrdelbach son of Ruaidrí Ó Conchobhair in 1225.[43] Three years later in 1228 he was expelled from the kingship and his younger brother, Aodh, was inaugurated at Carn Fraích 'as was customary with every king who had ruled over Connacht before him'.[44] Although not recorded in the annals, Aodh mac Feidhlimidh, on the testimony of the poet Giolla Brighde Mac Con Midhe, was also inaugurated there in 1264. In the poem 'Dearmad do fhágbhas ag Aodh', Giolla Brighde refers to Aodh as 'the stately-eyed king of Carn Fraoich' – a likely allusion to his having been inaugurated there.[45] Subsequent inauguration ceremonies at the mound are cited in *AC* for the years 1310, 1315 and 1407.[46]

There is no documentary evidence for inaugurations having taken place at Carn Fraích earlier than 1189. However, its adoption as a royal inauguration site may well have coincided with the emergence of the Uí Chonchobair as the leading family of Síol Muireadhaigh in the ninth century.

The appropriation of an antique landscape for tribal assembly and the ceremony of royal inauguration can also be seen in the case of Magh Adhair, the gathering place of the early medieval Dál Cais dynasty and their Uí Bhriain descendants in Thomond, Co. Clare. The place-name Magh Adhair means 'Adar's plain', which is mentioned in connection with the hero Adar in the legend of Carn Conaill.[47] The mound of Magh Adhair, which lies in the townland of Toonagh east of the village of Quin in southeast Co. Clare (a

---

40 Bieler 1979, 196–9. 41 Quiggin 1912, 169. 42 Dublin, Royal Irish Academy, MS. 490, 162; Simms 1987, 26–7. 43 *AC*, 9. 44 Ibid., 29. 45 Williams 1980, 163 [4]. 46 *AC*, 223, 233–5, 401. 47 Stokes 1894, 481; Gwynn 1913, iii, 443.

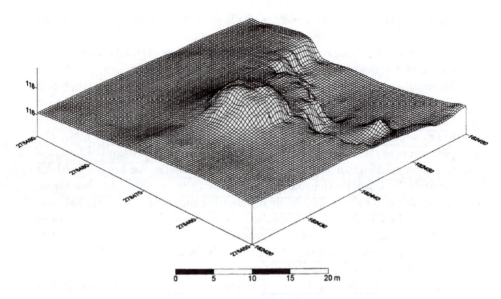

Figure 2.4 Topographical lattice model (vertical exaggeration × 2) of the mound identified as Carn Fraích by O'Donovan (drawing by J. Fenwick).

dominant feature in a greater complex of monuments), was the focus of royal assemblies and inaugurations from at least as early as the tenth century. Inauguration mounds by no means constitute a homogenous group. They are on the contrary quite heterogeneous, varying considerably in size and form, perhaps reflecting their origins, additions and alterations. In contrast to the alleged Carn Fraích, the mound of Magh Adhair is a large flat-topped earthwork, 4m high, with a basal diameter of 32m narrowing to 25m across its level summit (fig. 2.5). It is enclosed by a deep fosse and a denuded external bank. The summit is reached by a narrow ramped entrance or causeway that crosses the fosse at the west. In the late nineteenth century the antiquary T.J. Westropp noted 'a worn slab of limestone' on the north side of the summit of the mound which he proposed may have served as an inauguration stone (*leac*).[48]

    Although attempts have been made to classify Magh Adhair[49] and to describe suitable analogues for the mound,[50] this is an unusual earthwork for which no comparisons can be easily found. It does not present the appearance of an entirely prehistoric barrow or medieval mound, but is perhaps a marriage

48 Westropp 1896–8, 55, 57.   49 Grogan and Condit 2000, 23, propose that it 'conforms to the morphological description of a barrow'.   50 Herity 1993, 144–6.

Figure 2.5 The great mound of Magh Adhair with basin stone in foreground (photo courtesy of Wiltshire Collection, Department of Environment, Heritage and Local Government).

of the two – a prehistoric sepulchral heart with early medieval modifications for assembly purposes. The setting of the mound also places it apart from the hilltop locations of most of the other mounds attested as inauguration venues. It lies in what could be described as a natural amphitheatre. A semicircular ridge of limestone outcrop, called 'Cregnakeeroge' (*Craig na Ciaróge*, the 'rock of the clock or chafer'),[51] sweeps around the mound from north-west clockwise through to southeast.[52] The site is circumscribed on its west side by the 'Hell River' (*Abhainn Ifrinn*). There is no available explanation of the origin of this name, but it may hold otherworld connotations linked to inauguration rites, recalling the 'cave of Cruachu' which is portrayed in early Irish literary sources as one of the entrances to the otherworld – 'Ireland's gate of Hell'.[53] Within this area defined by the limestone ridge and the Hell River two additional archaeological features accompany the great mound. The first of these is a small roughly circular earth and stone mound, no more than 2m high

51 O'Donovan 1839, 64–5. 52 Westropp 1896–8, 60. 53 Stokes 1892, 449.

and 10m in diameter at base. It is heaped upon rock outcrop situated *c.*7m west of the great mound and overlooks the Hell River. Whether it is sepulchral or perhaps the former setting for the *bile* or sacred tree of Magh Adhair, or indeed a combination of both, is as yet unknown. The second feature of note is a large conglomerate boulder with porphyritic and quartzite inclusions uncharacter-istic of the otherwise limestone geology of the district (see fig. 2.5). It lies a little over 30m north-east of the great mound, just below the outcrop ridge. The upper surface of the boulder contains two basins, the larger, oval one of the two being artificial. Its function in respect of inauguration ritual is not known, but it is of interest that a small circular basin also occurs at Dunadd in Argyll, the inauguration site of the kings of Dál Riada between the seventh and ninth centuries.[54] Unlike the Magh Adhair basin stone, however, it is not freestanding but hollowed out on a seam of rock outcrop on the middle plateau of the nuclear fort.

The more unequivocal prehistoric dimension to the immediate landscape of Magh Adhair is indicated by the presence of an impressive standing stone situated mid-way down the north-facing slope of the field west of the Hell River. There may also have been a second standing stone between it and the river – in the late nineteenth century Westropp noted 'a shattered block' constituting its remains. A more recent study of this landscape also proposes that along with the standing stones, the presence of a number of *fulachta fiadh* (burnt mounds assumed to be cooking sites, generally datable to the Bronze Age), in the immediate vicinity of Magh Adhair, affords the great mound a prehistoric context.[55] These, however, may not necessarily be relics of a Bronze Age past left untouched during centuries of medieval assembly activity at Magh Adhair when one would expect feasting to have taken place.

In keeping with the appropriation of the vestiges of a prehistoric landscape for their assembly-place, in the tenth century the Dál Cais dynasty also assumed a 'new or revised prehistoric pedigree', with Cormac Cass son of Ailill Aulomm as their progenitor. This served to give them equal standing with the other loosely federated dynastic groups which constituted the powerful Munster Eóganacht who claimed Eógan Mór son of Ailill Aulomm as their eponymous ancestor.[56] The Dál Cais, or Déis Tuaiscirt as they were known prior to the tenth century, had invaded the east Clare region from their original homeland, south of the Shannon estuary in eastern Limerick, as early as the mid-eighth century. Their expansion and political dominance was consolidated perhaps a century-and-a-half before they are first mentioned in the native annals as Dál Cais in 934.[57] In that period their tribal name had

54 Campbell and Lane 1993, 52; *RCAHMS* 1988, 149–59.   55 Grogan and Condit 2000, 23.
56 Kelleher 1967, 234; Ó Corráin 1972, 1.   57 Ó Corráin 1979, 7–9.

changed, their pedigree had been upgraded and they had annexed new territory and established an assembly-place in the conquered region.

Their association with Magh Adhair is first noted in the chronicles for the year 981. In that year Máel Sechnaill, king of Tara plundered the territory of the Dál Cais, which was then ruled by Brian Bóraimhe (d. 1014). In the course of the raid a sacred tree (*bile*) called the *bile* of 'Aenach-Maighe-Adhair' was cut, after being dug from the earth with its roots.[58] The annalist's use of the word *aenach* (*óenach*) in the full title of Magh Adhair is significant, as it designates the site as a place of tribal assembly, distinguished by a hallowed meeting tree. Almost seventy years later, during the reign of Donnchad mac Briain (d. 1064), the *bile* was prostrated once again, from which we may deduce that either it had not been fully destroyed in the attack of 982 or it had been replaced by another tree which was flourishing by 1051.

Both of these events indicate the significance of the *bile* Magh Adhair to the Dál Cais kings and their enemies. Its uprooting was manifestly the greatest insult which either the king of Mide or Connacht could pay to the Ua Briain king of Dál Cais. Three additional sites in Ulster and Connacht, which are later recorded as inauguration places, also had sacred trees – a coincidence that argues for a strong association between *biledha* and king-making venues. The *biledha* Tulach Óg at the Uí Néill inauguration site were cut down in 1111[59] and the *bile* Cráeb Telcha at Crew, Co. Antrim was destroyed in 1099.[60] In 1129 the same fate was shared by the Ruadh-bheitheach (Red Birch) sacred to the kings of Uí Fhiachrach Aidhne in south Galway.[61]

By the thirteenth century Magh Adhair was well established as the inauguration site of the Uí Bhriain descendants of the early medieval Dál Cais. The *Caithréim Thoirdhealbhaigh* provides evidence for seven Uí Bhriain inaugurations at the site between 1242 and 1313, with the Mac Con Mara officiating at the ceremony in each case.[62] None of these references, however, record the details or exact location of the ceremony within the Magh Adhair complex.

Although the annals note a number of Uí Bhriain inaugurations after that of Donnchad Ó Briain in 1313, and throughout the fifteenth century, the place of inauguration is not mentioned in any of those entries. With no evidence to the contrary, it may reasonably be assumed that Magh Adhair continued to be the Uí Bhriain inauguration site in the later medieval period, endowing rival claimants with their inviolable right to the chieftainship well into the sixteenth century.

---

58 *AFM*, ii, 715; *AI*, 164–5; *Chron. Scot.*, 229. 59 *AFM*, ii, 991. 60 Ibid., ii, 963. 61 *Chron. Scot.*, 1129. 62 O'Grady 1929, 2, 5–6, 10, 32–3, 46–7, 48, 69.

INVENTING TRADITION

Where a genuine claim to the association of a particular mound with the progenitor of a dynastic group could not be made for inauguration purposes, it could instead be fabricated, or a new tradition created. The creation of such a tradition around the establishment of a new inauguration venue can be argued in the case of the Uí Dhubhda chiefs of Tír Fhiachrach – a small late medieval lordship in north Connacht in the west of Ireland. Prior to the settlement of north Connacht by Anglo-Norman families in the 1230s, that lordship formed part of the impressively large territory of Uí Fhiachrach Muaidhe which was coextensive with the boundaries of the diocese of Killala, and ruled by the Uí Dhubhda.[63] It covered the greater part of north Mayo incorporating Iorrus Domhnann (barony of Erris), Tír Amhalghaidh (barony of Tirawley), and Ceara (barony of Carra), and Tír Fhiachrach (barony of Tireragh) east of the river Moy in the present Co. Sligo.[64]

A tract on the inauguration of the Uí Dhubhda kings, inserted into the *Book of Lecan*,[65] claims that this dynasty had two inauguration sites frequented according to convenience, one on either side of the river Moy that divided their territory of Uí Fhiachrach Muaide into two halves (see fig. 2.1). The two sites in question are Carn inghine Briain, which lay east of the river in Tír Fhiachrach, and Carn Amhalghaidh to the west of the river in Tír Amhalghaidh. The tract reads:

> And there is one thing, should O'Dubhda happen to be in Tír Amhalghaidh he may repair to Carn Amhalghaidh to be nominated, so as that all the chiefs are about him: but should he happen to be at Carn inghine Briain it is not necessary for him to go over [the Moy] to have the title given to him, and it is not necessary for him to come across [to Carn inghine Briain] from Carn Amhalghaidh ...[66]

It would be most unusual for a sept to have had two inauguration sites in use simultaneously. This situation can be more easily explained by the mid-fourteenth century political circumstances in which the Uí Fhiachrach tract seems to have been compiled. Recent work on the tract suggests that it may well have been contrived as a piece of propagandist antiquarianism hearkening back to the pre-thirteenth century heyday of Uí Fhiachrach Muaide, which before the Anglo-Norman settlement had constituted a much larger territory. But in fact, the overlordship of Iorrus, Ceara and Tír Amhalghaidh was irrev-

63 Byrne 1987, 34.   64 Ó Corráin 1972, 10–12.   65 The excerpt from the tract cited here is part of a later recension of the Uí Fhiachrach prose tract compiled by Dubhaltach Mac Fir Bhisigh in *c*.1650.   66 O'Donovan 1844, 442–4.

ocably lost to the Uí Dhubhda after the Anglo-Norman settlement of Connacht. It was Tír Fhiachrach, east of the Moy estuary, alone, which was recovered by them in the second half of the fourteenth century and which subsequently became the entire extent of their lordship.[67] Nollaig Ó Muraíle suggests that rather than being 'a record of age-old traditions', the Tír Fhiachrach section of the tract may actually have been an attempt to create such traditions.[68] It seems likely then, that prior to the Anglo-Norman settlement, Carn Amhalghaidh was the regular inauguration site of this sept and that after the fourteenth-century reconquest of Tír Fhiachrach by the Uí Dhubhda, Carn inghine Briain may have been newly adopted as a suitable inauguration venue in their lordship east of the river Moy.

The nature of the two mounds that functioned as inauguration sites of the Uí Fhiachrach, in different times, is unclear. Little remains of Carn Amhalghaidh west of the River Moy in Tír Amhalghaidh, and the proposed location of Carn inghine Briain is somewhat speculative. Carn Amhalghaidh was identified by O'Donovan as 'Mullaghorn Fort' (*Mullach Chairn* – the mound on the summit) situated on the crest of an east-facing slope in the townland of Croghan near Killala, Co. Mayo.[69] The *carn* in question was levelled in the early twentieth century but not ploughed out, as the western half of the large enclosure which once delimited the site survives as a denuded scarp. Fortunately there are two antiquarian accounts that provide details of the mound. In the 1830s Caesar Otway visited the site and has left a detailed record of its appearance:

> We then walked westwards towards a rath [an earthen bank or rampart] that stood crowning with its lofty mound a considerable eminence. I was pleased to observe that it was dissimilar to most I have seen, for the circular mound was not, as is usual, entirely composed of earth, but was strengthened within by a stone wall. I have seen many raths entirely constructed of stones and multitudes composed of earth, but I don't recollect observing one before where a wall of stone is added to the defence of the earthen mound. From this rath there is an extensive view both seaward and inland ...[70]

To this description O'Donovan added that the internal diameter of the enclosure around the mound was *c*.24m and that it had an overall external diameter of *c*.74m. He too observed 'round stones of very great size placed circularly' on the inner side of the enclosure.[71] By the time Knox visited the

---

67 Byrne 1987, 34. 68 Ó Muraíle 2001, 236–7. 69 O'Donovan 1838, 261–3. 70 Otway 1845, 189. 71 O'Donovan 1838, 261–3.

site *c*.1911 it had been 'almost quite levelled'. The great stones that had lined the internal face of the enclosure had been thrown into a quarry, which had 'undermined and brought down part of the work'.[72]

The topographical lore relating to the genesis of this mound is curious, as it claims for it an early medieval origin. In a poem on the origins of Carn Amhalghaidh, in the twelfth-century metrical *Dindshenchas*, it is specified that it was Amhalghaidh who 'first trenched that carn ... in order to behold his long ships, and to have a place of assembly to dwell in'. The author of the poem adds that Amhalghaidh was laid in the carn.[73] In the Uí Fhiachrach prose tract in the *Book of Lecan*, this origin-tale is reiterated. The tract emphasizes that it was Amhalghaidh who raised that *carn* 'to serve as a place of tribal assembly and great meetings' (*do chum aonaigh agus ard-oireachtais*),[74] and the author goes on to say that:

> It was Amhalghaidh ... that raised that *carn* for himself, in order that he himself, and all those who should obtain the lordship after him, might receive the style of lord upon it. And it is in this *carn* that Amhalghaidh himself is interred, and it is from him it is named. And every king of the race of Fiachra that shall not be thus nominated, he shall have shortness of life, and his race or generations shall not be illustrious, and he shall never see the kingdom of God.[75]

In other words, no less than the progenitor of the race of Uí Fhiachrach is credited in these accounts with the erection of the enclosed mound, which he used as his place of inauguration and as the venue for tribal assembly and high-level meetings. He is also presented as designating the mound as his own burial place and consequently it becomes the only monument upon which his successors could legitimately receive their right to the kingship of Uí Fhiachrach. The genesis of Carn Amhalghaidh as given in both of these sources is explained in the manner of an origin-tale and must be understood as lore of place rather than factual account. Nonetheless it is telling of the importance which the compilers attributed to making a direct association between the eponymous ancestor of the sept and the place of inauguration of successive kings and chiefs drawn from the tribal group.

The archaeological monuments in the hinterland of the site may also hold clues to its origins. Like Carn Fraích and Magh Adhair there is a strong prehistoric dimension to the landscape of Carn Amhalghaidh. A short distance downhill to the southwest there is a group of burial mounds and a megalithic tomb the proximity of which intimates that the *carn* of Carn Amhalghaidh

---

72 Knox 1911, 95.   73 Gwynn 1913, iii, 422–3.   74 O'Donovan 1844, 100–1.   75 Ibid., 444.

may well have been a component of this sepulchral landscape.[76] The enclosure with its internal facing of large boulders is, however, unusual in the context of a barrow, and may have been a later modification of the monument. This type of revetment is known from a number of ringforts (generally attributed an early medieval date) in Co. Mayo. The most notable example is the impressive facing of boulders on the inner bank of a large ringfort near the village of Kilmaine in the south of the county, which was used as the inauguration place of the Mayo Burkes in the later medieval period.[77] But it must also be considered that the idea of building a mound for specific use as an assembly platform is quite valid. The tradition of erecting turf mounds for assembly, as well as re-using earlier sepulchral mounds, is well attested in Britain and continental Europe,[78] and there is no reason to assume that similar constructions would not have been erected specifically for royal ceremonial and assembly in early medieval Ireland.

While the basis for inaugurating the kings of Uí Fhiachrach on Carn Amhalghaidh may have been fabricated to enhance the legitimacy of their right to rule, the use of Carn inghine Briain for inaugurations in the post-Norman period appears to have been an invented tradition established to coincide with the re-conquest of Tír Fhiachrach by the Uí Dhubhda in the fourteenth century. The exact location of Carn inghine Briain ('the mound of Brian's daughter') is unrecorded. The Uí Fhiachrach tract simply states that it was east of the river Moy, in Tír Fhiachrach. Elsewhere I have argued that it may be identified with a curious two-tiered mound in the townland of Kilrusheighter on the southwest side of Aughris headland in Co. Sligo (see fig. 2.1).[79] The supporting evidence for this identification is based on a combination of place-name interpretation, the surface morphology of the mound itself, traditions of Lughnasa festival assemblies resonant of an *óenach*, horse-racing and political rallies on the headland, together with folk allusions to sovereignty, and the omnipresence of the Uí Dhubhda in local tales.

The mound has lost its more ancient name and is now known as Coggins' Hill. It lies towards the seaward side of a long, low grassy ridge on the coastline of Aughris offering a splendid view of the surrounding landscape and Sligo Bay. The most dominant presence on the eastern skyline is Knocknarea Mountain, which is crowned by a massive cairn attributed to Medb the legendary queen of Connacht. Coggins' Hill is one of three mounds of different character on the western side of Aughris headland which are each poised on the grassy cliffs above the Atlantic (see fig. 2.6). The most northerly and largest of the three is called Healy's Round Hill – a massive unenclosed

---

76 Record of monuments and places, County Mayo (MA015 –044). **77** FitzPatrick 2001a, 358–65. **78** Adkins and Petchey 1984, 243–51; Damell 1991, 291–6. **79** FitzPatrick 6, 67–105; 2001.

tumulus. It is separated from Coggins' Hill by Belturlin Bay and a tract of marshland. The third mound called 'Sheeaun' – a high conical earthwork with a small summit diameter – lies south of Coggins' Hill in the townland of Rathglass.

The unusual character of Coggins' Hill places it outside the standard classification of prehistoric sepulchral mounds and defensive earthworks. It is a steep-sided earthen mound, approximately circular in plan, 3m high, with a basal diameter of *c.*22m, narrowing to *c.*10m at the summit. A smaller oval mound, now no more than *c.*0.7m high, with a diameter of *c.*7.5m, crowns the centre of the summit (fig. 2.7). A shallow fosse, *c.*0.85m wide, and an external bank approximately 1m wide, enclose the upper eminence. There is also some evidence to suggest a step skirting the circumference of the mound about 1m above its base. This feature is quite discernible in the southeast quadrant where it manifests itself as a slight projection *c.*0.7m wide. It continues into the southwest quadrant but is imperceptible elsewhere. The results of a fluxgate gradiometry survey carried out in 1999 also register this feature and indicate its presence in the northeast quadrant as well as at south. Whether this can be construed as original to the architecture of the mound is difficult to say. It could be a purpose-built feature created to provide a third tier for participants in an inauguration ceremony. On the other hand, as the mound is sited on a ridge, it is quite conceivable that its lower half was actually created from the natural material of the ridge and that the projection which occurs 1m above the base of the mound is simply a register of old ground level. The entire mound is ringed at the base by a broad fosse, outside of which are the very degraded remains of a bank.

What makes this monument unusual is the presence of the small secondary mound on top. There is an interesting analogy between the arrangement of mound on mound and Queen Medb's cairn on the flat-topped summit of Knocknarea Mountain, which provides a dramatic eastern backdrop to Coggins' Hill (fig. 2.8). Was the 'architecture' of the mound contrived in conscious imitation of the profile of the mountain or was it simply a practical response to the choreographic requirements of royal inauguration? Ann Woodward in her study of British barrows draws attention to the way in which some barrows 'appear to represent in miniature the actual hills upon which they sit, or the profiles of hills visible directly from them'. The Giants' Grave long barrow on the edge of Salisbury Plain, for instance, has as its backdrop the 'dramatic whale-backed profile' of Martinsell Hill. In this setting, the long barrow appears as a scaled-down version of the hill.[80]

Some parallels for the arrangement of mound on mound at Coggins' Hill, however, can be detected at other inauguration sites. For instance, the mound of Sciath Gabhra near Lisnaskea, Co. Fermanagh, which was the inauguration place of the Méig Uidhir,[81] is crowned by a cairn of angular stones which gives

Sciath
Gabhra

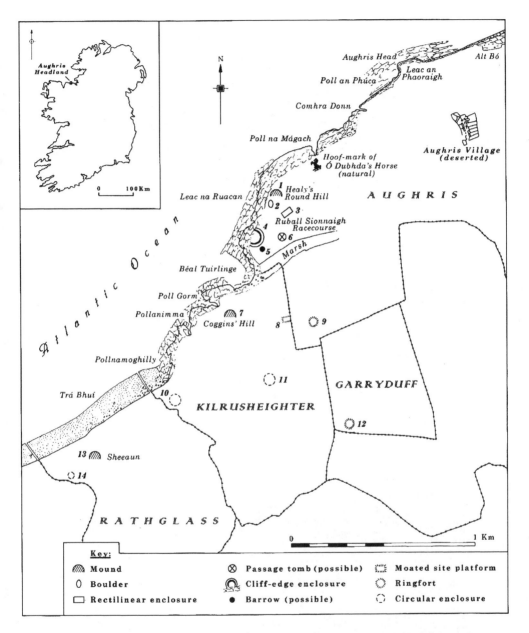

Figure 2.6 The western coastline of Aughris headland showing Coggins' Hill (7) and the archaeology of the immediate hinterland. Healy's Round Hill (1) and Sheeaun mound (13) are also shown (drawing by A. Gallagher).

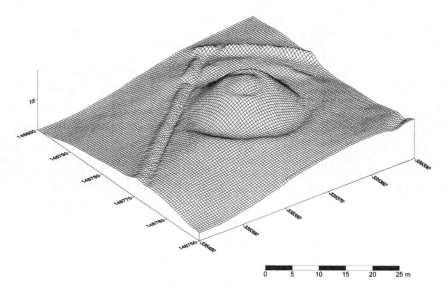

Figure 2.7 Topographical lattice model (vertical exaggeration × 2) of Coggins' Hill (drawing by J. Fenwick).

Figure 2.8 Coggins' Hill – the proposed site of Carn inghine Briain, Aughris, Co. Sligo. The profile of the two-tiered mound seems to echo the dramatic form of Queen Medb's cairn on the summit of Knocknarea Mountain, which can be seen behind the shoulder of the mound.

the monument a two-tiered profile (see fig. 2.2). Although significantly larger and more complex in its archaeology, the broad summit of Rathcroghan mound near Tulsk, Co. Roscommon also retains the very degraded remains of a sub-circular mound – the final feature added to the monument. In the eighteenth century Gabriel Beranger made a water-colour image of Rathcroghan showing this feature (fig. 2.9) which was then in a good state of preservation. As Waddell has explained, Beranger miscalculated the summit diameter of the greater mound with the result that it appears disproportionately broad in relation to its height.[82] In a caption to this drawing, Beranger described the smaller eminence on top as 'a small mount whose top has only 6 feet diameter, on which it is supposed the king had his station'.[83] The idea of the 'king's station' or throne-mound is a very valid interpretation of this little eminence on the greater mound, and the same purpose may have been served by the upper mound on Coggins' Hill. Although the Irish evidence is meagre as yet, a case can be made for the medieval use of small, possibly purpose-built mounds (or re-use of diminutive burial mounds on hilltops) which may in themselves have acted as the 'king's seat', or supported stone inauguration furniture.[84] There are also occurrences of two-tiered mounds at sites which have no certain connection with inauguration practices. A very large mound (with an enclosure attached to one side) is crowned by a smaller circular mound on the drumlin ridge of Knockadoobrusna, south of Boyle in north Co. Roscommon.[85] It is located in the territory of the Meic Dhiarmata of Magh Luirg.[86] The place-name Knockadoobrosna incorporates the Irish word *dumha*, which as Swift points out can apply to anything from a burial mound to a support for a hunting hut.[87]

Coggins' Hill could be a reused prehistoric monument or a medieval sepulchral mound, which was modified for assembly purposes by the addition of the upper mound. Alternatively it could have been newly constructed specifically to facilitate inauguration ceremonies in the later medieval period.

The place-name Carn inghine Briain holds the expectation that the later medieval inauguration place of the Uí Dhubhda was the burial mound of a royal woman of the Uí Fhiachrach – 'Brian's daughter'. But strangely the Uí Fhiachrach tract does not give the same attention to it as it does to Carn Amhalghaidh. Carn inghine Briain has no recorded history and no topographical lore attached to it. The absence of any commentary on its origins, in the tract, may serve to validate the view that its use as an inauguration site was in

80 Woodward 2000, 126. 81 *AFM*, vi, 1876–7; Greene 1972, 164–5. 82 Waddell 1983, 24. 83 Ibid., 24. 84 See for instance the contexts of the Ó Néill inauguration chair at Tulach Óg and the reputed Ó Néill Clann Aodha Buidhe chair at Castlereagh in FitzPatrick, 2003; FitzPatrick 2001a, 365–74 explores the evidence for an inauguration chair on a mound at Caher na nIarla in Co. Galway. 85 Condit 1993, 14–16. 86 *AC*, 239, 581. 87 Swift 2000, 115.

Figure 2.9 A view of Rathcroghan mound by Gabriel Beranger, 1779 (RIA MS. 3.c.30 [79]). The little mound on top (now quite degraded and best viewed from the air) is where Beranger supposed the 'king had his station' (by permission of the Royal Irish Academy © RIA).

fact a new tradition created for the Uí Dhubhda chiefs following their recovery of Tír Fhiachrach in the second half of the fourteenth century.

CONCLUSION

The criteria governing the choice of royal inauguration and assembly sites by the dynasts of early medieval tribal groups and later medieval septs were clearly influenced by the circumstances in which they emerged as politically dominant. In the case of the Dál Cais, the site they chose for their tribal assembly lay outside their original homeland in newly conquered territory to which they had begun to lay claim as early as the mid-eighth century. The reason they chose Magh Adhair as their tribal assembly-place is undocumented. It may be the case that the prehistoric aspect of the site and its associations with the legendary hero Adar provided the combination of 'antique' attributes requisite to a king-making site, into which they introduced their own modifications and additions. But the mound and its sacred tree may also have had prior significance for the indigenous Corcu Modruad people who had been driven into the Burren country of north Clare by the Dál Cais during their takeover. The adoption of the assembly-place of a conquered people by the victors would have proclaimed and consolidated the annexation of new territory. This can perhaps be more clearly demonstrated in respect of Tulach Og, which became the inauguration place of the Uí Néill kings of Ailech from at least as early as the mid-eleventh century. Hogan has very plausibly suggested that the attraction of Tulach Og for the kings of Ailech lay in the probability that it was the traditional inauguration site of the kings of Airghialla whom they had conquered by the early tenth century.[88]

Claims to a direct association with the antiquity of an inauguration site and legitimate right to rule were inextricably linked. Whether the claim was based in legend or historical fact mattered little, it seems. The Fraích saga as told in both *Táin Bó Fraích* and *Táin Bó Cúailnge* (Recension I), which may have been compiled, as O'Rahilly suggests, as early as the ninth century, was imprinted on the Connacht landscape. The alleged burial place of the hero Fraích became the mound upon which the Uí Chonchobhair dynasts of Síol Muireadhaigh were inaugurated 'as was customary with every king who had ruled over Connacht'. They attached themselves to the legendary hero Fraích and to a prehistoric landscape into which Fraích was placed.

That effecting a direct link between an inauguration site and the eponymous ancestor of the tribal group was seen as imperative to the legitimacy of kingship succession is evident in other circumstances. This practice is explicit in the case of those who documented the kingship ritual of the kings of Uí Fhiachrach Muaidhe. The compilers of the *Dindshenchas* or topographical lore relating to Carn Amhalghaidh, and the author of the Uí Fhiachrach tract, as set out in the *Book of Lecan*, emphasize its central place in the inauguration practices of the Uí Dhubhda kings of Uí Fhiachrach. Particular significance is attributed to Amhalghaidh as the creator of the inauguration mound, for his own election, his tribal assemblies and royal colloquies, and finally his burial place. The archaeology of the Carn Amhalghaidh landscape, however, suggests a possible prehistoric origin for the mound itself.

Just as the annexation of new territory required the establishment of a royal assembly place there, the re-conquest of part of a more ancient patrimony also warranted the adoption of a king-making site. With the Anglo-Norman settlement of Uí Fhiachrach Muaidhe in the thirteenth century and the recovery in

---

88 Hogan 1940, 422–3.

the fourteenth century of the lost Tír Fhiachrach portion of the once extensive kingdom, a site in the newly recovered territory was adopted as a regular
inauguration venue. Unlike Carn Amhalghaidh, the author of the Uí
Fhiachrach tract has no origin-tale to tell of Carn inghine Briain – the mound
of Brian's daughter – nor does he have an historical figure to attach to it. But
one wonders if in fact it refers to the fourteenth-century chief, Brian Ó
Dubhda, who did most to secure the re-conquest of Tír Fhiachrach. The use
of this mound for inaugurations appears to be a contrived tradition,
documented to coincide with the re-conquest of Tír Fhiachrach by the Uí
Dhubhda.

   In the cause of upgrading a dynasty or endorsing a king's right to rule over
a territory, genealogies could be fabricated and history made malleable.
Monuments and antique landscapes, some spanning millennia, played their
part too in the validation of royal succession in the kingdoms and lordships of
medieval Ireland. They were 'biographical landmarks'[89] where the ceremony
of king-making and the pedigree of a royal candidate could be visibly attached
to an illustrious past.

ACKNOWLEDGMENTS

I am indebted to Professor John Waddell for his invaluable comments on an
earlier draft of this paper, to Angela Gallagher for the maps which accompany
the text, and to Joseph Fenwick for the topographical lattice models of
Coggins' Hill and Carn Fraích.

ABBREVIATIONS

AC	*Annála Connacht* (AD 1224–1544), ed. and trans. A.M. Freeman.
AFM	*Annals of the kingdom of Ireland by the Four Masters*, ed. and trans. J. O'Donovan.
AI	*Annals of Inisfallen*, ed. and trans. S. Mac Airt.
ALC	*Annals of Loch Cé*, ed. and trans. S. Mac Airt.
AU	*The Annals of Ulster*, ed. S. Mac Airt and G. MacNiocaill.
Cal. S. P. Ire.	*Calendar of the state papers relating to Ireland* (24 vols) (London, 1860–1911).
Chron. Scot.	*Chronicum Scotorum*, ed. and trans. W.M. Hennessy.
DIL	*Dictionary of the Irish language*, Royal Irish Academy.

89 Waddell, Barton and Fenwick, forthcoming.

NLI   National Library of Ireland
RCAHMS   *Argyll: an inventory of the monuments, vol. 6 – Mid Argyll and Cowal*,
             Royal Commission on Ancient and Historic Monuments of Scotland.

REFERENCES

Adkins, R.A. and Petchey, M.R., 1984: 'Secklow hundred mound and other meeting place mounds in England', *Archaeological Journal* **141**, 243–51.

Bieler, L., 1979: *The Patrician texts in the Book of Armagh*. Dublin.

Bhreathnach, E., 1995: 'The topography of Tara: the documentary evidence', *Discovery Programme Reports* **2**, 68–76. Dublin.

Byrne, F.J., 1987: 'The trembling sod: Ireland in 1169', in A. Cosgrove (ed.), *Medieval Ireland, 1169–1534*, A *new history of Ireland*, vol. 2. Oxford. 1–42.

Campbell, E. and Lane, A., 1993: 'Celtic and Germanic interaction in Dalriada: the 7th-century metalworking site at Dunadd', in R. M. Spearman and J. Higgitt (eds), *The age of migrating ideas: early medieval art in Northern Britain and Ireland*. Edinburgh. 52–63.

Comerford, M., 1883: *Collections relating to the diocese of Kildare and Leighlin* (3 vols.). Dublin.

Condit, T., 1993: 'Ritual enclosures near Boyle, Co. Roscommon', *Archaeology Ireland* **7/1**, 14–16.

Damell, D., 1991: 'Fornsigtuna: a royal seat and precursor of an urban settlement', in K. Jennbert, L. Larsson, R. Petré and B. Wyszomirska-Werbart (eds), *Regions and reflections: in honour of Märta Strömberg*, Acta Archaeologica Lundensia, **8/20**. Lund. 291–6.

Dillon, M., 1961: 'The inauguration of O'Conor', in J.A. Watt, J.B. Morrall and F.X. Martin (eds), *Medieval studies presented to Aubrey Gwynn*. Dublin. 186–202.

Elliot, C.B., 1835: *Travels in Austria, Russia and Turkey*, vol. 1. London.

Fenwick, J. and Delaney, F., 1995: 'Carnfree mound', *Archaeogeophysical Imaging Project Newsletter* **3**, 6.

FitzPatrick, E., 1998: 'The inauguration of Tairdelbach Ó Conchobair at Áth an Termoinn', *Peritia* **12**, 351–7.

FitzPatrick, E., 2001: 'Assembly and inauguration places of the Burkes in Late Medieval Connacht', in P.J. Duffy, D. Edwards and E. FitzPatrick (eds), *Gaelic Ireland c.1250 –c.1650: land, lordship and settlement*. Dublin. 357–74.

FitzPatrick, E., 2001a: 'The gathering place of Tír Fhiachrach?: archaeological and folkloric investigations at Aughris, Co. Sligo', *Proceedings of the Royal Irish Academy*, **101c**, 67–105.

FitzPatrick, E., 2003: '*Leaca* and Gaelic inauguration ritual in medieval Ireland', in R. Welander, D. Breeze and T. Clancy (eds), *The Stone of Destiny: artefact and icon*. Edinburgh.

Freeman, A.M. (ed and trans),1944: *Annála Connacht* (AD 1224–1544). Dublin.

Greene, D. (ed.), 1972: *Duanaire Mhéig Uidhir*. Dublin.

Grogan, E. and Condit, T., 2000: 'The funerary landscape of Clare in space and time', in C. Ó Murchadha (ed.), *County Clare studies*. Ennis. 9–29.

Gwynn, E. (ed.), 1913: *The metrical Dindshenchas*, part 3. Dublin (reprint 1991).

Hennessy, W.M. (ed and trans), 1866: *Chronicum Scotorum*. London.

Herity, M., 1993: 'Motes and mounds at royal Sites in Ireland', *Journal of the Royal Society of Antiquaries of Ireland* **123**, 127–51.

Hogan, J., 1940: 'The Ua Briain kingship of Telach Óc', in J. Ryan (ed.), *Essays and studies presented to Eoin MacNeill*. Dublin. 406–41.

Jones, W.A., 1922–3: 'The proclamation stone of the Connaught kings', *Journal of the Galway Archaeological and Historical Society* **12**, 46.

Kelleher, J.V., 1967: 'The rise of the Dál Cais', in E. Rynne (ed.), *North Munster studies: essays in commemoration of Monsignor Michael Moloney*. Limerick. 230–41.

Knox, H.T., 1911: 'The Croghans and some Connacht raths and motes', *Journal of the Royal Society of Antiquaries of Ireland* **41**, 93–116, 301–42.

Knox, H.T., 1915: 'Carnfree and Carnabreckna', *Journal of the Galway Archaeological and Historical Society* **9**, 1–33.

Lynn, C.J. (ed.), 1997: *Excavations at Navan fort 1961–71: D. M. Waterman*. Belfast.

Mac Airt, S. (ed and trans), 1951: *Annals of Inisfallen*. Dublin.

Mac Airt, S. (ed and trans), 1951: *Annals of Loch Cé*. Dublin.

Mac Airt, S. and MacNiocaill, G. (ed and trans), 1983: *The annals of Ulster*. Dublin.

Meid, W. (ed.), 1974: *Táin Bó Fraích*. Dublin.

Newman, C., 1997: *Tara: an archaeological survey*, Discovery Programme Monograph **2**. Dublin.

Ó Cathasaigh, T., 1977–8: 'The semantics of "Síd"', *Éigse* **17**, 137–55.

Ó Corráin, D., 1972: *Ireland before the Normans*. Dublin.

Ó Doibhlin, E., 1971: 'O'Neill's "own country" and its families', *Seanchas Ard Mhacha* **6/1**, 3–23.

O'Donovan, J., 1837: *Letters containing information relative to the antiquities of the County of Roscommon: collected during the progress of the Ordnance Survey in 1837*, ed. M. O'Flanagan, 1927. Bray.

O'Donovan, J., 1838: *Letters containing information relative to the antiquities of the County of Mayo: collected during the progress of the Ordnance Survey in 1838*, ed. M. O'Flanagan, 1927. Bray.

O'Donovan, J., 1839: *Ordnance Survey name books, County Clare: parish of Clooney*, ed. M. O'Flanagan, 1927. Bray.

O'Donovan, J. (ed.), 1844: *The genealogies, tribes and customs of Hy-Fhiachrach*. Dublin.

O'Donovan, J. (ed and trans), 1851: *Annals of the kingdom of Ireland by the four masters* (7 vols). Dublin.

O'Grady, S.H. (ed and trans), 1892: *Silva Gadelica (I–XXXI): A Collection of tales in Irish with extracts illustrating persons and places* (2 vols.). New York (reprint 1970).

O'Grady, S.H. (ed.), 1929: *Caithréim Thoirdhealbhaigh* (2 vols.), Irish Texts Society **27**. London.

Ó hÓgáin, D., 1988: *Fionn mac Cumhaill: images of the Gaelic hero*. Dublin.

Ó Muraíle, N., 2001: 'Settlement and place-names', in P.J. Duffy, D. Edwards and E.

FitzPatrick (eds), *Gaelic Ireland c.1250–c.1650: land, lordship and settlement*. Dublin. 223–45.

O'Rahilly, C. (ed.), 1961: *The Stowe version of Táin Bó Cúailnge*. Dublin.

O'Rahilly, C. (ed.), 1976: *Táin Bó Cúailnge*. Dublin.

Orpen, G.H., 1911: 'Croghans and Norman motes', *Journal of the Royal Society of Antiquaries of Ireland* 41, 267–76.

Otway, C., 1845: *Sketches in Erris and Tyrawley*. Dublin.

Quiggin, E.C., 1912: 'A poem by Gilbride MacNamee in praise of Cathal O'Conor', in O. Bergin and C. Marstrander (eds), *Miscellany presented to Kuno Meyer*. Halle. 167–77.

RCAHMS, 1988: *Argyll: an inventory of the monuments, vol. 6 – Mid Argyll and Cowal*. Edinburgh.

Record of monuments and places: County Mayo. (National Monuments and Historic Properties Service, 1996).

Royal Irish Academy, 1990: *Dictionary of the Irish language*. Dublin.

Sims-Williams, P., 1990: 'Some Celtic otherworld terms', in A.T.E. Matonis and D.F. Melia (eds), *Celtic language, Celtic culture: a festschrift for Eric P. Hamp*. Van Nuys. 57–81.

Simms, K., 1980: '"Gabh umad a Fheidhlimidh" – A fifteenth-century inauguration Ode?', *Ériu* 31, 132–45.

Simms, K., 1987: *From kings to warlords: the changing political structure of Gaelic Ireland in the later middle ages*. Woodbridge (reprint 2000).

Stokes, W., 1892: 'The battle of Mag Mucrime', *Revue Celtique* 13, 426–74.

Stokes, W.,1894: 'The prose tales in the Rennes Dindshenchas', *Revue Celtique* 15, 27–336, 418–84.

Stokes, W., 1895: 'The prose tales in the Rennes Dindshenchas', *Revue Celtique* 16, 31–83, 135–67, 269–310.

Stokes, W. and Windisch, E. (eds), 1900: 'Acallam na Senórach', in *Irische Texte*. Leipzig. 1–224.

Swift, C., 1996: 'Pagan monuments and Christian legal centres in early Meath', *Ríocht na Midhe* 9/2, 1–21.

Swift, C., 2000: '*Óenach Tailten*, the Blackwater Valley and the Uí Néill Kings of Tara', in A.P. Smyth (ed.), *Seanchas: studies in early and medieval Irish archaeology, history and literature in honour of Francis J. Byrne*. Dublin. 109–20.

Waddell, J., 1983: 'Rathcroghan – A royal site in Connacht', *Journal of Irish Archaeology* 1, 21–46.

Waddell, J., Barton, K. and Fenwick, J., forthcoming: *Rathcroghan: archaeological and geophysical survey in a ritual landscape*.

Wagner, H., 1970: 'Studies in the origins of early Celtic civilisation', *Zeitschrift für Celtische Philologie* 31, 1–58.

Wailes, B., 1982: 'The Irish "royal sites" in history and archaeology', *Cambridge Medieval Celtic Studies* 3, 1–23.

Warner, R.B., 1988: 'The archaeology of early historic Irish kingship', in S.T. Driscoll and M.R. Nieke (eds), *Power and politics in early medieval Britain and Ireland*. Edinburgh. 47–68.

Westropp, T.J., 1896–8: 'Magh Adhair, Co. Clare: The place of inauguration of the
    Dalcassian kings', *Proceedings of the Royal Irish Academy* **4C**, 55–60.
Williams, N.J.A., 1980: *The poems of Giolla Brighde Mac Con Midhe*, Irish Texts Society
    51. Dublin.
Woodward, A., 2000: *British barrows: a matter of life and death*. Stroud.

The archaeological context of assembly in early medieval Scotland – Scone and its comparanda

STEPHEN T. DRISCOLL

It is a common supposition that Scone is Scotland's Tara and that the inaugurations there of the kings of Scots were part of an ancient tradition that stretched back to Pictish times and beyond into prehistory. There is a certain geographical logic to this; Scone is in the centre of the east midlands of Scotland, in the heartlands of the southern Picts. There is, however, no contemporary evidence for the royal status of Scone prior to the foundation of the Gaelic kingdom of Alba in the later ninth century. This paper will investigate whether Scone is indeed ancient or a new creation of the ninth to tenth century by examining its historical and landscape context and by comparison with other places of assembly in Scotland, beginning with the hillforts of the Iron Age.

Given the symbolical significance of Scone, it has inspired a remarkably slim body of archaeological scholarship, a situation it shared with Tara until recently.[1] Fortunately the return of the Stone of Destiny in 1996 has stimulated scholarly interest in the stone and Scone.[2] Although nothing like as rich as Tara's, there is a well-developed historical literature relating to Scone, which takes as its centrepiece a medieval account of the Scone inauguration of the juvenile Alexander III in 1249.[3] In the past considerable attention has been focused on what appear to be archaic aspects of this ceremony. The poet, 'a certain highland Scot', who performed the critical duty of reading the royal genealogy at the culmination of the ceremony, has been regarded as the embodiment of an ancient, traditional practice, which lends the inauguration

---

1 Compare the level of detail in the recent Discovery Programme volume by Conor Newman 1997, with the brief entry in RCAHMS 1994, 124–7. 2 As will become plain, I owe a considerable debt to various contributors to the Historic Scotland and the Society of Antiquaries of Scotland symposium on the Stone of Destiny, which represents a major advance in our understanding of the stone and its historic setting. The collected papers, along with additional contributions, were published by Welander, Breeze and Clancy 2003. 3 The account is found in Walter Bower's *Scotichronicon* in Taylor et al. 1990 Vol. 5: Books IX and X, 290–7. The most often cited recent account of the inauguration is found in Duncan 1975, 552–8.

ceremony an air of archaism redolent of the Dark Ages.[4] It is likely that some
of the traditions were in fact ancient in the thirteenth century, but even so we
should be sensitive to how 'traditions' can be manipulated to make ceremonies
appear timeless and beyond challenge.

The earliest mention of Scone comes from the 'Chronicle of the Kings of
Alba', a late tenth-century compilation drawing upon contemporary annals,
which describes an assembly which took place in 906.[5]

> And in his sixth year King Constantine [II son of Áed] and Bishop
> Cellach vowed together with the Gaels [*Scotti*], to maintain the laws and
> disciplines of the faith and the rights of churches and of gospel-books on
> the Hill of Faith close to the royal *civitas* of Scone.[6]

This first reported event at Scone records the public declaration of a legal
decree. Although sometimes interpreted as part of a royal inauguration, this is
unlikely since Constantine had already been king for six years. In the opinion
of Thomas Charles-Edwards, what is recorded is the proclamation of an ecclesiastical law (*cáin*), an act which was a 'collaboration of king and people',[7] and
therefore must have been witnessed by an assembly of the Gaels. Scone may
have been chosen as a suitable site for this assembly because the ecclesiastic
content of the decree required that it take place at a church of some significance. In his translation Charles-Edwards chooses to leave *civitas* untranslated;
in contemporary Irish usage the word generally describes a church settlement,
but occasionally *civitas* describes an important royal site.[8] Both meanings are
possible here and it is widely believed that there was a religious community at
Scone prior to the foundation of an Augustinian abbey in *c*.1114–20 by
Alexander I. There is no evidence to support the traditional suggestion of a *céli
dé* foundation,[9] so the presence of an old and important church at Scone is

4 John Bannerman 1989, 120–49. 5 This chronicle has previously been referred to as The
Chronicle of the Kings of Scotland, The Old Scottish Chronicle and the Poppleton Manuscript.
The earliest reference to Scone has sometimes been confused with the location of a battle at
Caislen-Credi which took place in 729 (as I myself did in 1998c, 173), but as A.O. Anderson 1922
(vol. 1, 224, nn. 1 and 2) made clear, there are no good reasons to accept such an identification.
6 Translation of this passage is disputed – the original Latin is ambiguous. The translation
followed here comes from Charles-Edwards 1999, 60–1. It differs in a number of significant ways
from the more familiar translation of Anderson 1922 (repr. 1990), vol. I, 445. For the Latin text
see Anderson 1980, 251.   7 Crucially Charles-Edwards takes '*cum scotti*' to refer to participants
in the event rather than describing the laws enacted as in A.O. Anderson's phrase '... in
conformity with [the customs of] the Scots'.   8 Etchingham 1999, 93–9; Hudson 1998, 156, n.1.
9 Kenneth Veitch 2001 reassesses Alexander I's contribution as a patron of reformed monasticism and provides the best account of the founding of Scone. Veitch promotes the view that
eleventh-century Scone was principally a secular royal centre (2001, 138–9). Fawcett's 2002
account of the buildings of Scone is the most comprehensive survey of its architectural history.

indicated only by the presence of an *annat* place-name in the vicinity. The Annaty Burn is the major stream of the parish and runs through the centre of the village of New Scone, 1.5 km to the south of the abbey and old village of Scone. As Thomas Clancy has shown, *annat* names relate to a period prior to the development of a fully fledged parochial system and describe a 'mother church' with a superior relationship over other neighbouring churches.[10]

There is no indication that Scone was a royal residence in the Pictish period, indeed the admittedly sparse evidence points instead to Forteviot as the pre-eminent royal centre in this area until at least the mid-ninth century. Cinaed mac Alpíne died at the Pictish palace of Forteviot in 858 and did not become associated with Scone until long after his death.[11] The annalistic notice of the death of Donald, Cinead's brother and successor, in 862 at *Rathinveramon* ('rath at the mouth of the Almond'), appears to indicate the location of the nearest royal centre.[12] Rathinveralmond presumably refers to a reoccupation of the Roman fort at Bertha. Thus, in the absence of other evidence, it seems that there was no royal residence at Scone itself until much later after the foundation of the abbey.[13] Scone was a royal *thanage*, which indicates a royal interest in the lands of Scone after the endowment of the church, but on linguistic grounds this administrative construct is likely to have been coined in the tenth century or later.[14] This is reinforced by the name of the place which is not Pictish, but Gaelic.[15]

The earliest historical evidence for Scone suggests that it was not always a place of royal inauguration, while revealing the early presence of a significant church and hinting at royal estates. In trying to understand when and why Scone became the site of royal assemblies, the landscape is a valuable starting place. By comparing Scone's topographical and archaeological features with those seen at other Iron Age tribal centres, I hope to make clear that Scone marks a departure from tradition. This alone is a good reason to consider Scone's landscape setting.

A second reason for looking at the landscape is the growing realization that the inauguration rites at Scone were not static, but were modified as need dictated. This is particularly clear in the thirteenth century, but this innovative approach to royal ceremonial events arguably began in 906. The most obvious

There is no archaeological evidence for an early church, but as the RCAHMS 1994, 124–7 account makes plain, there has been little archaeological investigation. **10** Clancy 1995, 91–115. **11** Dauvit Broun 1999a, 172, notes that Cinead was known to contemporaries as *rex Pictorum* and argues that the link between Cinead and his Pictish predecessors was only broken in the mid- to late-tenth century. It is from that point that Scone was introduced into the account of how Cinead destroyed the Picts. **12** Anderson 1980, 267; MacDonald 1982. 51–3, n. 1 prefers to locate Rathinveralmond at Crammond Roman fort at the mouth of the Forth Almond, but this seems remote from the sphere of the other activity noted in the Chronicles of the Kings of Alba. **13** Anderson 1980, 274–5. **14** Barrow 1973, 1–68. **15** Taylor 1995, 426.

force for ceremonial development was the Church which assumed increasing importance as Scone became the site of royal assemblies at which the kings were publicly acknowledged by the political community of Alba. The physical characteristics of the site have the potential to reveal changes in the ceremonies which are hinted at in the documentary evidence and are revealed in the form and treatment of the Stone of Destiny.

As we will see, Scone is at the physical centre of the kingdom; but it is also the symbolic centre, and as such its landscape setting can be expected to be rich in historical associations. These meanings in the landscape contribute to shaping what Dauvit Broun has termed the 'Irish identity of the kingdom of the Scots'[16] and contribute to the notion of sovereignty that the kingship of Scone sustained. This identity was constructed in part from the raw material of the landscape and from human modification to it; moving through the landscape was one of the shared experiences of the assembly and arguably this experience of royal space was the most widely accessible expression of royal ideology.[17]

IRON AGE RELIGION AND PLACES OF ASSEMBLY

As an aid to thinking about how Scone came into being, it is valuable to consider earlier traditions of assembly in northern Britain and how prehistoric assembly-places relate to their wider archaeological and natural landscape. There is a disparate but extensive body of evidence that testifies to the special interest of prehistoric peoples in the high places of Scotland. This should not surprise us: given the natural topography, an interest in mountains or prominent hills is understandable. Despite numerous studies of individual hillforts, few modern archaeologists have examined the topic at a more general level. Since the mid-1960s there has been relatively little interest in Iron Age tribal assembly-places.[18] This reluctance is probably because the large-scale excavations which would be required to produce firm conclusions have never materialized. As a result the search for Iron Age tribal centres among the hillforts of northern Britain has more than an air of antiquarian speculation about it.

How are we to identify which, among so many, are the significant hills? Remarkably, modern place-names can provide one indication of Iron Age religious tribal affiliations. For instance, Schiehallion, a prominent conical

16 Broun 1999a and 1999b. 17 Alcock (2003, 154–7) has assessed the size of the armies, the largest of which might have consisted of six thousand men. This figure offers a crude guide to the potential scale of a Scottish royal assembly and suggests that the crowds at a royal assembly should be reckoned in the thousands. 18 Feachem 1966, 59–87.

peak in Perthshire, means '(fairy) hill of the Caledonians', and Loudon Hill (Ayrshire) probably comes from *Lugudunon*, 'fort of (the god) Lugos'. Dumyat, a hillfort that glowers over Stirling, is named for the Iron Age people of the Forth valley, the *Maeatae* and, perhaps most striking is the name Carn Smeart, a Sutherland hill, which retains the name of the *Smertae*, a people otherwise known only from Ptolemy's map.[19] The presence of ritual monuments like the prominent cairns which crown Tinto (Lanarkshire), Knockjargon (Ayrshire) and East Lomond (Fife) are further important clues, but the most important type of hilltop structures, earth- or stone-built hillforts, are too ubiquitous to be indicative without qualification.[20] No systematic methodology for the identification of religious, ethnic or political affiliation is proposed here: the task of analysing Scottish hillforts remains to be done. In what follows I merely note that specific peaks were the focal point for ritual activity in the Iron Age. Such hills may be identified by the presence of hilltop enclosures, cairns and pools, sometimes all of these together. Religious gatherings appear to have taken place both on the summits and at the feet of these hills. In a few instances such activities survived in some form late enough to be captured in the linguistic record, as in the case of Finavon (Angus), the vitrified hillfort whose name probably comes from *fid-nemed*, 'wood sanctuary'.[21] Alas, there is no equivalent to Ireland's Croagh Patrick, a mountain set in a wider prehistoric ritual landscape, which pilgrims still climb annually in veneration of St Patrick.

There are a number of instances where firm archaeological evidence indicates Iron Age religious activity associated with a particular hillfort. Possibly the most familiar example is Arthur's Seat, Edinburgh and the adjacent Duddingston Loch. The hill itself has no fewer than four prehistoric enclosures, none of which display particularly defensive qualities, while the loch has produced one of the most important Iron Age hoards in northern Britain.[22] The unique underground cistern at Burghead, the great Pictish promontory fort on the Moray coast, may have had a pagan cult purpose and the same may be true of certain wells or artificial pools, for instance at Finavon, Traprain Law, and, as we shall see, Moncrieffe Hill near Scone.[23]

One of the best-attested examples is the triple-peaked Eildon Hill, which overlooks the Tweed at Melrose. Its Iron Age importance is reflected in the siting at its foot of the Roman fort of Trimontium (modern Newstead). The

19 Watson 1926, 21, 199, 59, 17. 20 Apart from a trickle of radiocarbon dates from small-scale excavations there has been no work to replace Feacham's 1966 overview or his 1963 gazetteer. Euan MacKie's 1976 review of the vitrified forts, including his work at Finavon, was of value for this category of hillfort. However recent work on the Angus hillforts by Ian Ralston, Derek Alexander and colleagues demonstrates that a great deal remains still to be done before these monuments are fully understood. 21 Watson 1926, 250. 22 Stevenson 1949, 186–97; Piggott 1953, 68–123. 23 Edwards and Ralston 1978.

Tweed Valley probably experienced the longest period of Roman occupation of any place north of Hadrian's Wall. Trimontium was one of the most consistently manned of the northern forts and maintained its garrison even after the troop withdrawal associated with the abandonment of the Antonine Wall. On the highest of Eildon's three peaks stands one of the largest hillforts in Scotland, crowned with at least 296 house stances enclosed in ramparts over 2 km long. Small-scale excavation has produced radiocarbon evidence which suggests two main periods of activity in the late Bronze Age and again in the late Iron Age.[24] Roman pottery can be dated to the first, second and fourth centuries. Despite the almost urban density of house platforms on Eildon (for once Feachem's use of the term *oppidum* seems acceptable) the altitude makes it highly unlikely that this was a permanent year-round settlement.[25] In addition to the house platforms, the summit is crowned by a structure represented by postholes and enclosed by a circular bank, evidence of intense burning and Roman pottery. This structure has been interpreted as a Roman signal station, but a small temple seems equally plausible, even probable, given the location and the discoveries made in Trimontium below.

The excavations of the complex of forts, camps and annexes at Newstead produced some of the most remarkable evidence for cult activity anywhere in Roman Britain.[26] Despite primitive excavation techniques, over one hundred pits, shafts and wells between 1 and 13m deep were discovered. Many of these contained votive offerings, which, although they consist largely of Roman military material (altars, helmets and weapons), are conspicuously Celtic in their use of water-filled shafts.[27] The richness of the ritual expressions represented by the Newstead pits has recently been reaffirmed by the work of Simon Clark.[28]

It seems quite likely that the extraordinary Roman interest in the site was due in no small part to its religious importance. Indeed, the concentration of shafts and wells within the confines of the military precinct could be interpreted as evidence that the Roman authorities sought to control access to the sacred area. There can be little room for doubt that during the Iron Age the Eildons were the major focal point in the Tweed basin and the tribal gathering place of the Selgovae. This alone would explain Roman interest in managing the site.

The transformation from paganism to Christianity in Scotland is poorly understood, not least because of the apparent chronological gaps in the archaeological record. Moderate encouragement that such gaps are not fatal to an understanding of how Iron Age religious centres influenced the early medieval religious and political landscape comes from Fraser Hunter's comprehensive

24 Owen 1992, 21–72. 25 Ibid., 66. 26 Curle 1911. 27 Ross and Feachem 1976, 229–38.
28 Clarke 1994, 73–81; Clarke 1997, 72–82.

review of Iron Age hoarding, the main source of evidence for ritual activity in northern Britain. His work has revealed that the deposition of hoards was an episodic activity, going in and out of fashion over the centuries.[29] This means that the chronological gaps in deposition need not necessarily imply neglect, rather phases of alternative devotional activity. In this respect the presence at Newstead of Roman pottery dating from the fourth century makes it only a short chronological jump to the establishment of an important early Christian monastery at Old Melrose a mere kilometre away. Little is known about the origins of Old Melrose, apart from its subsequent association with St Cuthbert[30] who becomes the primary cult figure in the Borders in the Middle Ages.

Not too far from Melrose is another place where we may be able to identify an active Iron Age assembly-site at the dawn of the Christian period. Bede recounts the missionary triumph of Paulinus at Yeavering, where so great was the enthusiasm of the natives that he spent a continuous thirty-six days instructing and baptizing the crowd in the river Glen.[31] Understandably Bede does not dwell on the setting, apart from reporting that *Adgefrin* was the site of a royal vill. This may (or may not) be a deliberate attempt to downplay the reason for such a gathering in the first place. The place-name *Adgefrin* is a straightforward borrowing into English of British 'goat hill'. Towering over the site of the Northumbrian royal estate are the Cheviots and prominent among them is Yeavering Bell, which contains a hillfort of simiiar proportions to Eildon.[32] The great crowd which was conveniently on hand to be baptized may have gathered at Yeavering on some other more traditional business. Perhaps Paulinus was taking advantage of a long-standing assembly or religious festival.

These few examples will have to stand for the many (less spectacular) others which provide clear evidence that regional gatherings took place during the first millennium in Scotland at sites of heightened religious significance (fig. 3.1). Here we are not concerned with the theology of Iron Age religion, but with the key physical traits: striking topographic settings, frequently accompanied by prehistoric burial monuments, which juxtapose high places, often impressively enclosed, with wet places where offerings might be made.

A final example, which is of immediate relevance to Scone, is Moncrieffe Hill, which stands seven kilometres down the Tay at its confluence with the Earn (fig. 3.2). Moncrieffe Hill is the isolated southern tail of the Sidlaws, a range of hills running south-west through Strathmore. The Tay cuts through the Sidlaws to create impressive cliffs, which visually dominate the eastern end of Strathearn. It is above such cliffs that the main hillfort on Moncrieffe Hill

29 Hunter 1997, 108–33. **30** Thomas 1971, 35–6. **31** *HE* II, 14. **32** Hope-Taylor 1977, 6–7, 18–19.

Figure 3.1 View of Moncrieffe Hill from the south. The fort occupies the rounded summit above the tree line to the right of the craggs (photograph: author).

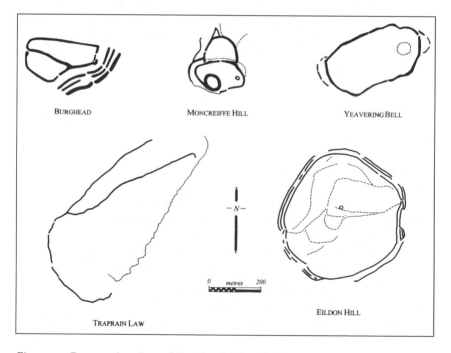

Figure 3.2 Comparative plans of Burghead, Moncrieffe Hill, Yeavering Bell, Traprain Law, Eildon Hill.

sits. It is a large multi-vallate hillfort, which shows evidence of several phases of construction. Within its main enclosure is an impressive well or artificial pool. The name Moncrieffe has been interpreted by W.J. Watson as meaning 'hill of the tree', which he believed signified a 'conspicuous ... possibly tribal tree'.[33] Such sacred trees are a familiar feature of Irish assembly-places and so its etymology strengthens the impression that Moncrieffe too was an assembly-place. Moncrieffe has been identified as the location of the Battle Mónad Croib in 729 (Annals of Ulster *s.a.* 728) between two rivals for the kingship of Fortriu. It has been suggested that the protagonists may have deliberately chosen to meet in battle at a place with appropriate associations of royal inauguration.

SCONE TOPOGRAPHY, TOPONYMICS AND TRADITION

Scone sits in the Gowrie between Strathearn, Strathmore and Fife and thus can be said to occupy the geographical centre of Alba, the tenth-century kingdom of the Scots (fig. 3.3). Scone and Perth lie a distance apart on opposite banks of the Tay at its upper tidal limit, its highest medieval navigable point and lowest crossing-place. Scone is on the east bank opposite the Tay's confluence with the river Almond. There is a ford at this point, which in Roman times was protected by a fort on the western side at Bertha. No traces remain of the Roman bridge which is presumed to have stood there. The tributaries of the Earn and the Almond swell the Tay from a stony highland river into a broad firth, thus Scone is not just at a crossroads, but is also a place which is easily connected to the wider world.

The focal point of Scone is not a mountain, but an artificial mound known as the 'Moot Hill'. The flat-topped, oval mound stands adjacent to Scone Palace, the nineteenth-century country seat of the Earl of Mansfield, which probably occupies the site of the guest house of the Augustinian abbey. The mound is located on the edge of a natural terrace 30m above the Tay. Although not especially high, the view from the mound was unobstructed to the west and north and before the Palace was built the Moot Hill enjoyed a magnificent panorama across the Tay, up Strathearn and to the Braes of Angus. The view embraces most of the kingdom of Fortriu and the Gowrie, although Moncrieffe is obscured by an intervening hill.

It is sometimes suggested that the Moot Hill has been shaped from a prehistoric barrow, and this is an intriguing possibility (fig. 3.4). The flat-topped mound stands about 4m above the surrounding ground, its sides sloping

33 Watson 1926, 401.

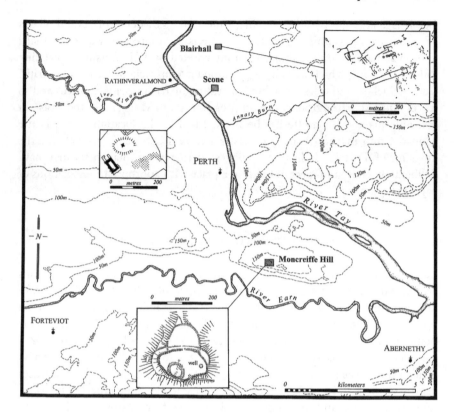

Figure 3.3 Map showing locations of Moncrieffe Hill, Scone and the Blairhall cropmarks. Inset detail of Scone shows positions of the Moot Hill, the palace and approximate location of the abbey.

outwards at 45 degrees. It has clearly been modified in modern times, apart from the nineteenth-century burial chapel on its summit (utilizing the remains of the post-medieval parish church) and the existing steps, it may also have been tidied up in the eighteenth century when the policies were laid out.[34]

The Moot Hill belongs to a large class of monuments in Britain that can be described as 'court hills'. G.W.S. Barrow has made a study of these in Scotland, with particular emphasis on the place-name evidence.[35] There has been no systematic study of the archaeology of these places. There are some clear examples of the appropriation of prehistoric burial monuments for this purpose,[36] but natural rock formations have also been used and in England it has long been known that court hills might be purpose built. Although there

34 Fawcett 2003, for fuller account of the later and post-medieval history of Scone. 35 Barrow 1992, 217–46. 36 Stevenson 1995, 197–236.

Figure 3.4 View of Moot Hill, Scone from the west with modern steps leading to the mausoleum showing through the snow (photograph: author).

are religious and indeed supernatural associations with such hills, the context to emphasize here is the legal one, because what little we know of the function of such places is bound up with legal performance. Early medieval law in Scotland, as elsewhere, was fundamentally a public matter, based ultimately on oral testimony and conducted in the open. One of the key places where this occurred was the court hill.

In terms of the setting and form of the Moot Hill, there are strong comparisons to be drawn with Irish medieval inauguration sites, as Elizabeth FitzPatrick has recognized.[37] In medieval Ireland inauguration most frequently took place on mounds which were generally flat-topped and rather less frequently were associated with stone structures, either a *leac* (flagstone) or a stone chair.[38] The preference for higher ground, and an association with special trees, are frequently embodied in the place-names. Horse symbolism figures prominently in Celtic royal mythology and this interest is often manifest in the racing of horses at royal assemblies.[39] Intriguingly, the Perth Hunt Races are held on a course set out on the low plain to the north of the Moot Hill. Whether the Scone Park racecourse occupies a more ancient course is unknown; the earliest records of the Perth races go back no further than 1613.[40]

---

37 FitzPatrick 1997, 76–7, 139–40. 38 Ibid., 50–78. 39 Binchy 1958, 113–38; Binchy 1970; Swift 2000, 24–50. 40 Martin 1999, 163–9.

A significant feature of the wider landscape of Scone is the exceptional concentration of prehistoric monuments on the first ridge to the north of the Moot Hill (fig. 3.5). The cropmarks at Blairhall consist of a barrow cemetery, cursus, and other features, which probably span the Neolithic to the Bronze Age. Although now ploughed flat, they would probably have still been partially upstanding and conspicuous in the tenth century. Apart from Kilmartin, it is difficult to think of a concentration in mainland Scotland that compares in scale, particularly when one embraces the cropmarks of Neolithic ritual monuments in the Huntingtower complex on the western approach to the crossing of the Tay.

There is a reasonable amount of evidence (and more will surely be found if people look) to show that there was renewed activity around ancient monuments in the early Middle Ages in Scotland. I have argued elsewhere that this appropriation and revitalization of ancient monuments played an active role in the development of kingship at this time.[41] Comparisons between Dunadd and Kilmartin in Argyll and Scone reveal a common interest in the deep, mythological past. In its political dimension this interest is comparable to the interest in deep genealogies and mytho-historical origin accounts which were used to legitimate volatile contemporary political realities. The notion of a deliberately archaising aspect to the ideology of kingship is one which Dauvit Broun has explored through the royal genealogies[42] and which is here echoed in the archaeology.

The inaugural ceremony at Scone, as understood from the earliest evidence, that is from the mid-thirteenth century, involved the incumbent sitting on the Stone of Destiny. The stone is an ancient object which has clearly gone through several physical changes conveying new ideological messages and fulfilling particular ceremonial requirements over time. The return of the Stone to Scotland in 1996 inspired the first substantial scholarly investigations since the nineteenth century.[43] Geological analysis reveals the Stone to be a block of sandstone quarried in the immediate Scone vicinity.[44] Visually it is unexciting, but on close inspection it is possible to see that it has been modified on many different occasions (fig. 3.6). Initially it was dressed in a Roman manner and has subsequently been modified by trimming, the cutting of grooves and the addition of iron rings. Presumably the rings allowed the Stone to be moved more easily from within Scone Abbey for use out in the open air. The final treatment of the stone, a smoothing off of the upper surface, presumably relates to its placement in the timber throne following its removal to Westminster Abbey by Edward I.[45]

---

41 Driscoll 1998a, 142–58.   42 Broun 1999a.   43 A symposium in 1997 spawned the publication of Welander, Breeze and Clancy 2003.   44 Fortey et al. 1998, 145–52.   45 Steane 1993, 38–40.

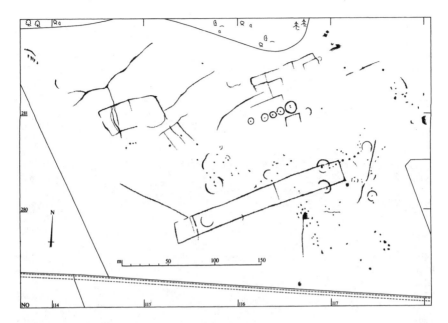

Figure 3.5 Transcription of Blairhall cropmarks (courtesy of Royal Commission on the Ancient and Historical Monuments of Scotland).

Unfortunately the modifications to the Stone are too prosaic to reveal the associations through which it acquired its royal aura. From the many possible explanations for the observations about its physical condition, two alternative origins have been suggested.[46] One possibility is that the stone was cut from an natural outcrop which had served as a *leac*. This would be consistent with a belief that Scone was heir to royal rituals, perhaps akin to the inauguration traditions of the Scots in Dál Ríada as reflected in the carvings at Dunadd which point to a standing posture.[47] The transformation from *leac* into a seat would also accord with FitzPatrick's evidence for an evolution from an initial standing posture on a *leac* (flagstone) to a sitting posture on a block or chair in Ireland.[48]

The alternative is that stone was originally quarried for use in a building and was later selected to be sat upon. Stone buildings are known from both of the Roman forts on the Tay (Bertha and Carpow) and stone could also have been used in a church, indeed a handy ashlar block could easily have found its way from one of these Roman forts into the nearby royal churches at Abernethy and Scone. If Scone as a royal centre is a construct of the tenth

46 Campbell 2003. 47 Campbell 2003; Lane and Campbell 2000, 247–9. 48 FitzPatrick 1997, FitzPatrick 2003.

Figure 3.6 The Stone of Destiny (courtesy of Historic Scotland, crown copyright).

century, then logically there can have been no ancient *leac*. On balance it seems more likely that the Stone was taken from a structure with significant royal attributes and that it was always intended to serve as a royal seat, in the manner of an Imperial throne.

The rings set into the Stone may be more than just convenient handles. In ideological terms the portability of the stone was one of its most important properties, since although in fact the Stone is local, medieval tradition claimed it had been transported to Scone from the ancestral centre at Tara by the incoming Scots.[49] Portability was a handy attribute: it allowed rulers to draw on existing symbols of Gaelic royal legitimacy which proved particularly valuable as the ruling dynasty of what had become Alba ceased to think of itself as Pictish and began to regard itself as Gaelic.

CEREMONIAL CONTINUITY AND INNOVATION

The celebrated inauguration of the seven year-old Alexander III in 1249 has been regarded as providing a window on Dark Age ceremony.[50] The accounts of this event which have found their way into various medieval histories (Melrose Chronicle, Fordun and Bower) have recently been reassessed by Dauvit Broun.[51] He has reconstructed an original account, composed before the end of the thirteenth century, which can be further illuminated by two thirteenth-century seals: Alexander's own seal and that of Scone Abbey. The latter depicts the inauguration ceremony itself; both show the king enthroned.[52] The seals are more or less contemporary representations, unlike the more famous image from Bower's *Scotichronicon* which was executed in the 1440s[53] but which, nevertheless, contributes to the interpretation of the tiny figures on the Scone Abbey seal.

In Broun's reconstruction of the ceremony of 1249, the Church has only a background role. The principal actors are the two leading magnates of the kingdom, the Mormaers (Earls) of Fife and Strathearn, who place Alexander on the royal seat adorned with silk cloths. Only then was Alexander consecrated by the bishop of St Andrews. Finally, the royal poet reads out the king's genealogy in the 'mother tongue' (i.e. in Gaelic) back to the dynasty's Irish progenitor. Significantly the ceremony is said to have been conducted near to

49 Broun 2003. 50 Bannerman 1989. 51 Broun 2003. 52 Bannerman 1989; Duncan 1975, 552–8; Duncan 2002. 53 Chapter 10 of the Corpus Christi College's *Scotichronicon* (Cambridge MS 171, fo. 206) begins with a drawing of Alexander III seated between two figures (the Mormaers of Fife and Strathearn) upon or before a flat-topped mound upon which stands a cross. In the foreground the king's poet recites his ancestry. Reproduced as Figure 1 in Watt 1987 and discussed in detail in notes 435–441.

a cross *outside* the east end of the church. Although the precise location of the Abbey is not known to this day, the Moot Hill stands to the north-west of the presumed site. Broun regards this use of the church, although no more than a backdrop, and the Episcopal consecration, as innovations of the thirteenth century and sees in them evidence of the Scots' frustrated desire to follow the established practice of anointing and crowning the king as enjoyed by other sovereign nations. Papal refusal of permission to anoint was no obstacle to the seal cutter, however, who shows Alexander looking every bit the medieval European king. Probably the best sense of what a Scone assembly might have been like comes from an even later account, although again found in Bower.[54] The coronation of Robert III took place at Scone in August 1390 and the festivities around the ceremony lasted for several days:

> everyone passed these days of festival most pleasantly. So great was the crowd from every part of the kingdom that gathered for the king's coronation that all the standing crops of the monastery ... and in other places ... round about were ruined by the horses.[55]

The point of this story (and the one that follows in *Scotichronicon*) is to emphasize the king's sound conscience and love of justice. After being shamed by sarcastic political theatrics, Robert III agrees to hear the case relating to the damaged crops and in the end judges himself responsible for the damage, since the crowds were drawn to celebrate his inauguration. The tone of the story suggests that the gathering was somewhat unruly and playful, but also seems to indicate that king took care of royal business there, including the settling of legal disputes. The rule of law is thus an important element of the portrait of good royal practice being painted here. In the fifteenth century Scone was understood as a place where people came to acclaim their king, to have some fun and to settle disputes. This legal dimension returns us to the theme of the earliest reference to Scone, as a platform for the promulgation of legal judgment and decree. Possibly the most striking observations to emerge from this reconsideration of the Scone inauguration ceremony concern the dynamic that existed between a desire to appeal to tradition and antiquity and at the same time a willingness to introduce new practices as circumstance required.

AN EARLY MEDIEVAL CONTEXT: POST-VIKING POWER CENTRES

Apart from the Stone of Destiny, the most distinctive feature at Scone is the Moot Hill. We are beginning to appreciate that similar flat-topped mounds

54 Watt 1987, 3–7; McGavin 1995, 144–58. 55 Watt 1987, 3.

have a wide currency in what may be termed the Irish Sea province. Moreover, they seem to appear at about the same time: towards the end of the Viking Age.

Given that other contributors are addressing the Irish and Manx material, we can focus on one particular example which helps to illuminate Scone. Until 1851 a great flat-topped, stepped mound, known as the Doomster Hill, stood at Govan now subsumed within the city of Glasgow (fig. 3.7).[56] Govan did not emerge as the pre-eminent royal centre in the region until after the sack of Dumbarton Rock by Dublin Vikings in 870. It is about this time that an extraordinary body of sculpture began to accumulate there including some exceptional hogback burial monuments, which exhibit a strong Norse influence.[57] It is possible to reconstruct a royal complex at Govan which was at the heart of the tenth- and eleventh-century kingdom of the Strathclyde Britons. Ironically we can see the geography of this complex more clearly in post-industrial Govan than we can at rural Scone. The Doomster Hill and the church with its royal cemetery are in Govan proper, on the south bank of the Clyde, opposite the confluence of the Kelvin. Across the river, but still within the medieval parish and connected by a ford, was the royal estate of Partick. My excavations have provided radiocarbon dates that show that a Christian cemetery was in existence at the site by the fifth to sixth century, and that the pear-shaped plan of the modern churchyard derives from a bank and ditch constructed no later than the eighth to ninth century.[58] The existing church is the third post-Reformation building on the spot, but evidence for an early medieval church was also found partially underlying them. The excavations also revealed a road running from the church to the Doomster Hill, a connection fossilized in the street plan as Pearce Lane and, of course, paralleled at Tynwald. There is no close dating evidence for the construction of the mound, but a date in the tenth century would seem reasonable given the rest of this evidence.

On the model of Govan we might expect that the Moot Hill at Scone had been in some way linked to the Abbey. It is interesting that the position of Rathinveralmond, vis-à-vis Scone is analogous to the relative position of Partick, although prudence cautions us from pressing this physical comparison too far, especially as there is no evidence to suggest that Scone had a royal cemetery. None the less, we are entitled to imagine that Scone, like Govan, consisted of a complex of structures which were designed to create an exceptional stage for royal ceremonies.

56 For further detail see Driscoll 1998b, 95–114. 57 Ritchie 1994. 58 For the radiocarbon dates and a fuller summary of the archaeological evidence see Driscoll 2003.

Figure 3.7 View of Govan in 1758 from the north side of the Clyde by Robert Paul. The Doomster Hill stands to the left of the ferry landing and Govan Old parish church is mostly hidden by the trees on the right (copyright Glasgow City Libraries).

CONCLUSIONS

The Moot Hill at Scone is not without its own mythology. Its *dindshenchas* (place-name lore) on first glance seems modern and trivial. The Moot Hill is also known as 'Boot Hill', and is so labelled on Ordnance Survey maps. The name is said to come from the mound being made up of soil emptied from the boots of the king's loyal supporters and is thus composed of earth from all parts of Scotland. This account is of dubious antiquity, but nevertheless alerts us to the symbolic potential created by the physical structures used in royal inaugurations. The raising of Boot Hill provides a physical metaphor for the popular approval of legitimate rule and support for the rule of law. The reference to footwear is also intriguing, as the single shoe was a device widely associated with Irish inauguration ceremonies.

It would appear that in Pictish times the focus of political authority in Strathearn was Moncrieffe Hill, which, as we have seen is a complex late Iron Age hillfort with a well and tribal tree. In its final stages Moncrieffe acquired a massive dun (dry-stone fortified dwelling) which would have been an appropriate royal residence during ceremonial occasions or assemblies. Scone on the other hand has no Pictish history. Instead its development can be linked to the appearance of new Gaelic political forces following the ninth-century depredations of the Vikings. There is an apparent shift in the monumental setting away from the ancient hillfort of Moncrieffe, which may be seen as an effort to create a new ideological landscape. A landscape that has its direct analogue in the genealogical constructs of the tenth to eleventh century, which sought to connect the dynasty of Cinead mac Alpíne to Ireland. Some of the key features of Scone resemble those at Govan and also reflect developments seen at other places in the medieval Celtic world. The use of monuments such as the Moot Hill and the increasingly closer involvement of the Church are ceremonial innovations, significant signals about the sort of sovereignty they sustained.

At Scone the early formation of a European state can be read in the physical layout. The prehistoric monuments provide an ancestral backdrop, but in the foreground are structures that symbolize the rule of law, through the Moot Hill with its repository of supernatural connotations, and administrative government, in the form of a royal monastery where the clerics were also clerks. Scone also makes it clear that sovereignty is not a static concept. By the thirteenth century the church was architecturally more prominent and played a more central ceremonial role. The political value of open-air public acclamation, symbolized by the clashing of 'melodious shields'[59], had been replaced by more conventional European ceremonies.

In one respect Scone is like Tara as it was ten years ago: it is clear that much of our understanding of Scone is based upon comparative guesswork. Until there is more systematic fieldwork, comparable to the Discovery Programme's work at Tara, Scone will remain a largely mythological place.[60]

ABBREVIATIONS

HE   Bede, *A history of the English church and people*, see Sherley-Price, L. (trans) 1995. London.

RCAHMS   Royal Commission on the Ancient and Historical Monuments of Scotland.

59 As it is called in the eleventh-century poem *The Prophecy of Berchan*. See Duncan 1975, 115 and Anderson 1922, I 519.   **60** This paper has benefited from discussions with many colleagues at the Oxford symposium and subsequently at the First Millennia Research Group (Edinburgh) and a Glasgow-Strathclyde School of Scottish Studies seminar. My interest in Scone was rekindled by Sally Foster's invitation to contribute to her 1998 collection on the St Andrews Sarcophagus, and has been fuelled in part by correspondence with Mark Hall (Perth Museum). My greatest intellectual debt in preparing this paper for publication is once again to Katherine Forsyth. Thank you all.

REFERENCES

Alcock, L., 2003: *Kings and warriors, craftsmen and priests in Northern Britain AD 550–850*. Edinburgh.

Alexander, D. with Ralston, I.B.M., 1999: 'Survey work on Turin Hill, Angus', *Tayside and Fife Archaeological Journal* 5, 36–49.

Anderson, A.O., 1922: *Early sources of Scottish history A.D. 500–1286*. Edinburgh (reprint Stamford 1990).

Anderson, M.O., 1980: *Kings and kingship in early Scotland*. Edinburgh.

Bannerman, J., 1989: 'The King's poet and the inauguration of Alexander III', *Scottish Historical Review* 68, 120–49.

Barrow, G.W.S., 1973: 'Prefeudal shires and thanes', in G.W.S. Barrow, *The kingdom of the Scots*. London. 1–68.

Barrow, G.W.S., 1992: 'Popular courts', in G.W.S. Barrow, *Scotland and its neighbours in the middle ages*. London. 217–46.

Binchy, D., 1958: 'The fair of Tailtiu and the feast of Tara', *Eiru* 18, 113–38.

Binchy, D., 1970: *Celtic and Anglo-Saxon kingship*. Oxford.

Broun, D., 1999a: *The Irish identity of the kingdom of the Scots in the twelfth and thirteenth centuries*. Woodbridge.

Broun, D., 1999b: 'Dunkeld and the origins of Scottish identity', in D. Broun and T.O. Clancy (eds), *Spes Scotorum: hope of Scots: Saint Columba, Iona and Scotland*. Edinburgh. 95–114.

Broun, D., 2003: 'The origins of the stone of Scone as a national icon', in Welander et al., *The Stone of Destiny*, 183–98.

Campbell, E., 2002: 'Royal inauguration in Dál Ríata and the Stone of Destiny', in Welander et al., *The Stone of Destiny*, 43–60.

Charles-Edwards, T.M., 1999: *The early medieval Gaelic lawyer*, Quiggin Pamphlet No. 4. Cambridge.

Clancy, T.O., 1995: 'Annat place-names in Scotland and the origins of the Parish', *Innes Review* 46, 91–115.

Clarke, S., 1994: 'Abandonment, rubbish disposal and "special" deposits at Newstead', in S. Cottam, S. Scott and J. Taylor (eds), *Proceedings of the Fourth Annual Theoretical Roman Archaeology Conference*. Oxford. 73–81.

Clarke, S., 1997: 'A quantitative analysis of the finds from the Roman fort at Newstead – some preliminary findings', in K. Meadows, C. Lemke and J. Heron (eds), *Proceedings of the Sixth Annual Theoretical Roman Archaeology Conference*. Oxford. 72–82.

Curle, J., 1911: A *Roman frontier post and its people: the fort at Newstead*. Glasgow.

Driscoll, S.T., 1998a: 'Picts and prehistory: cultural resource management in early medieval Scotland', *World Archaeology* 30 (1), 142–58.

Driscoll, S.T., 1998b: 'Church archaeology in Glasgow and the kingdom of Strathclyde', *Innes Review* 49, 95–114.

Driscoll, S.T., 1998c: 'Political discourse and the growth of Christian ceremonialism in Pictland: the place of the St Andrews sarcophagus', in S. Foster (ed.), *The St Andrews sarcophagus: a Pictish masterpiece and its international connections*. Dublin. 168–78.

Driscoll, S.T., 2003: 'Govan: an early medieval royal centre on the Clyde', in Welander et al., *The Stone of Destiny*, 77–84.

Duncan, A.M.M., 1975: *Scotland: the making of the kingdom*. Edinburgh.

Duncan, A.M.M., 2003: 'Before coronation: making a king at Scone in the thirteenth century', in Welander et al., *The Stone of Destiny*, 139–68.

Edwards, K. and Ralston, I., 1978: 'New dating and environmental evidence from Burghead Fort, Moray', *Proceedings of the Society of Antiquaries of Scotland* **109**, 202–10.

Etchingham, C., 1999: *Church organisation in Ireland AD 650 to 1000*. Maynooth.

Fawcett, R., 2003: 'The buildings of Scone abbey', in Welander et al., *The Stone of Destiny*, 169–81.

Feacham, R., 1963: *Guide to prehistoric Scotland*. London.

Feachem, R., 1966: 'The hill-forts of Northern Britain', in A.L.F. Rivet (ed.), *The Iron Age in northern Britain*. Edinburgh. 59–87.

FitzPatrick, E., 1997: *The practice and siting of royal inauguration in medieval Ireland*. Unpublished PhD thesis, Trinity College Dublin.

FitzPatrick, E., 2003: 'Some Ulster inauguration chairs', in Welander et al., *The Stone of Destiny*, 107–22.

Fortey, N.J. et al., 1998: 'A Geological Perspective on the Stone of Destiny', *Scottish Journal of Geology* **34 (2)**, 145–52.

Foster, S. (ed.), 1998: *The St Andrews sarcophagus: a Pictish masterpiece and its international connections*. Dublin.

Hope-Taylor, B., 1977: *Yeavering: an Anglo-British centre of early Northumbria*. London.

Hudson, B., 1998: 'The Scottish Chronicle', *Scottish Historical Review* **72**, 129–61.

Hunter, F., 1997: 'Iron Age hoarding in Scotland and Northern England', in A. Gwilt and C. Haselgrove (eds), *Reconstructing Iron Age societies*. Oxford. 108–33.

Lane, A. and Campbell, E., 2000: *Dunadd: An early Dalriadic capital*. Oxford.

MacDonald, A., 1982: 'Caiseal, Dun, Lios and Rath in Scotland II', *Bulletin of the Ulster Place-Name Society* (ser. 2) **4**, 32–57.

MacKie, E., 1976: 'The vitrified forts of Scotland', in D.W. Harding (ed.), *Hillforts and later prehistoric earthworks in Britain and Ireland*. London. 205–36.

McGavin, J. J., 1995: 'Robert III's "Rough Music": charivari and diplomacy in a medieval Scottish court', *Scottish Historical Review* **74**, 144–58.

Martin, P., 1999: 'An early 19th century racecourse stand at Uthrogle, near Cupar, Fife', *Tayside and Fife Archaeological Journal* **5**, 163–9.

Newman, C., 1997: *Tara: an archaeological survey*. Dublin.

Owen, O., 1992: 'Eildon Hill North', in J.S. Rideout, O.A. Owen and E. Halpin (eds), *Hillforts in southern Scotland*. Edinburgh. 21–72.

Piggott, S., 1953: 'Three metalwork hoards from southern Scotland', *Proceedings of the Society of Antiquaries of Scotland* **87**, 68–123.

RCAHMS 1994: *South-east Perth: an archaeological landscape*. Edinburgh.

Ritchie, A. (ed.), 1994: *Govan and its early medieval sculpture*. Stroud.

Ross, A. and Feachem, R., 1976: 'Ritual rubbish? The Newstead pits', in J.V.S. Megaw (ed.), *To illustrate the monuments*. London. 229–38.

Steane, J., 1993: *The archaeology of the medieval English monarchy*. London.

Stevenson, R.B.K., 1949: 'The nuclear fort of Dalmahoy and other Dark Age capitals', *Proceedings of the Society of Antiquaries of Scotland* 83, 186–97.

Stevenson, S., 1995: 'Excavation of a kerbed cairn at Beechhill House, Coupar Angus, Perthshire', *Proceedings of the Society of Antiquaries of Scotland* 125, 197–236.

Swift, K., 2000: 'The local context of *Óenach Tailten*', *Ríocht na Midhe* 11, 24–50.

Taylor, S., 1995: 'Settlement-names of Fife'. Unpublished PhD thesis, University of St Andrews.

Taylor, S., Watt, D.E.R. and Scott, B. (eds), 1990: *Scotichronicon* (vol. 5, books IX and X). Aberdeen.

Thomas, C., 1971: *The early Christian archaeology of North Britain*. Glasgow.

Veitch, K., 2001: '"Replanting paradise": Alexander I and the reform of religious life in Scotland', *Innes Review* 52, 136–66.

Watson, W.J., 1926: *Celtic place-names of Scotland*. Edinburgh.

Watt, D.E.R. (ed.), 1987: *Scotichronicon* (vol. 8, books XV and XVI). Aberdeen.

Welander, R., Breeze, D. and Clancy, T.O. (eds) 2003: *The Stone of Destiny: artefact and icon*. Edinburgh.

Gorsedd, *dadl*, and *llys*: assemblies and courts in medieval Wales

T.M. CHARLES-EDWARDS

This short contribution has a limited purpose: to make available to English readers some brilliant work by the leading student of medieval Welsh literature in the first half of the twentieth century, Sir Ifor Williams, and to add some further reflections on the legal material. There is a desperate need for further work on Welsh place-names and, *via* such names, on the archaeology of assembly sites; but here I shall confine myself to words and to texts. So far as the words are concerned, I shall look at three: *gorsedd*, *llys*, and *dadl*; as for the texts, my main hunting ground will be the Welsh laws of the twelfth and thirteenth centuries, although I shall stray sometimes into later legal texts and also into non-legal texts.

LLYS

In 1930 Ifor Williams, Professor of Welsh at Bangor, brought out an edition of the best-known work of medieval Welsh prose literature, 'The Four Branches of the Mabinogi', *Pedeir Keinc y Mabinogi*.[1] These are four linked tales of uncertain date; my own preference is for the late-eleventh or early-twelfth century, but some scholars are either agnostic or prefer a later date.[2] All four tales concern themselves, to a greater or lesser extent, with royal courts and their rulers; they also espouse a particular courtly ethic.[3] In the first and third of the Four Branches the court in question is that of Arberth, a 'chief court' of the ruler of Dyfed, namely Pembrokeshire and western Carmarthenshire.[4]

---

1 Williams 1930. English-language editions exist of the first two branches: Thomson 1957; Thomson 1961. The Fourth Branch has recently been edited by I. Hughes: Hughes 2000. Convenient translations include Jones and Jones 1949, and Gantz 1976. 2 Sims-Williams 1991; Charles-Edwards 1970. 3 Phillips 2000 concentrates mainly on *Chwedyl Gereint vab Erbin*, one of the Welsh Romances, but note 356–7. 4 National Grid Reference SN108144 (church); the English form Narberth is from *yn Arberth* 'in Arberth'. The implication of the passage is that a Welsh king might have more than one 'chief court'.

The term used by these tales for 'court' is *llys*, also well-attested in the twelfth-and thirteenth-century lawbooks. It had, at that period, a double meaning: for a complex of buildings built to receive the king and his entourage as they made their circuit round the kingdom and also for the royal entourage itself. *Llys* was both people and place.[5]

A crucial thing to appreciate at the outset is that Middle Welsh had no term that corresponded to modern English 'court'.[6] The English term ties together something political (the royal court) with something which is part of a judicial organization; the latter – the judicial court as I shall term it – has, itself, a double meaning, for the people who constitute the court and the building in which a case is heard (No. 1 Court in the Old Bailey, for example). The closest thing in Welsh is *llys*, the term we have already met, itself with its own double meaning; but it had a quite different background, being cognate with Old Irish *less*, Modern Irish *lios*, roughly 'an enclosed space embracing domestic and agricultural buildings', widely attested in names for 'ring-forts' in the northern half of Ireland.[7] Moreover, it would be quite wrong to suppose that a medieval Welsh judicial court needed a building such as the Old Bailey in which to conduct its proceedings. *Llys* began as an enclosed complex of buildings; it acquired the sense of a royal entourage only secondarily. That entourage included the judge of the court, *ynad llys*, but that still did not make the *llys* into a judicial court rather than a set of buildings designed to receive the king and his companions.

The term *llys*, therefore, can rapidly be dismissed. What makes one think that it might have been used in the thirteenth century for a court of law as well as a royal court is that legal disputes may be heard at the *llys* of the commote or *cantref*. Yet such a *llys* was the royal centre of an administrative district. It just happened to be the case that cases might be heard at such a centre; it was not *per se* a judicial forum. In some parts of Wales there was a judge of a commote, and he is likely often to have judged cases in the vicinity of the *llys*, but the *llys* as such was not his court. When the term *llys* takes on a somewhat more judicial aspect in late-medieval texts that may be under the influence of Latin *curia*.

GORSEDD

In the first and third Branches a major role was performed, in addition to the *llys* at Arberth, by the *Gorsedd Arberth*. Ifor Williams's note on *gorsedd* is what provides my starting-point.[8] He notes that *gorsedd* may be translated 'mound',

---

5 Jones 2000. 6 Stephenson 1980 is helpful on record sources for Welsh legal procedure.
7 Flanagan 1980–1. 8 Williams 1930, 120–1, on p. 9, l. 3 of the text.

'tumulus', or 'barrow', and points, first, to a collection of place-names from Flintshire which include the term;[9] secondly, he cites examples in the laws where it has been translated 'court' or 'session'; and, thirdly, he invokes parallels such as the Tynwald on the Isle of Man, as well as Mawer's *Place-names and history* on open-air courts and assemblies situated at places chosen 'because of the presence of some ancient barrow, some cross or stone, some sacred object hallowed by time and superstition'. Williams also cited Mawer on the role of Old English *hlāw* and *beorg* as well as Old Norse *haugr* in the names of assembly-places. This explains, concluded Ifor Williams, the double meaning of *gorsedd*: on the one hand 'mound, barrow' and, on the other, 'court, judicial assembly'.

In the last paragraph of his note, however, Williams introduced another comparison, this time not with Germanic counterparts but with Irish *síd*, sometimes translated 'elf-mound' (in anglicized place-names often 'Fairymount'). The reason was that the *gorsedd* of the Four Branches was 'a centre of magic'. In early Irish literature such otherworld mounds were perceived as the residences of pre-Christian deities. They might be artificial mounds or natural eminences; and the same is true of Welsh *gorsedd*.[10] This Irish comparison introduced a certain tension into Williams's account of *gorsedd*: a tension between comparing the Welsh term with such historical institutions as the Tynwald and Anglo-Saxon assemblies and comparing it with Irish elf-mounds. Yet the Irish parallel does not exclude the earlier comparison with English mounds used as assembly places, since, in Ireland, a site graced with prehistoric mounds might be used as a place of assembly while at the same time being portrayed as a residence of pre-Christian gods.[11] This-worldliness and other-worldliness were, in this instance, intertwined. However, his Irish comparison would have had a more historical and less mythological slant if he had cited the Irish cognate of *gorsedd*, namely *forad*, discussed above.[12]

Before beginning a more detailed examination of the legal evidence, it will be helpful to take a quick look at the *Gorsedd Arberth*. It is introduced towards the beginning of the second sub-tale of *Pwyll Pendefig Dyfed*, namely the first of the Four Branches. This sub-tale was the story of how Pwyll, lord of Dyfed, won his bride, Rhiannon daughter of Efeydd Hen. It began with an after-dinner stroll from the *llys* at Arberth to 'the top of a *gorsedd* which was adjacent

---

9 Ifor Williams cites the examples of *gorsedd* standing for a mound in Hemp 1921–2. A more recent publication is Owen 1994, index p. 313. 10 For a natural eminence see Owen 1994, 260. 11 A good example is Rathcroghan, Old Irish Cruachain, in Co. Roscommon, well known as a site where this world and the otherworld might meet, as in the Old Irish saga *Echtra Nerai* (Meyer 1889; Meyer 1890), but also used as the site for assemblies (e.g. the Annals of Ulster *s.a.* 783, 814 (corrected dates): Mac Airt and Mac Niocaill 1983). 12 FitzPatrick, Warner this volume.

to the court; it was called *Gorsedd Arberth*'.[13] Pwyll was warned by an unnamed person from the *llys* that it was a peculiar quality of the *gorsedd* that 'whatever aristocrat should sit on it would not leave it without one of two things: either a wound or losses or else he would see some marvel'. Pwyll was not put off and went to the top of the *gorsedd* and sat there. It was while they were sitting that they saw Rhiannon riding past on her horse – and those who wish to know why a young woman ambling past a mound on her horse might count as a marvel may read the tale for themselves. It is noticeable, however, that, in full accordance with the etymological meaning of *gorsedd* – 'over-seat' – there is much talk in this passage of sitting upon the *gorsedd* and using it as a vantage-point. Apart from that, all we need to know is that scholars have discerned extra marvels for themselves, not from Gorsedd Arberth but from their armchairs. One or two of these are so close to the surface of the story that they half appear even on a first reading and are likely to have been at least as apparent to a medieval audience; others, however, require the black arts of the philologist and the student of comparative Celtic literature. For example, the name of the horsewoman, Rhiannon, is derived from a British *rīgantonā*, generally translated 'divine queen'.[14] It thus becomes entirely possible to see Rhiannon as a sovereignty goddess; the Third Branch opens with a dialogue in which Pryderi, Pwyll's son and heir, offers the hand of his mother to Manawydan, saying: 'The seven cantreds of Dyfed were left to me, and Rhiannon my mother is there. I shall give her to you, and possession of the seven cantreds with her. And although the title of the realm may be mine, its enjoyment shall be yours and Rhiannon's'.[15] Gorsedd Arberth only makes its appearance in passages which have to do with the marriage of Pwyll, lord of Dyfed, and the 'Divine Queen', whether as prelude or as consequence, right up to the final section of the Third Branch, when Manawydan takes the thievish mouse he has captured to Gorsedd Arberth and sets up a gallows on the very summit. We know next to nothing about Welsh royal inaugurations, but if, in Dyfed, they had involved Gorsedd Arberth, there would have been a conjunction of ritual and site similar to other cases discussed in this volume; unfortunately, in the Welsh case, this remains wholly speculative.[16]

   From this proposed execution of a thief, fictional but very much in accordance with the law, we may turn to the laws themselves. A preliminary point to bear in mind is that legal proceedings were different in South Wales, on the one hand, and in Gwynedd and parts of Powys on the other. The south was the home of the communal court, in which men might be judges 'by privilege of

13 Williams 1930, 9.   14 The suffix *–on–* also appears in *Matrona*, 'Mother Goddess', *Maponos* (Welsh Mabon), 'Son–God', and *Epona*, 'Horse Goddess'.   15 Williams 1930, 49–50. 16 However, Andrews shows from the poetry of the period that ideas of kingship as a marriage between king and country were still current in the thirteenth century: Andrews 1976–8.

land' and recourse was often had to 'the elders of the country'.[17] As far as we can tell, a northerner might pursue a case arising from a broken contract by going to the judge's house, where most of the proceedings might take place.[18] Such a case is always perceived at this period as taking place 'before the judge' rather than in some place set aside for hearing legal cases.[19] If the case was about land, however, it was expected to be heard on the land in dispute:[20]

> And at that adjudged date it is proper for all to come to the land, both them and their aid. And then it is proper to make two parties and to sit legally. This is how they sit legally: the King, or the man who is in his place, sits with his back to the sun or the weather (lest the weather should disturb his face), with the court justice or the commote justice (whichever is the senior) sitting in front of him, with the other justice or justices who may be present on his left hand, and the priest (if any) or priests on his right hand; and next to the King his two elders, with his goodmen[21] from there on, on either side of him. From there a gangway for the justices, facing them, for them to proceed to their judgement-seat.

This description of the arrangement of 'the parties' in dispute and those who will hear the case goes on until it is clarified by a diagram. This is repeated, with modifications, in other texts and is fundamental to how the Welsh lawyers saw this special form of judicial assembly (the arrows mark the direction in which people were facing.[22]

↓ Noble	Noble	Elder	King	Elder	Noble	Noble ↓
↓		Priest(s)	senior Judge	junior Judge(s)		↓
↑ Assistant	Defendant	Advocate		Advocate	Claimant	Assistant ↑
↑ Serjeant				Serjeant		↑

17 Davies 1986. 18 *AL* XIV. xlv. 1 (from a fourteenth–century MS). 19 A case concerning contracts and suretyship was heard 'before the two knees of a judge', namely before a judge who was himself seated: *Ior*, §§ 61/2, 67/2. Cf. the picture of the court judge, seated and in action: Huws 1988, 2. 20 Jenkins 1986, 84–5. This is a translation of part of *Ior*, § 73, an early thirteenth-century text. 21 Namely, nobles. 22 Note, however, that the diagram as it appears in MS *B*, the base MS used by Wiliam in his edition (*Ior*, § 72), was a later scribe's addition in a gap which had been left by the first scribe. It was not consistent with the rules given in the text, which D. Jenkins has used to correct the diagram given in *Law Texts from Medieval Wales*: Jenkins 1986, 85 (and see note on 85. 10–16). The (contemporary) diagram in MS *A* can be seen in Gwenogvryn Evans, 1909; it is accurate except that the back row is one position too far to the left. This is correct in *E*, another thirteenth-century MS, which, however, gets the positions of 'the parties' quite wrong. The remaining thirteenth-century MS (*C*) is defective at this point and does not contain the diagram.

The line dividing those around the king, facing away from the sun or the weather, and the parties facing in the opposite direction is found in MS *A*. That the parties were facing the king and those people to his left and right is demonstrated by the statement of the relationship of the advocates to the central gangway, which comes immediately after the text given above.[23] All were sitting except for the serjeants at the back. This arrangement distinguishes clearly between judicial authority and the parties. The former – I shall call it the bench – included the judges and also the king, his elders and nobles, and the priest who accompanied the judges, both in what we may call the court and when they went out of the court to take counsel among themselves. The back row of the bench, the king and his great men, remained seated throughout a case;[24] only the row in front, judges and priest, could move away to take private counsel. All those associated with judicial authority were facing, like the king, away from the sun or the weather. The central gangway divided the parties from each other and also provided a way for the judges and the priests to come and go. This court, therefore, was not a place as such, but a plan: we may call it a seating-plan of people in judgment and in dispute.

The distinction between the judicial section (sitting with their backs to sun or weather) and the parties could be expressed by using *gorsedd* for the former; and in this sense we may translate *gorsedd* by 'the bench'.[25] A text preserved in two fifteenth-century manuscripts talks of the king 'scattering' (namely dismissing) 'the *gorsedd* and the parties' at the conclusion of a day's proceedings.[26] Here the term *gorsedd* has shifted from the place where the king, elders, nobles, judges and priests sat to those persons themselves, viewed collectively and distinguished from the parties; the same shift of meaning is found in the English phrase 'a bench of magistrates'. When an early Welsh triad refers to 'the three silent ones of the *gorsedd*' it may again be referring to this set of people.[27]

However, *gorsedd* could also be used of all those included within the seating-plan of the court, the parties as well as the bench. In one early fourteenth-century manuscript a simplified seating-plan is introduced by the words, 'And thus they sit in their *gorsedd*'.[28] The notion of a *gorsedd* as somewhere where people sit is still preserved; what has vanished is the significance of *gor-* 'over'. By the time of the fifteenth-century collection of model plaints emanating from the lordship of Llandovery (Cantref Bychan), *gorsedd* was an entirely natural term for a court.[29] By then, also, *gorseddog* was employed for the president of the court (the lord or, more usually, his steward)

---

23 *Ior*, § 73/5–6; hence the diagram in a fifteenth-century MS (given in the frontispiece to Jenkins 1986), which makes the advocates face each other, is inaccurate.   24 *AL* IX. xvi. 27; XIV. xlv. 21.   25 As Aneurin Owen sometimes did: e.g. *AL* IX. xvi. 6.   26 *AL* VI. i. 84; cf. VI. i. 41.   27 Wade–Evans 1909, 125.12.   28 *AL* VIII. xi. 17.   29 *AL* XII.

and *gorseddwr* ('*gorsedd*-man') for someone who owed suit of court and was thus subject to that particular lord's jurisdiction.[30] Broadly, then, *gorsedd* came to be used considerably more commonly in the later texts, and this seems to be associated with an extension of its meaning from 'the bench' to the whole court, initially, perhaps, conceived as seated in a certain prescribed plan.

DADL, DADLEU

The third term in my triad is *dadl*, a word also found in Breton and Cornish, and, more remotely, in Irish (*dál*). Its existence in this range of languages, as well as the way it was formed, indicate that it is an ancient term, with at least two millennia of history behind it before we meet it in the Welsh lawbooks. In the twelfth and thirteenth centuries, however, it underwent changes, perhaps partly under the influence of Latin *placitum*.

When it occurs in Old Welsh, Old Cornish, and Old Breton (approximately before 1100), it signifies various forms of assembly-place.[31] It glosses Latin *forum*, *curia*, and *concio*. A man who makes speeches in an assembly is, in Old Cornish, a *datheluur*, a '*dathel*-man'. A *dadl* appears to be a collection of people assembled together in one place to speechify and to argue. There is nothing to indicate that they thought of a *dadl* as normally occurring in a building, although the Bretons may sometimes have thought that Latin *curia* and *forum* were buildings: they gloss them as '*dadl*-house', whereas the Welsh glossator working on a manuscript of Ovid's *Art of love* explains *fora* as *dadl*-places.[32] As it happens, in that particular passage of Ovid, the *fora* in question were used as places in which to hold judicial courts. There may be the odd slight difference of opinion about the physical nature of a *forum* or a *curia* in the classical Latin texts; but the meaning of *dadl* in the Brittonic languages and of *dál* in Irish was, to all intents and purposes, the same, a meeting or assembly.

Once we get to Welsh texts of the twelfth and thirteenth centuries, however, change is evident, although it has gone further in some parts of Wales than in others. Since the Old Welsh glosses belonged to the ninth and early tenth centuries, over two centuries had intervened before the period in the late twelfth century to which the earliest lawbook has been dated.[33] In an early thirteenth-century lawbook from Gwynedd, 'The Book of Iorwerth', *dadl* only occurs in what, historically, is a plural form, *dadleu*. The same is true of another Gwynedd text of the same century, 'The Book of Pleading', and

---

30 With these terms we enter the Marcher world described by Davies: Davies 1978: chap. 7, 'Judicial Lordship'. 31 Lambert, 1996: 16–8; Falileyev, 2000: 41; Fleuriot, 1964: 127; Campanile, 1974: 36. 32 Hunt, 1961: f. 38r10 = line 79 of Ovid's text. In the next line *foro* is glossed by *dadl*. 33 Pryce 1986, 154.

almost entirely true of a third, 'The Book of Cases'.[34] Moreover, it is clear that, in some cases at least, this historically plural form was now felt as singular.[35] Usually, it means 'case' (or 'cases') in the same double sense as the English word bears when used in a legal context: it might signify either the whole case as considered by a judge or judges, including the arguments and testimonies advanced from both sides, or it might signify simply the case put by one side. It can mean 'dispute' (not necessarily yet taken to court), as in the following example:[36]

> Every dispute (*dadl*) which may arise between them on their own (sc. between the members of a church community), judges from the community are entitled to adjudicate for them.

In four examples, however, from the Book of Iorwerth, *dadleu* refers to the legal proceedings conducted on a certain day in a certain place, potentially including more than one case; in this sense, 'sessions' has been adopted as the best English translation.[37] This is presumably a large part of the explanation for the dominance in Gwynedd of the historically plural form, *dadleu*: we can see it as an onion – the sessions on a given day may include more than one case; and such a case would itself include both the plaintiff's arguments and those of the defendant. The semantic range of *dadl* and *dadleu* thus embraced the entire onion: sessions, case and argument. Another, purely grammatical shift confirms that change was affecting the word. Some examples show what gender *dadleu* had once it had come to be felt as a singular noun; and they demonstrate that, whereas *dadl* had been feminine, *dadleu* was masculine.[38]

In South Wales we have a situation intermediate between the Old Welsh (and Old Breton and Cornish) singular noun standing for an assembly and this new, North-Welsh usage. The intermediate character of South-Welsh *dadl* is indicated immediately by the presence of both singular (and feminine) forms alongside historic plurals which, sometimes, yielded new singular masculines. We thus have all stages laid out before us: feminine singular *dadl*, plural *dadleu*, and new masculine singular *dadleu*. Moreover, we also have (as we did not have in the North-Welsh lawbooks) new plurals, *dadleueu* and *dadleuoed*.[39] The

---

34 *AL* VII. and IV–VII. respectively; of the latter, Bks. IV–V are mostly in the thirteenth–century MS *Col* and were printed by D. Jenkins: Jenkins 1973. **35** This phenomenon was the subject of another important note by Sir Ifor Williams in his edition of *Pedeir Keinc y Mabinogi*: Williams 1930, 189 (on p. 38, l. 14). His account is much to be preferred to that in *Geiriadur Prifysgol Cymru*, which obscures the historical development, and does not advert to any direct connection between *dadl* and *dadlau*. **36** *AL* IV. i. 28. This is also the modern sense registered in Fynes–Clinton 1913, 70. **37** *Ior*, 81/8, 91/1, 94/1, 113/5; trans. Jenkins 1986, 96. 122, 125, 159. **38** *Dadl* is singular and feminine in *Bleg*, 117. 17; the formerly plural form *dadleu* is singular and masculine at 116. 26. **39** *Bleg*, 13. 16; 126. 22 (and see the *L* variant).

difference between the south and the north may be because the South-Welsh lawbooks were more accumulations of text – some old, some recent – while the North-Welsh lawbooks were reshapings of old material involving a fairly thorough rewriting.

In the South-Welsh lawbooks, *dadl* did not mean 'assembly' but 'dispute' or 'case'.[40] It was as much an encounter between arguments as a meeting between people. The contrast may, however, be overdrawn because of an aspect of the Old Welsh evidence. For the most part, Old Welsh survives as a collection of glosses. Archbishop Dunstan, when he was still bishop of Worcester, had a composite manuscript now called 'St Dunstan's Classbook'.[41] Two of the sections that came to form part of this book were Welsh, of which one was the handsome copy of Ovid's 'Art of Love', Book I, mentioned above, in which *fora* was explained as *datl-locou*, '*dadl*-places'. The places were Roman, the poem written for a Roman audience – all equally remote from our Welsh glossator working in the late-ninth or early-tenth century. He may have appreciated that the forum in question was one in which legal cases were heard, but we cannot be sure. Nor can we expect to recover the full range of meanings possessed by Old Welsh *datl* by scrutinising a couple of glosses. When, however, we put together Old Irish *dál* (: *dadl*) and the Middle Welsh material, we can extract a more likely account. *Dál* regularly means 'meeting', but alongside this standard sense there was a second, 'law-suit' or 'legal case'. Given the history of Welsh *dadl* after 1100, it is highly likely that, before 1100, there was a dual meaning similar to that of Old Irish *dál*.

The benefit of taking into consideration different terms is that they provide different vantage-points from which to examine assumptions made about courts and assemblies. Of our triad of terms, *llys* was an instructive cul-de-sac for the purpose of judicial assemblies: in the thirteenth century at least, it was a political not a judicial court. *Gorsedd* was much more helpful. Since *gorsedd* means, literally, 'over-seat', it looks as though it had some connection with the conception of a judicial court as a seating-plan. Most probably it referred to the king's party, the two lines, first of king, elders and nobles, and secondly of judge(s) and priest(s). These are likely to have occupied a higher position than 'the parties' facing them. This might be because they used a natural or artificial mound, as the semantic history of *gorsedd* implies, or because a form of dais was used. By the early fourteenth century, and perhaps earlier, *gorsedd* had come also to be used of all those seated according to the plan, for the parties as much as for the bench; this suggests that the place-name usage may predate the

---

40 The Latin lawbooks use *lis*, *placitum* and *causa*, e.g. *Latin Texts* 319.20: *causa* = *dadyl* in *Bleg*, 6.26; *Latin Texts*, 374.37–8: *lis*, = *dadyl* in *Bleg*, 117.13; *Latin Texts*, 385.32: *placitum* = *dadyl* in *Bleg*, 70.6; *Latin Texts* 390.35: *placitum* = *dadleu* (sg.) in *Bleg*, 83.20.   **41** *Saint Dunstan's Classbook* ed. Hunt 1961, f. 38a.

fourteenth century. *Dadl* and *dadlau* had a different background, starting life as a meeting of people and developing towards a meeting of arguments in a single case or in the sessions of an entire day. While the other terms long remain attached to their roots as terms for types of place, *dadl* has more to do with men and disputes.

ABBREVIATIONS

AL	*The ancient laws and institutes of Wales*, ed. A. Owen.
Bleg	*Llyfr Blegywryd*, ed. S.J. Williams, and J.E. Powell.
Ior	*Llyfr Iorwerth*, ed. A.Rh. Wiliam.
Latin Texts	*The Latin texts of the Welsh laws*, ed. H.D. Emanuel.

REFERENCES

Andrews, Rh., 1976–8: 'Rhai agweddau ar sofraniaeth yng ngherddi'r Gogynfeirdd', *Bulletin of the Board of Celtic Studies* **27**, 23–30.

Campanile, E., 1974: *Profilo etimologico del cornico antico.* Pisa.

Charles-Edwards, T.M., 1970: 'The date of the Four Branches of the Mabinogi', *Transactions of the Honourable Society of Cymmrodorion*, 263–98.

Davies, R.R., 1978: *Lordship and society in the march of Wales, 1282–1400.* Oxford.

Davies, R.R., 1986: 'The administration of law in medieval Wales: the role of the *Ynad Cwmwd* (Judex Patrie)', in T. M. Charles-Edwards et al., (eds), *Lawyers and laymen: studies in the history of law presented to Professor Dafydd Jenkins.* Cardiff. 258–73.

Emanuel, H.D. (ed.), 1967: *The Latin texts of the Welsh laws.* Cardiff.

Falileyev, A., 2000: *Etymological glossary of Old Welsh.* Tübingen.

Flanagan, D., 1980–1: 'Common elements in Irish placenames: *dún, ráth, lios*', *Bulletin of the Ulster Place-Name Society* (2nd series) **3**, 16–29.

Fleuriot, L., 1964: *Dictionnaire des gloses en vieux breton.* Paris.

Fynes-Clinton, O.H., 1913: *The Welsh vocabulary of the Bangor district.* London.

Gantz, J., 1976: *The Mabinogion.* London.

Gwenogvryn Evans, J. (ed.), 1909: *Facsimile of the Chirk codex of the Welsh laws.* Llanbedrog.

Hemp, W. J., 1921–2: 'A list of mounds, cairns and circles of the Northern Flintshire plateau', *Bulletin of the Board of Celtic Studies* **1**, 358–67.

Hughes, I. (ed.), 2000: *Math uab Mathonwy: pedwaredd gainc y Mabinogi.* Aberystwyth.

Hunt, R.W. (ed.), 1961: *Saint Dunstan's classbook from Glastonbury*, Umbrae Codicum Occidentalium IV. Amsterdam.

Huws, D., 1988: *Peniarth 28: Darluniau o lyfr cyfraith Hywel Dda/Illustrations from a Welsh lawbook.* Aberystwyth.

Jenkins, D., 1973: *Damweiniau colan.* Aberystwyth.

Jenkins, D., 1986: *The law of Hywel Dda: law texts from medieval Wales.* Llandysul.

Jones, G.R.J., 2000: '*Llys* and *Maerdref*', in Charles-Edwards et al., (eds), *The Welsh king and his court*. Cardiff. 296–318.

Jones, G., and Jones, T., 1949: *The Mabinogion*. London.

Lambert, P.-Y., 1996: *Lexique étymologique de l'irlandais ancien de J. Vendryes*. Dublin.

Mac Airt, S. and Mac Niocaill, G. (eds), 1983: *The annals of Ulster (to AD 1131)*. Dublin.

Meyer, K. (ed.), 1889: '*Echtra Nerai*', *Revue Celtique* **10**, 212–28.

Meyer, K. (ed.), 1890: '*Echtra Nerai*', *Revue Celtique*, **11**, 209–10.

Owen, A. (ed.), 1841: *The ancient laws and institutes of Wales*. London.

Owen, H.W., 1994: *The place-names of East Flintshire*. Cardiff.

Phillips, M., 2000: 'Defod a moes y llys', in T.M. Charles-Edwards et al. (eds), *The Welsh king and his court*. Cardiff. 347–61.

Pryce, H., 1986: 'The prologues to the Welsh lawbooks', *Bulletin of the Board of Celtic Studies* **33**, 151–82.

Sims-Williams, P., 1991: 'The submission of Irish kings in fact and fiction: Henry II, Bendigeidfran, and the dating of *The Four Branches of the Mabinogi*', *Cambrian Medieval Celtic Studies* **22**, 31–61.

Stephenson, D., 1980: *Medieval Welsh law-Courts*. Aberystwyth.

Thomson, D.S. (ed.), 1961: *Branwen Uerch Lyr*. Dublin.

Thomson, R.L. (ed.), 1957: *Pwyll Pendeuic Dyuet*. Dublin.

Wade-Evans, A.W. (ed.), 1909: *Welsh medieval law*. Oxford.

Wiliam, A.Rh. (ed.), 1960: *Llyfr Iorwerth*. Cardiff.

Williams, I. (ed.), 1930: *Pedeir Keinc y Mabinogi*. Cardiff.

Williams, S.J. and Powell, J.E. (eds), 1961: *Llyfr Blegywryd*. Cardiff.

PART II

England

Assembling the dead

HOWARD WILLIAMS

The end of direct Roman administration of the province of Britannia in the early fifth century AD led to the immigration of Germanic groups and a major re-orientation of society and ideology in eastern England.[1] Archaeologists and historians have long debated the ethnic, religious and social character of communities and kingdoms during this time of upheaval, including whether the tyrants and kings of these centuries held public assemblies. For many eighteenth- and nineteenth-century Anglo-Saxon scholars, assembly was an institution that reflected the racial characteristics of all the primitive Teutonic races, and consequently it was believed to be present among 'Anglo-Saxon' groups before, during, and after the migrations to Britain.[2] However, this premise is based upon an out-moded racial paradigm and relies on wishful thinking more than evidence. Written sources fail to provide us with the precise nature of kingdoms in this period, and inevitably, public assemblies are rarely mentioned.[3] It is also clear that assemblies were not static institutions and may have had very different forms with varying social functions and physical contexts as society developed through the Anglo-Saxon period.[4]

The period is much better served by a rich database of archaeological evidence, yet identifying the physical signature of infrequent gathering places is a challenge for archaeologists both in Britain and elsewhere. This situation does not rule out the possible existence of assembly-places in early Anglo-Saxon England, since despite the rich place-name and documentary evidence, the archaeology of later Anglo-Saxon assemblies in many areas is also limited, fragmentary and ambiguous.[5] Yet equally, the absence of a distinctive archaeological site-type may indicate that assemblies took different forms in the early period, or perhaps assembly functions were integral parts of other types of site already known to archaeologists and historians.

1 Esmonde Cleary 1989. 2 For a review of late eighteenth- and nineteenth-century Anglo-Saxonism, see MacDougall 1982. 3 Loyn 1984, 3–29, 131–48; Stenton 1971, 298–301; Reynolds 1999, 76–81. 4 Bullough 2000; Loyn 1984, 142; Sawyer 1998, 134–5. 5 Adkins and Petchey, 1984; Pantos 2002; Reynolds 1999, 76–81.

It has been suggested that assemblies in early Anglo-Saxon England occurred at pagan sanctuaries, and that later Anglo-Saxon assembly-places continued at sites of earlier pagan religious practices.[6] Given the 'grandstand' structure excavated by Brian Hope-Taylor at the royal palace of Yeavering in Northumberland, elite residences have also been argued to have functioned as places of assembly.[7] However, the nature of pagan temples remains untested by systematic archaeological investigation, and both temples and elite settlements are difficult to identify with any certainty before the seventh century.[8] No pattern for assembly in the fifth and sixth centuries has yet been forthcoming.[9] An obvious response to this situation would be to argue that we cannot reconstruct the locations and character of assemblies in the fifth and sixth centuries. However, this paper suggests that a distinctive and well-known category of archaeological site might have served as assembly-places during this period.

Graves and cemeteries continue to dominate our archaeological knowledge of the fifth to seventh centuries AD in eastern England. In recent years early medieval burial sites have been used in discussions of social structures,[10] symbolic systems and ideologies[11] as well as more traditional debates concerning ethnic and cultural identities and religious practices.[12] These approaches focus upon the human remains, artefacts, grave structures and monuments, but rarely address the roles, functions and significance of cemeteries *as places*.[13] This paper will consider the possibility that a small group of large cremation cemeteries in the East Midlands and East Anglia were more than collections of graves, but instead acted as sacred and social foci where assemblies may have been held.

ANGLO-SAXON CEMETERIES AS PLACES

Long ago, E.T. Leeds observed that 'There is no reason to suppose that the pagan grave-field was enshrouded by any less degree of sanctity than "God's acre" ...'[14] Despite this statement, only recently have attempts been made to

6 Loyn 1984, 143–4; Meaney 1995; Reynolds 1999, 77; Sawyer 1998, 332; Semple this volume; Whitelock 1952, 24. 7 Reynolds 1999, 51–2; Semple this volume. 8 For a review of elite settlements see Reynolds 1999; Welch 1992. Hines 1997 has made the suggestion that pagan sanctuaries need not reflect places of religious congregation in the fifth and sixth centuries, but instead may have evolved during the seventh century in a context of increasing political complexity and religious conflict. See also Blair 1995 for some possible ritual or mortuary structures dating to this period. 9 But see Semple this volume. 10 Härke 1997; Richards 1987; Stoodley 1999. 11 Pader 1982; Richards 1992; Williams 1997; 1998. 12 Härke 1990; Wilson 1992; Williams 2001, 2002. 13 But see Bullough 1983; Härke 2001; Lucy 1998; Semple this volume. 14 Leeds 1913, 11.

address the social and sacred character of cemeteries in the early Anglo-Saxon landscape. These approaches have been inspired by an increasing interest in the roles of monuments and funerary sites in past sacred geographies by landscape archaeologists utilizing social theory and phenomenological perspectives.[15] Among these studies are those that focus specifically on the landscape context of burial sites and cemeteries in past societies.[16] Debates rage over both the theory and methodology of these studies,[17] yet they provide inspiration for new perspectives upon the study of early medieval mortuary practices in relation to space, place and landscape.[18] They encourage us to see burial sites as contexts for a wide range of mortuary and ancestral rites beyond their narrow function as locations for the disposal of dead bodies. In this context we might investigate the choice of burial location and the use of burial sites as meaningful for the ways past communities constructed and reproduced their identities, social memories and perceptions of the world around them.

In order to illustrate the value of these perspectives I wish to focus upon one early Anglo-Saxon burial site and its possible role as a central place in the wider context of other cemeteries. The site in question is Loveden Hill in the parish of Hough-on-the-Hill in the region of Kesteven in southern Lincolnshire (figs. 5.1 & 5.2).[19] In the 1920s, excavations were conducted both in and around a possible barrow on the hill-top. More extensive excavations took place in the late 1950s directed by Kenneth Fennell and in the early 1970s by Nigel Kerr.[20] The excavations produced burials dating to between the mid-fifth and mid-seventh centuries AD. It is estimated that around 1800 graves were uncovered, 95% of which were cremation burials.[21] Originally at least 2000 graves may have been present on the site.[22] Although only partially excavated and the results unpublished, Loveden Hill is the second largest early medieval cemetery known from England.[23]

---

15 E.g. Bradley 1998; Cummings 2000a; Tilley 1994; Richards 1996. **16** Only a few studies have focused upon the symbolic, ideological and social significance of burial location. These include for Bronze Age Crete, Branigan 1998; for Iron Age square barrows in East Yorkshire, Bevan 1999; for the Iron Age in southern Jutland, Parker Pearson 1993; for Romano-British burials, Esmonde Cleary 2000. **17** Brück 1998; Cummings 2000b; Fleming 1999. **18** Lucy 1998; Thäte 1996; Theuws 1999; Williams 1997; 1998; 1999a. **19** The study of the landscape context of the Loveden Hill cemetery forms part of a broader project investigating the location of cremation cemeteries in the East Midlands and East Anglia: Williams 2002b. **20** Fennell 1964; 1974; undated; Leahy 1993, 40; Meaney 1964, 158–9; Wilson 1959; Webster 1973; Wilkinson 1980; Lincoln SMR record 30289. **21** A 'cremation burial' is the term used by archaeologists to describe material taken from the pyre site after cremation and given a formalized, ritual disposal elsewhere: McKinley 1997. **22** Fennell 1974. **23** In early Anglo-Saxon England, cremation burials include human bone, the remains of sacrificed animals (mainly sheep, horses, cattle and pigs) as well as fragments of artefacts retrieved from the pyre. These remains were usually placed in a ceramic urn that frequently bore elaborate decoration. These were then interred in formal cemeteries like Loveden Hill. For overviews of early Anglo-Saxon cremation

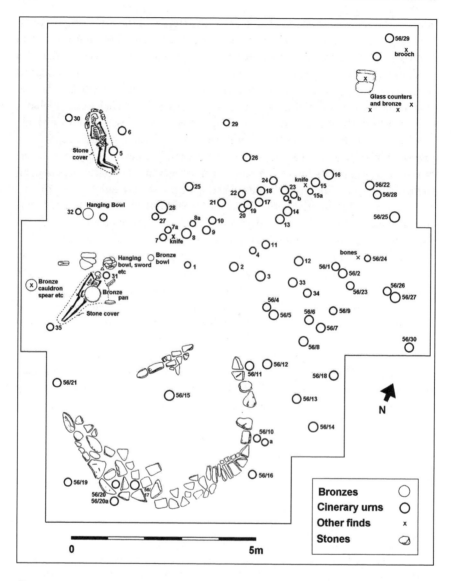

Figure 5.1 Section of Fennell's excavations of the Loveden Hill cemetery showing one concentration of cremation burials in ceramic and bronze vessels. The curving stone arrangement may have been the foundations of a funerary structure (redrawn after Fennell unpublished). Not to scale.

The Loveden Hill burial site is not a typical early Anglo-Saxon cemetery. The site is one of a distinctive class of cemetery in which cremation predominates and inhumation occurs infrequently. These cemeteries are much larger than contemporary inhumation and mixed-rite burial sites and are found in a

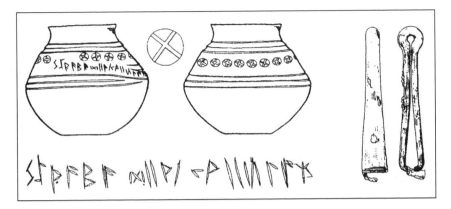

Figure 5.2 Cinerary urn with stamped and runic decoration from Loveden Hill with tweezers (A.11/251, redrawn after Fennell 1964: 324a). Not to scale.

discrete distribution through East Anglia, the East Midlands and East Yorkshire.[24] Other well-known sites include Cleatham in Lincolnshire,[25] Newark in Nottinghamshire,[26] and Sancton in East Yorkshire.[27] Only one of these sites, Spong Hill in Norfolk, has received near-complete excavation and publication.[28] Although inhumation graves are usually present at these sites they represent only a minority rite.[29] Elsewhere, cremation burials appear as a minority rite in inhumation-dominant cemeteries and in roughly equal proportions to inhumation graves in mixed-rite cemeteries, but the predominance of cremation and the size of these cemeteries sets them apart.[30]

ASSEMBLIES FOR THE LIVING AND THE DEAD

The size of these cemeteries has frequently led archaeologists to regard them as central burial places serving many settlements and farms and perhaps related to a defined 'tribal' territory.[31] For Spong Hill, McKinley estimates that at least 2700 individuals were cremated and buried, and Loveden Hill may have been of a comparable size.[32] Even accounting for the possibility that these

practices, see Bond 1996; Lucy 2000; McKinley 1994; Richards 1987; 1992; 1995; Wilkinson 1980; Williams 2001, 2002. **24** Williams 2000. **25** Leahy 1998. **26** Kinsley 1989. **27** Myres and Southern 1973; Timby 1993. **28** Hills 1977; 1980. **29** E.g. At Spong Hill there were a small number of inhumation graves in a discrete area of the site: Hills et al. 1984. **30** This definition of 'cremation cemeteries' differs from the traditional one adopted by Myres and Green 1973 and Meaney 1964 and rests on arguments developed in Williams 2000; 2001b. **31** Arnold 1997, 55; Dark 2000; Eagles 1989; Leahy 1993; 1999; McKinley 1994, 66–71; Williamson 1993, 65–8. **32** McKinley 1994, 66.

two sites were exceptionally large,[33] most other cremation cemeteries may have contained anywhere between 500 and 2000 burials and were therefore usually at least twice the size of the largest known inhumation burial sites.[34] The size of these sites is unprecedented for pre-Christian rural populations and suggests a special form of mortuary organization and the gathering together of the living and the dead from a large area.

McKinley estimates that between fifty-six and ninety-six 'families', each averaging eight individuals, may have used the Spong Hill cemetery. The adjacent settlement, although only partially excavated, appears too small to have contained this number of households.[35] The study of the cinerary urns supports this. The variety of pot stamps and fabrics seems to suggest that social groups from different places in the environs were burying their dead at the cemetery. In rarer cases, the stamps and fabrics suggest pots (and hence perhaps mourners or even the dead contained within the urn) had come from outside the locality.[36] Although pyre sites have been identified at cremation cemeteries,[37] the absence of pyre debris from most urns suggests that cremation often took place elsewhere. Whether the corpse was carried long distances to the pyre and the cremation took place at a discrete site near the cemetery, or cremation occurred near the settlement and the ashes were transported, the cemeteries clearly had large catchment areas.[38] Processions with the corpse or ashes may have used specific pathways linking the cemetery to settlements, making the burial site a focus for different communities to come together during mortuary practices and forge relationships with the place of burial, the dead, and each other.

Contrary to some suggestions, there are indications that cremation cemeteries were not the final destination of everyone living in a particular territory, and hence were not literally 'tribal' burial sites. Smaller inhumation and mixed-rite cemeteries were also established across eastern England and sometimes these were in close proximity to the larger cremation cemeteries.[39]

---

33 McKinley 1994, 70 cautiously regards Spong Hill as exceptionally large. However, it may be exceptional only in relation to the scale and longevity of well-recorded antiquarian and archaeological investigations. Other cremation cemeteries may have approached a similar size but remain only partially investigated.   34 Inhumation cemeteries rarely contain more than three hundred graves where completely excavated. Examples of small cemeteries in which cremation is the dominant rite are exceptionally rare and most of these are best explained as excavated fractions of much larger burial sites.   35 McKinley 1994, 70; Williamson 1993, 65.   36 Arnold 1997; Brisbane 1980, 215; Williams and Vince 1997.   37 Carnegie and Filmer-Sankey 1993; see discussion in Williams 2000.   38 McKinley 1994, 85, pers comm. The absence of pyre debris may however reflect post-cremation rituals: McKinley 1994, 86. See Williams 2000 for a summary of the evidence and the argument that the cremation pyres of some individuals were on areas adjacent to the cemetery.   39 For example, both Loveden Hill and Spong Hill appear to have broadly contemporary inhumation cemeteries within the same parish: see below and Hills 1977, 30–1.

In south Lincolnshire large cremation and small inhumation cemeteries are interspersed and although the inhumation burial sites may have been later additions to the mortuary organization of the region by perhaps as much as one or even two generations, once established these smaller burial sites continued in use alongside the earlier cremation cemeteries throughout the late fifth and sixth centuries.[40] It may be the case that access to the larger cremation cemeteries like Loveden Hill was restricted to selected social groups or households living over a wide territory whereas other groups in these areas either preferred to inhume their dead and inter in smaller cemeteries, or else were deliberately excluded from the larger cremation-dominated burial sites.[41] Therefore it appears that Loveden Hill and other cremation cemeteries represent a different sphere of mortuary organization which was maintained for well over a century despite overlapping geographically and temporally with smaller inhumation and mixed-rite burial sites.

This evidence suggests that cremation cemeteries had a special role in society. As significant places for the dead from dispersed communities over a wide area they would have become places of assembly for large numbers of people. These would potentially include not only close kin and friends of the deceased, but many other individuals owing allegiance to the deceased and mourners, as well as those with more specific duties, roles and obligations to enact. Early Anglo-Saxon funerals are often portrayed in illustrations as small, intimate, family-led occasions, yet this may be a romanticized view drawing more upon nineteenth- and twentieth-century patterns of mourning than upon a likely scenario for early Anglo-Saxon mortuary practices.[42] Evidence from later medieval documentary sources and ethnographic analogies from other pre-industrial societies, illuminate the ways that funerals can frequently involve hundreds, sometimes thousands of individuals, on occasions including different socio-economic, political and ethnic groups.[43] In addition, funerals are often occasions for a range of social activities including feasting, settling disputes and forming alliances through gift giving. Such activities may also have been enmeshed with early Anglo-Saxon funerary rites making cemeteries special locations for assembly. The size and character of the cemetery would have required a distinctive mortuary organization. Indeed, Joan Kirk observed

40 See Williams 2001 for a discussion of the relationships between inhumation/mixed-rite cemeteries and cremation cemeteries in eastern England. 41 In other words, cremation cemeteries may not have served discrete territories as suggested by Williamson 1993, 67. 42 Popular illustrations of Anglo-Saxon grave-side scenes focus upon the interaction of a small number of close relatives to the deceased laid out in the grave, or upon the act of depositing the cremation urn. For example see the illustrations of non-royal funerals in Carver 1998, 108; Dark 2000 plate 7. 43 See Williams 1999b. Norse sagas give an impression of large congregations at funerals, e.g. the feast held by Unn the Deep-Minded in *Laxdæla Saga*: Magnusson and Pálsson 1969, 55–7. See also the account of Ibn Fablan: Jones 1984, 425–30.

fifty years ago that, for the early Anglo-Saxon cemeteries of the Thames valley, cremation rites may have involved particular ritual specialists presiding over the cremation and post-cremation procedures.[44]

These arguments suggest that cremation cemeteries acted as places of assembly because they were locations where many different communities may have gathered for mortuary rites, perhaps under the supervision or control of a political and religious elite. As a result, burial rites at sites like Loveden Hill may have encouraged common concepts of community, group identity and social memories to be expressed and reproduced.[45] Having examined the implications of the size of these cremation cemeteries, let us now move on to consider the nature of the cremation rite itself.

PLACE AND CREMATION

The characteristics of the cremation rites at Loveden Hill and other cemeteries provide support for the significance of cemeteries as places of assembly. Ethnographic accounts of cremation rites from India and south-east Asia,[46] together with portrayals of cremation in early medieval literary sources, such as *Beowulf* and the description of a Viking funeral by Ibn Fablan,[47] illustrate the ways in which cremation can be a powerful spectacle, laden with symbolism and experienced by large groups of people. Unfortunately, such accounts frequently focus attention upon the act of cremation rather than the significance of post-cremation rites.[48] However, while the cremation can be an important moment of social, cosmological and ontological transformation for the deceased and for mourners, in many cultures, both past and present, it also facilitates a range of post-cremation rites. The 'cremains' can be left at the pyre site,[49] but cremation is rarely the end of the obsequies.[50] Sometimes the pyre site is commemorated, or alternatively mourners may try to retrieve fragments of bone and objects from the pyre. These 'cremains' may then be dealt with in a number of ways. For instance, they may be dispersed among mourners,[51] scattered at holy or sacred places and temples,[52] immersed in the sea, rivers or pools,[53] kept in the home of kin,[54] or incorporated into above-ground memorials for the dead.[55] In some societies, cremated remains are carried in clothing as a sign of mourning,[56] while in others, they are eaten by

44 Kirk 1956, 126–7. For a different view, see Fennell 1964 who regards cremation as unspecialized where timber is plentiful: Fennell 1964, 104. 45 See Edmonds 1999 for a comparable argument for early Neolithic causewayed enclosures. 46 Covarrubias 1937, 359–88; Downes 1999; Geertz 1984; 1993, 36–9; Habenstein and Lamers 1960; Hobert 1978; Parry 1982; 1994; Wales 1931. 47 Wylie 1855. 48 Williams 2000. 49 Rivers 1906. 50 Williams 2000. 51 Toynbee 1971. 52 Habenstein and Lamers 1960. 53 Parry 1994; Monnerie 1995. 54 Davies 1997. 55 Kan 1989; Rishøj Pedersen 1974/5. 56 MacLeod 1925.

close relatives during a funerary feast.[57] They need not receive any one destination but can be divided up and dispersed in different locales and ritual settings. The collection and burial of cremated remains in formal cemeteries is, therefore, only one possible option for the disposal of ashes in communities past and present. Where it does occur, burying cremated remains is often used to forge strong relationships with the landscape, and serves to articulate relationships between the living community and the newly dead as well as with ancestors and the place of disposal. The timing of the burial, the choice of location and the character of cinerary containers and structures can all be shown to have both social and cosmological significance.[58]

Following the ideas discussed by Hertz and Van Gennep, death rituals can be seen as rites of passage with a number of distinct stages. First the rites encourage a break with the living (rites of initiation or separation), followed by a period of time when mourners and the dead are between states (liminality). These rites are often followed by further practices that are intended to forge and stabilize new identities and roles for both mourners and the deceased (i.e. rites of incorporation).[59] These last rites often emphasize symbols of regeneration and embodiment so that post-cremation rites frequently attempt to construct a new 'body' for the deceased. These general themes vary considerably between societies and cannot always explain the structure of rituals surrounding death completely, but they do provide a starting point for understanding the logic and ordering of cremation rites. In many societies the cremation process is not simply destructive. Instead, rites serving to dissolve bodily integrity are followed by strategies that emphasize the reconstitution and regeneration of the dead and post-cremation rites can be understood in this context. They enable the proper transition of the spirit and soul of the deceased into a new state of being through the manipulation of the human remains, material culture, space and place. In this context cemeteries are repositories where identities are repeatedly materialized and fixed. In this sense, they can be regarded either as conduits to otherworlds, or places where the dead are believed to reside.[60] In either case, cemeteries can have a role as

57 Chagnon 1968, 50–1. 58 For the eschatological and cosmological significance of post-cremation rites, see Downes 1999; Hobert 1978; Parry 1994. Sergei Kan has discussed the significance of the grave structures and containers within which cremated remains were placed, as well as the location of the cemetery as a 'village for the dead' among the Tlingit Indians of the American North-West Coast: Kan 1989, 38–41, 54, 106, 115–18. 59 Bloch and Parry 1982; Hertz 1960; Huntingdon and Metcalf 1991; Parry 1994; Van Gennep 1960. Both Van Gennep (1960) and Hertz (1960) use cremation rites from Indian and south-east Asia to discuss death as a rite of passage and a social process. 60 As Tilley (1994) has noted, ethnographic and anthropological accounts rarely provide detailed accounts of the spatial and landscape context within which rituals and other activities take place in contemporary non-Western societies. There are however some studies that provide useful analogies for the situation in early Anglo-Saxon England: Babu 1994; Kan 1989; Vitebsky 1993.

simultaneously conceptually 'central' to the social world of the living and their cosmologies but as 'liminal': existing between worlds.

The archaeological remains of cremation burials from early Anglo–Saxon England and sites like Loveden Hill can be usefully interpreted in this regard. The burial rites served in the reconstitution of the deceased's 'body' and the incorporation of the deceased into a community of ancestors. In Anglo–Saxon post-cremation rites no attempt is made to 'represent' the deceased, neither is the new form necessarily 'individual' – burials may include elements of animals and sometimes the remains of more than one human skeleton[61] – but the retrieval and selective inclusion of objects can be argued to articulate the building of the 'body' for the new identity and personhood of the dead. Elsewhere I have argued from the nature and treatment of the grave goods, ceramic containers and bones, that they all had active and key roles in the reconstitution of the identity of the dead person in relation to both survivors and ancestors.[62] This interpretation stands in contrast with existing symbolic and social explanations of the cremation rite which argue that cinerary urns, grave goods and animal remains reflected the identity of the deceased in a direct way.[63] This re-membering and rebuilding of the dead has implications for the way cemeteries were perceived. They were places where the living gathered, but also where the dead reached a new state of being.

The construction of a place for the assembled dead would also be mediated through the use of monuments over burials. Archaeological excavation rarely produces evidence of substantial grave markers over the cremated remains due to disturbance, differential presentation and poor excavation. At many cemeteries, however, there are hints that single graves or groups of burials were commemorated with above-ground structures. At Loveden Hill and other sites, small mounds of stones and earth, lines of posts and timber grave houses may have marked graves and simultaneously acted as foci for ceremonies and further burials.[64] Most studies of the relationship between place and burial rites focus upon the way monuments transform the experience of place and create an enduring focus for remembrance.[65] Yet these grave structures may not have been particularly 'monumental' and many could have been short-lived. Only in combination might they have created a distinctive experience for visitors to the cemetery. For well over a century, each new burial added further visible features to the cemetery and may have served to map genealogies and histories. Loveden Hill would appear as an area scattered with

---

61 Williams 2000; 2001; 2002a; 2002b. For a useful discussion of the construction of personhood through the mortuary treatment of bones see Fowler 2001.   62 There are many societies across the world where the cremated remains are made into an image, effigy or memorial representing the deceased.   63 Richards 1987; 1992; 1995; Ravn 1999.   64 Williams 2000.   65 Bradley 1998.

the remains of mounds and grave structures in varying states of disrepair, covering single or groups of graves – some remembered, some forgotten by the community. The biographies of the place were constructed through the repeated addition of graves, testified by referencing of earlier visible structures and charted through the decay of the visible, modest grave monuments. For the different groups using Loveden Hill, the ephemeral structures marking individual burials or groups of graves would articulate and reproduce group biographies and relations with ancestors, rather than celebrating and remembering the dead as a host of discrete individuals.[66]

A further factor to consider is the spatial character of the site. While Loveden Hill received thousands of cremation burials, the small size of the cinerary urns allowed them to be placed in relatively close proximity (fig. 5.1). In this way, cremation cemeteries created a distinctive spatial and physical experience for mourners attending the burial rite that would have contrasted markedly with the acts of grave digging, and the use of space in inhumation and mixed-rite cemeteries. The proximity of graves to one another may have further emphasized the cemetery as a place where the new social person was constructed in relation to memories of earlier funerals and the identities of those already buried.

THE LOCATION OF CREMATION CEMETERIES

The study of the topography and environs of these cemeteries adds further evidence to support their role as places of assembly. In many cases we know disappointingly little about the hinterlands of cremation cemeteries and the archaeological investigation of their surroundings is a priority for future research.[67] However, a preliminary survey reveals some interesting results. While there appears to be no uniform pattern in cremation cemetery location, equally sites do not seem to have been located at random.[68] Cemeteries can be shown to be situated in relation to distinctive topography, major routes, existing monuments and structures, as well as centres of late Roman political authority.[69]

In the case of Loveden Hill, the top of a prominent hill was selected as the burial site (figs 5.3 and 5.4).[70] It is situated west of the main Lincolnshire

66 Barrett 1994; Williams 2000. 67 Williams 2002b. 68 Fieldwork carried out with support of the research fund of the School of Archaeology, Trinity College Carmarthen in August 2001 supported by visits to the SMRs at Lincoln, Scunthorpe, Matlock, West Bridgford and Grimsby. 69 Leahy 1993, 36; Williamson 1993 observed the relationship between major Roman settlements and cremation cemeteries in the East Midlands and East Anglia, drawing upon observations by J.N.L. Myres (1969; 1986) and Clark (1940). 70 Fennell 1964.

Figure 5.3 View of Loveden Hill looking south-south-west from Brandon Road showing how the hill dominates its local landscape (photograph: author).

Figure 5.4 Loveden Hill looking west from the high ground close to the village of Hough-on-the-Hill illustrating the expanse of the Witham valley overlooked by the hill (photograph: author).

escarpment and consequently enjoys wide views over the Witham plain to the north, west and south. Although the land is higher to the east, the hill is one of most striking and easily recognized landmarks in the vicinity. The choice of this hill therefore suggests a desire for the site to be intervisible with settlements spread out to the west around the river Witham and on the higher ground around the villages of Gelston and Hough-on-the-Hill. This hypothesis is supported by recent finds of Anglo-Saxon metalwork indicating settlements and/or cemeteries in the adjacent parishes of Carlton Scroop, Normanton, Hougham, Foston and Barkston (those with known findspots and closest to Loveden Hill are marked on the map: fig. 5.5).[71] All of these sites would be visible from Loveden Hill, and Loveden Hill may have dominated their horizon. Furthermore, fieldwalking conducted by Nigel Kerr identified a spread of Saxon pottery overlying the site of a Roman villa immediately to the north of the hill.[72] One inhumation grave excavated by Fennell on Loveden Hill was covered with part of a Roman column (presumably re-used from the villa), seemingly materializing the relationship between the cemetery and the nearby settlement.[73] While it may remain difficult to 'prove' where those buried on Loveden Hill lived out their days, the topography illustrates that the relationship between probable settlement sites and the cemetery was more than one of spatial proximity. The dead were placed where they would be intervisible with contemporary settlement sites. Pathways probably also linked many of the settlements with the hill; paths meant for both the living and the dead to follow. Similar patterns have been identified at other cremation cemeteries in the East Midlands, including that on Hall Hill in West Keal parish, Lincolnshire. Here, fieldwalking by the Fenland Survey has shown that the cemetery was located on a prominent hill overlooking a number of contemporary settlement sites that it may have served.[74]

The spatial and visual relationship between cemetery and settlements is supported by the discovery of a sixth-century small-long brooch found about two kilometres to the west of Loveden Hill. This brooch was fragmented and distorted by fire and may represent a rare example where the site of a pyre serving the cemetery on the hill to the east has been identified. If this is the case, then it provides support for a picture of dispersed funerary activity across the landscape surrounding the cemetery. This further illustrates how the sequence of funerary rites inscribed meanings onto places and the routes between them.

Furthermore, as mentioned above, burial in the area was clearly not restricted to the use of the cremation cemetery. Only three kilometres to the east of the Loveden Hill cemetery in Normanton parish, a sixth-century inhumation cemetery of at least thirty graves has recently been uncovered.[75] Loveden Hill was clearly only one choice of burial site for people living in the

71 Early Anglo-Saxon period small finds recorded in the area of Loveden Hill with the Scunthorpe SMR recorded in August 2001: NLM 779 – Fosten – sixth-century brooch; NLM 782 – Fosten, Fragment of sixth-century Square Headed brooch; NLM 2102 – Carlton Scoop – cruciform brooch; NLM 3455 – Hougham – cremated remains of a small-long brooch (see map); NLM 3462 – Fosten – sixth-century rivet; NLM 3463 – Fosten – sixth-century spearhead; NLM 3480 – Hougham – cruciform brooch (see map); NLM 3481 – Hougham – cruciform brooch (see map); NLM 3873 – Barkston – cruciform brooch. Also an early Anglo-Saxon spearhead was found at Temple Hill Farm in Hough-on-the-Hill parish: Lincoln SMR record 30286 (see map). 72 Lincoln SMR record 30285; Williams 2002b. 73 Fennell 1964. 74 Hall and Coles 1994, 127–8; Lane and Hayes 1993, 59; Williams 2002b. 75 Lincoln SMR record 35401.

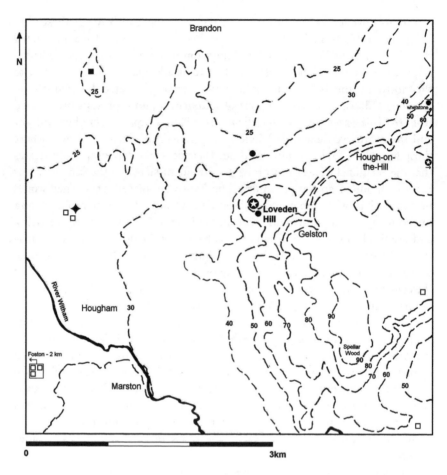

Figure 5.5 The Loveden Hill cemetery (dot with star) and its local landscape in the early Anglo-Saxon period. The contours illustrate the prominent position of the hill on the edge of the Lincolnshire cliff and symbols mark findspots of early Anglo-Saxon objects. Further metal-detector finds of fifth–sixth century objects are known from the area but their exact provenance is unknown.

vicinity. The place may have been special for selected groups or communities who defined their identities in relation to the hill and the gatherings which took place upon it. For these groups, travelling to the cemetery would mean that the site would be visible over considerable distances while the dead may have 'overlooked' the living during their everyday lives.

Other archaeological features provide hints that Loveden Hill may have been a special focus beyond its use as a burial site. Initially it was thought that the burial site focused upon a prehistoric mound.[76] A later excavator, Nigel Kerr, considered this to be a natural knoll, but whilst this may be so, the early Anglo-Saxons may well have regarded the feature as an ancient burial mound.[77] There are a number of cases where early medieval burial sites focus upon mound-like natural features in the same way that prehistoric barrows are re-used.[78] In addition, Fennell suggested that the feature may have been enlarged in the early medieval period, although the evidence is unclear,[79] while, aerial photographs hint at the presence of other undated mounds close to the cemetery on the hilltop. It has been argued that ancient barrows were re-used as burial sites because they had come to be regarded as the dwellings or burials of 'ancestors' or 'supernatural' groups.[80] Their association with the past and the dead made them liminal places between this and other worlds, places of intercession with the sacred, and places important in defining social memories. The fragmentary evidence hints at the possibility that these features could have attracted burials to Loveden Hill and the mounds may have been foci for gatherings and ceremonies.[81] If this was the case, the earlier structures provided a common monumental focus to the cemetery and a ready-made 'stage' for ritual performances, as well as providing a tangible link to imagined pasts and ancestors.

Aerial photographs also suggest a series of enclosures associated with the cemetery. Although undated, these could also be associated with early medieval activities on the hill. There are tentative hints of enclosures associated with other cremation cemeteries, maybe reflecting settlement or ritual activity close to the cremation burial site.[82] It is possible that they represent corrals for animals brought either for sacrifice or for exchange by mourners. Only excavation around cremation cemeteries will reveal the date and character of such features, but they hint that the 'site' extended beyond the area used for burial to include other arenas of social activity.

The possibility that the area around Loveden Hill may have had special functions in the early Anglo-Saxon period is also raised by the discovery of a whetstone or sceptre from nearby in the parish of Hough-on-the-Hill to the north-east of the modern village. The terminal is formed in the shape of a human head and shoulders and the piece is made from stone that may derive from southern Scotland. Comparisons with whetstones from Uncleby and Sutton Hoo suggest a seventh-century date, and a ceremonial and royal

---

76 Fennell 1964, 78. Also, an Abercromby type A Beaker has been recovered from the parish (Hough-on-the-Hill) and may have come from Loveden Hill: Lincoln SMR record 30290. 77 Semple 1998, Thäte 1996; Williams 1997. 78 Williams 1997; Hall and Whyman 1996, 117–18. 79 Fennell 1964, 80–2. 80 Williams 1997. 81 Lincoln SMR record 30284 and 30288. 82 Lincoln SMR record 30284 and 30288; Hills 1977, 31; Leahy 1998, 94; Leahy pers comm; Williams 2002b.

function has long been proposed for such objects.[83] This object is most closely paralleled by the whetstone from mound 1 at Sutton Hoo and may indicate that upon Loveden Hill, or close by, was a centre of political authority in the pre-Viking period. Inevitably, the evidence is fragmentary, but it may be no coincidence that the neighbourhood of the hill was a wapentake meeting place in the later Anglo-Saxon period.[84]

Other sites support the interpretation of cremation cemeteries as operating, in part, as central places of assembly (figs. 5.6 and 5.7). Some also utilize prominent hills (e.g. Hall Hill, West Keal), while elsewhere the tops of ridges with wide views in certain directions were chosen (e.g. Cleatham)[85], or locations next to important routes (i.e. Roman roads – e.g. Baston,[86] Newark,[87] Thurmaston)[88]. Some of these sites seem to focus upon pre-existing monuments. Also, as mentioned earlier, many cremation cemeteries (although by no means all) seem to be associated with important Roman-period settlements. Examples of cemeteries close to Roman centres include sites seemingly precisely placed outside the walls of Roman towns and often overlying Roman cemeteries at York,[89] Ancaster, Lincolnshire,[90] Longthorpe, Cambridgeshire,[91] Great Casterton, Rutland,[92] and Caistor St Edmund, Norfolk.[93] Meanwhile close relationships exist with major Roman roadside settlements at Newark, Nottinghamshire,[94] Brettenham[95] and Great Walsingham,[96] in Norfolk, and Lackford in Suffolk.[97] Such relationships are usually explained as evidence for 'continuity' in settlement patterns between the Roman and early medieval periods,[98] or else are related to the political and military geography of Germanic invasion and settlement in which 'Anglo-Saxon' mercenaries first gained a foothold through agreed settlement with British tyrants whose power centred on these sites.[99] An alternative interpretation of this pattern may instead focus upon the potential for abandoned Roman towns to act as enclosures for assembly, with mortuary functions forming only part of their broader socio-political and economic roles. There is little evidence that Roman towns retained their social and administrative functions beyond the early fifth century. Rather than being concentrations of

83 Everson and Stocker 1999, 182–6; Evison 1975; Simpson 1979. 84 Fennell 1964, 74; Sawyer 1998, 51; Pantos 2002, 110; Lincoln SMR Record No. 35331. A further relevant relationship might be possible continuities between the location of cremation cemeteries and soke centres. This is a point discussed by Paul Everson (1993, 98) and Kevin Leahy (1999, 130). 85 Mayes and Dean 1976. 86 Kinsley 1989. 87 Williams 1983. 88 Stead 1956. 89 Leahy 1993, 39; Meaney 1964, 151. Note that Meaney regards this as a cremation cemetery overlying Roman inhumations and cremations; Leahy sees it as a 'mixed-rite' cemetery. This author follows Meaney in this case. 90 Frere and St Joseph 1974. 91 Grainger and Mahany unpublished. 92 Myres and Green 1973; Penn 2000. 93 Kinsley 1989. 94 Bagnall Smith 1999; Clarke 1937; Gurney 1995; Meaney 1964, 169–70. 95 Meaney 1964, 184. 96 Lethbridge 1951. 97 E.g. Williamson 1993. 98 Myres 1969; 1986; Higham 1992. 99 Myres and Green 1973.

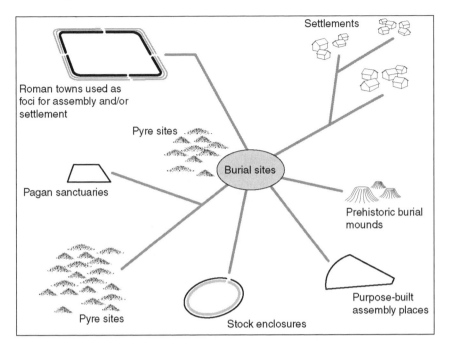

Settlements

Roman towns used as
foci for assembly and/or
settlement

Pyre sites

Burial sites

Pagan sanctuaries

Prehistoric burial
mounds

Purpose-built
assembly places

Pyre sites

Stock enclosures

Figure 5.6 Model of possible spatial relationships between early Anglo-Saxon
assembly, settlement, sacred places and cremation cemeteries.

population, they may have been used as places of meeting, their association
with an existing or earlier centre of political authority giving legitimacy to
meetings held there.

The best case of this relationship is at Caistor St Edmund in Norfolk where
two large and well-known cremation cemeteries were placed in situations
overlooking the site of the Roman civitas capital of the *Iceni* in the fifth and
sixth centuries.[100] Little evidence has been found for activity within the Roman
town at this time, but by the late seventh century, metal-detected and excavated
finds suggest that adjacent to Caistor was a 'productive site'; perhaps a high
status residence, trading place or even an early unrecorded monastic site.[101]
This may have been a new foundation sometime during the seventh century,
but equally it could represent the development of an existing central place
whose presence became archaeologically visible with changing patterns in the
circulation and deposition of coins and other copper and iron items.[102] The
area of the town may have been a place of continued political authority,

100 Scull 1992, 12; Penn 2000. 101 A similar argument has been put forward by Williamson
1993, 67. 102 Leahy 2000; Ulmschneider 2000.

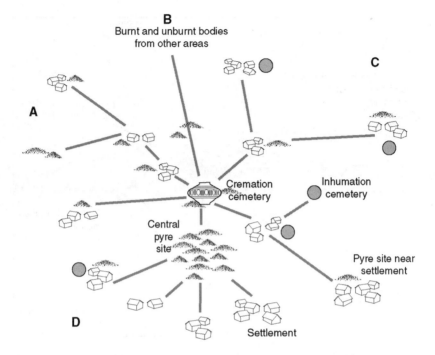

Figure 5.7 Cremation cemeteries as places for assembling the dead. Hypothetical models of relationships and pathways between early Anglo-Saxon settlements, pyre sites, inhumation cemeteries and large cremation cemeteries. Area A suggests a model of cremation at or near settlements before the remains are transported to a central cemetery. Area B illustrates the possibility that some individuals may have travelled long distances before being buried at a large cremation cemetery. Area C suggests the possibility that settlements could use different burial sites, some corpses being inhumed in the locality of settlements, while other dead individuals are taken to large cremation cemeteries. Area D adds the possibility that there were separate, centrally located, pyre sites where corpses were taken before a procession led to the cemetery. Scenarios are not mutually exclusive, and all may have involved some cremations taking place close to the cemetery. Areas A and C reflect the pattern most likely to have taken place around Loveden Hill.

assembly and ritual practices in the fifth and sixth centuries even if it was abandoned as a centre of population.

CONCLUSIONS

This essay has argued that we need to re-think the way we understand early Anglo-Saxon cemeteries. I would argue that although the term 'cemetery' is useful, it can lead us to make certain assumptions which may not be appropriate when applied to the large cremation cemeteries of the East Midlands and East Anglia. This special group of burial sites can be regarded as places of assembly in two ways.

It can be argued that cremation cemeteries were places for the assembly of the dead on a scale that is unprecedented for rural communities in the British Isles before the construction of parish churches towards the end of the first millennium AD. In this sense, the size of the cemeteries, the post-cremation rites enacted at them, and the use of distinctive and prominent topographic locations combined to allow the sites to serve as places of assembly. These were not only assemblies for the living, but also places for assembling and burying the dead in order to create the impression of communality and ancestors in the landscape.

Discussions of central and sacred places in other periods tend to focus upon the significance of large-scale monument-building programmes. In this light, it may seem difficult to regard the collection of small urns and burnt bones as comparable evidence. Yet the size of the cemeteries, the social significance of cremation, and the nature of the cremation burial rite combine to illustrate the importance of these places in the early Anglo-Saxon landscape. This relationship with place was emphasized by selecting specific sites with sacred associations – the use of ancient monuments and distinctive hill-top locations as at Loveden Hill are simply two of a series of options available and utilized by cremation cemeteries of this period. In other instances, the ruined enclosure of a defended Roman small town may have been used as a focus with the cremation cemetery re-using the location of an extra-mural Roman cemetery.

Related to the funerary use of the site, cremation cemeteries could have been places of assembly in addition to gatherings for mortuary practices yielding few archaeological traces. Unlike communities of the late seventh and eighth centuries AD, communities of the fifth, sixth and early seventh centuries did not have available large numbers of portable artefacts likely to be lost or left at sites of exchange, trade, and other kinds of gathering away from settlements. Such meetings remain archaeologically invisible. If we cannot even find the pyre sites associated with the cremation cemeteries, we must keep open the possibility that other activities taking place close by may have yet to be identified archaeologically. In this sense, it may be possible that the burial area at cremation cemeteries constitutes the only visible part of a larger central place, or one of a series of closely related locations for select communities in fifth- to seventh-century England. There is every possibility that in proximity to cremation cemeteries are social, religious and political foci interlocked with this central burial place. To develop this argument in future would require new fieldwork in the environs of these important early medieval burial sites.[103]

103 Vince 2001.

ACKNOWLEDGMENTS

Thanks to the staff of the East Midlands Sites and Monuments Records including Virginia Baddeley (West Bridgford), Ed Dickinson (Grimsby), Andy Myers (Matlock), Sarah Grundy and Jill Stephenson (Lincoln), Mike Hemblade (Scunthorpe), Richard Knox and Peter Liddle (Leicester) for courteously providing information. Special thanks must go to Kevin Leahy (North Lincolnshire Museum, Scunthorpe) for valuable discussions, hospitality, good humour and making time to accompany me to the sites of Lincolnshire cremation cemeteries. Vicki Cummings and Seán Goddard helped with illustrations. I appreciate the comments of Vicki Cummings, Cathy Lloyd, Jackie McKinley, Kevin Leahy and Elizabeth Wilson who read earlier drafts of the paper. Aliki Pantos and Sarah Semple gave generous support and advice as well as editorial rigour. This research was conducted with the financial and logistical support of Trinity College Carmarthen. All errors are my own responsibility.

REFERENCES

Adkins, R.A. and Petchey, M.R., 1984: 'Secklow hundred mound and other meeting place mounds in England', *Archaeological Journal* **141**, 243–51.

Arnold, C.J., 1997: *An archaeology of the early Anglo-Saxon kingdoms.* London.

Babu, M.M., 1994: 'Post-cremation-urn-burial of the Phayengs (Manipur): a study of mortuary behaviour', *Eastern Anthropologist* **47(2)**, 157–71.

Bagnall Smith, J., 1999: 'Votive objects and objects of votive significance from Great Walsingham', *Britannia* **30**, 21–56.

Barrett, J., 1994: *Fragments from antiquity: an archaeology of social life in Britain, 2900–1200 BC.* Oxford.

Bevan, W., 1999: 'The landscape context of the Iron-Age square-barrow burials, East Yorkshire', in J. Downes and T. Pollard (eds), *The loved body's corruption.* Glasgow. 69–93.

Blair, W.J., 1995: 'Anglo-Saxon pagan shrines and their prototypes', *Anglo-Saxon Studies in Archaeology and History* **8**, 1–28.

Bloch, M. and Parry, J., (eds), 1982: *Death and the regeneration of life.* Cambridge.

Bond, J. 1996: 'Burnt offerings: animal bone in Anglo-Saxon cremations', *World Archaeology* **28**:1, 76–88.

Bradley, R., 1998: *The significance of monuments.* London.

Branigan, K., 1998: 'The nearness of you: proximity and distance in early Minoan funerary landscapes', in K. Branigan (ed.) *Cemetery and society in the Aegean Bronze Age.* Sheffield. 14–26.

Brisbane, M. 1980: 'Anglo-Saxon burials: pottery, production and social structure', in

P. Rahtz, T. Dickinson and L. Watts (eds), *Anglo-Saxon cemeteries 1979*. Oxford. 209–16.

Brück, J., 1998: 'In the footsteps of the ancestors: a review of Christopher Tilley's "A phenomenology of landscape: places, paths and monuments"', *Archaeological Review from Cambridge* 15:1, 23–36.

Bullough, D.A., 1983: 'Burial, community and belief in the early medieval west', in P. Wormald (ed.), *Ideal and reality in Frankish and Anglo-Saxon society*. Oxford. 175–201.

Bullough, D.A., 2000: 'Anglo-Saxon institutions and early English society', in D. Pelteret (ed.), *Anglo-Saxon history – basic readings*. London. 1–20.

Carnegie, S. and Filmer-Sankey, W., 1993: 'A Saxon "cremation pyre" from the Snape Anglo-Saxon cemetery, Suffolk', *Anglo-Saxon Studies in Archaeology and History* 6, 106–11.

Carver, M., 1998: *Sutton Hoo: burial ground of kings?* London.

Chagnon, N., 1968: *Yanomamö: the fierce people*. London.

Clarke, R., 1937: 'The Roman villages at Brettenham and Needham and the contemporary road system', *Norfolk Archaeological Society* 26, 123–63.

Covarrubias, M. 1937: *Island of Bali*. London.

Cummings, V., 2000a: 'Myth, memory and metaphor: the significance of place, space and the landscape in Mesolithic Pembrokeshire', in R. Young (ed.), *Mesolithic lifeways: current research from Britain and Ireland*. Leicester. 87–95.

Cummings, V. 2000b: 'Landscapes in motion: interactive computer imagery and the Neolithic landscapes of the Outer Hebrides', in C. Buck, V. Cummings, C. Henley, S. Mills and S. Trick (eds), *UK chapter of computer applications and quantitative methods in archaeology*, B.A.R. International Series 844. Oxford. 11–20.

Dark, K., 2000: *Britain and the end of the Roman empire*. Stroud.

Davies, D.J., 1997: *Death, ritual and belief: the rhetoric of funerary rites*. London.

Downes, J., 1999: 'Cremation: a spectacle and a journey', in J. Downes and T. Pollard (eds), *The loved body's corruption: archaeological contributions to the study of human mortality*. Glasgow. 19–30.

Eagles, B., 1989: 'Lindsey', in S. Bassett (ed.). *The origins of Anglo-Saxon kingdoms*. Leicester. 202–12.

Edmonds, M., 1999: *Ancestral geographies in the Neolithic*. London.

Esmonde Cleary, S., 1989: *The ending of Roman Britain*. London.

Esmonde Cleary, S., 2000: 'Putting the dead in their place: burial location in Roman Britain', in J. Pearce, M. Millett and M. Struck (eds), *Burial, society and context in the Roman world*. Oxford. 127–42.

Everson, P. 1993: 'Pre-Viking settlement in Lindsey', in A. Vince (ed.), *Pre-Viking Lindsey*. Lincoln. 91–100.

Everson, P. and Stocker, D., 1999: *Corpus of Anglo-Saxon stone sculpture. Volume V: Lincolnshire*. Oxford.

Evison, V.I. 1975: 'Pagan Saxon whetstones', *Antiquaries Journal* 55, 70–85.

Fennell, K.R., undated: *Excavation of an Anglo-Saxon cemetery at Hough-on-the-Hill, Lincolnshire*. Unpublished Report, Lincoln Sites and Monuments Record.

Fennell, K.R., 1964: 'The Anglo-Saxon cemetery at Loveden Hill (Hough-on-the-

Hill) Lincolnshire and its significance in relation to the Dark Age settlement of the East Midlands'. Unpublished PhD thesis, University of Nottingham.

Fennell, K.R., 1974: 'Pagan Saxon Lincolnshire', *Archaeological Journal* 131, 283–88.

Fleming, A., 1999: 'Phenomenology and the megaliths of Wales: a dreaming too far?', *Oxford Journal of Archaeology* 18(2), 119–25.

Fowler, C., 2001: 'Personhood and social relations in the British Neolithic with a study from the Isle of Man', *Journal of Material Culture* 6/2, 137–63.

Frere, S.S. and St Joseph, J.K., 1974: 'The Roman fortress at Longthorpe', *Britannia* 5, 1–70.

Geertz. C., 1984: *Negara: the theatre state in nineteenth-century Bali.* London.

Geertz, C., 1993: *Local knowledge.* London.

Grainger, G. and Mahany, C., unpublished: 'Roman and Anglo-Saxon burials, and a Roman kiln, excavated at Great Casterton in 1966'. Leicester.

Gurney, D., 1995: 'Small towns and villages in Roman Norfolk: the evidence of surface and metal-detector finds', in A.E. Brown (ed.), *Roman small towns in Eastern England and beyond.* Oxford. 53–67.

Habenstein, R.W. and Lamers, W.M., 1963: *Funeral customs the world over.* (2nd edn.). London.

Hall, D. and Coles, J., 1994: *Fenland survey: an essay in landscape and persistance.* London.

Hall, R.A. and Whyman, M., 1996: 'Settlement and monasticism at Ripon, North Yorkshire, from the 7th to 11th centuries AD', *Medieval Archaeology* 40, 62–150.

Härke, H., 1990: '"Warrior graves"? The background of the Anglo-Saxon weapon burial rite', *Past & Present* 126, 22–43.

Härke, H., 1997: 'Early Anglo-Saxon social structure', in J. Hines (ed.), *The Anglo-Saxons from the migration to the eighth century: an ethnographic perspective.* Woodbridge. 125–70.

Härke, H., 2001: 'Cemeteries as places of power', in M. De Jong, T. Theuws with C. van Rhijn (eds) *Topographies of power in the early middle ages.* Leiden. 9–30.

Hertz, R.,1960: *Death and the right hand.* London.

Higham, N., 1992: *Rome, Britain and the Anglo-Saxons.* London.

Hills, C., 1977: *The Anglo-Saxon cemetery at Spong Hill, North Elmham. Part I: catalogue of cremations.* Dereham.

Hills, C., Penn, K. and Rickett, R., 1984: *The Anglo-Saxon cemetery at Spong Hill, North Elmham. Part III: catalogue of inhumations.* Dereham.

Hines, J., 1997: 'Religion: the limits of knowledge', in J. Hines (ed.), *The Anglo-Saxons from the migration to the eighth century: an ethnographic perspective.* Woodbridge.

Hobert, M., 1978: 'The path of the soul: the legitimacy of nature in Balinese conceptions of space', in G.B. Milner (ed.), *Natural symbols in South East Asia.* London. 5–29.

Huntingdon, R. and Metcalf, D., 1991: *Celebrations of death.* Cambridge.

Jones, G., 1984: *A history of the Vikings.* Oxford.

Kan, S., 1989: *Symbolic immortality: the Tlingit potlatch of the nineteenth century.* Washington.

Kinsley, A., 1989: *The Anglo-Saxon cemetery at Millgate, Newark-on-Trent, Nottinghamshire.* Nottingham.

Kirk, J., 1956: 'Anglo-Saxon cremation and inhumation in the Upper Thames Valley in pagan times', in D. Harden (ed.), *Dark Age Britain*. London.

Lane, T.W. with Hayes, P., 1993: *The Fenland project No. 8: Lincolnshire survey, the northern fen-edge*, East Anglian Archaeology 66. Sleaford.

Leahy, K., 1993: 'The Anglo-Saxon settlement of Lindsey', in A. Vince (ed.), *Pre-Viking Lindsey*. Lincoln.

Leahy, K., 1998: 'Cleatham, North Lincolnshire, the "Kirton in Lindsey" cemetery', *Medieval Archaeology* 42, 94–5.

Leahy, K., 1999: 'The formation of the Anglo-Saxon kingdom of Lindsey', *Anglo-Saxon Studies in Archaeology and History* 10, 127–34.

Leahy, K., 2000: 'Middle Anglo-Saxon metalwork from South Newbald and the "productive site" phenomenon in Yorkshire', in H. Geake and J. Kenny (eds), *Early Deira: archaeological studies of the East Riding in the fourth to ninth centuries AD*. Oxford. 51–82.

Leeds, E.T., 1913: *The archaeology of the Anglo-Saxon settlements*. Oxford.

Lethbridge, T.C., 1951: *A cemetery at Lackford, Suffolk*. Cambridge.

Loyn, H.R., 1984: *The governance of Anglo-Saxon England, 500–1087*. London.

Lucy, S., 1998: *The early Anglo-Saxon cemeteries of East Yorkshire: an analysis and reinterpretation*. Oxford.

Lucy, S., 2000: *The Anglo-Saxon way of death*. Stroud.

MacDougall, H.A., 1982: *Racial myth in English history: Trojans, Teutons, and Anglo-Saxons*. Montreal.

Macleod, W.C., 1925: 'Certain mortuary aspects of North-West coast culture', *American Anthropologist* 27, 122–49.

Magnusson, M. and Pálsson, H. (trans), 1969: *Laxdæla Saga*. London.

Mayes, P. and Dean, M.J., 1976: *An Anglo-Saxon cemetery at Baston, Lincolnshire*. Sleaford.

McKinley, J., 1994: *The Anglo-Saxon cemetery at Spong Hill, North Elmham. Part VII: the cremations*. Dereham.

McKinley, J., 1997: 'Bronze Age "barrows", funerary rites and rituals of cremation', *Proceedings of the Prehistoric Society* 63, 129–45.

Meaney, A.L., 1964: *A gazetteer of early Anglo-Saxon burial sites*. Oxford.

Meaney, A.L., 1995: 'Pagan English sanctuaries, place-names and hundred meeting places', *Anglo-Saxon Studies in Archaeology and History* 8, 29–42.

Monnerie, D., 1995: 'On "grandmothers", "grandfathers" and ancestors: conceptualizing the universe in Mono-Alu, Solomen Islands', in D. de Coppet and A. Iteanu (eds), *Cosmos and society in Oceania*. Oxford. 105–35.

Myres, J.N.L., 1969: *Anglo-Saxon pottery and the settlement of England*. Oxford.

Myres, J.N.L., 1986: *The English settlements*. Oxford.

Myres, J.N.L. and Green, B., 1973: *The Anglo-Saxon cemeteries of Caistor-by-Norwich and Markshall*. London.

Myres, J.N.L. and Southern, W.H., 1973: *The Anglo-Saxon cremation cemetery at Sancton, East Yorkshire*. Hull.

Pader, E.J., 1982: *Symbolism, social relations and the interpretation of mortuary remains*. Oxford.

Pantos, A., 2002: 'Assembly-places in the Anglo-Saxon period: aspects of form and location'. Unpublished DPhil thesis, University of Oxford.

Parker Pearson, M., 1993: 'The powerful dead: relationships between the living and the dead', *Cambridge Archaeological Journal* 3, 203–29.

Parry, J., 1982: 'Sacrificial death and the necrophagus ascetic', in M. Bloch and J. Parry (eds), *Death and the regeneration of life*. Cambridge. 74–110.

Parry, J., 1994: *Death in Benares*. Cambridge.

Penn, K., 2000: *Excavations on the Norwich Southern bypass, 1989–1991. Part II: The Anglo-Saxon cemetery at Harford Farm, Caistor St Edmund, Norfolk*, East Anglian Archaeology Report 92. Gressenhall.

Ravn, M., 1999: 'Theoretical and methodological approaches to Migration Period burials', in M. Rundkvist (ed.), *Grave matters: eight studies of first millennium AD burials in Crimea, England and southern Scandinavia*. Oxford.

Reynolds, A., 1999: *Later Anglo-Saxon England: life and landscape*. Stroud.

Richards, C., 1996: 'Monuments as landscape: creating the centre of the world in late Neolithic Orkney', *World Archaeology* 28, 190–208.

Richards, J., 1987: *The significance of form and decoration of Anglo-Saxon cremation urns*. Oxford.

Richards, J., 1992: 'Anglo-Saxon symbolism', in M. Carver (ed.), *The age of Sutton Hoo*. Woodbridge. 131–48.

Richards, J., 1995: 'An archaeology of Anglo-Saxon England', in G. Ausenda (ed.), *After Empire: towards an ethnology of Europe's barbarians*. Woodbridge. 51–66.

Rishøj Pedersen, L., 1974/5: 'Religious activities during the dry season among the Lao Song Dam, Thailand', *Folk* 16–17, 345–81.

Rivers, W.H.R., 1906: *The Todas*. London.

Sawyer, P., 1998: *Anglo-Saxon Lincolnshire*. Lincoln.

Scull, C., 1992: 'Before Sutton Hoo: structures of power and society in early East Anglia', in M. Carver (ed.), *The age of Sutton Hoo*. Woodbridge. 3–23.

Semple, S., 1998: 'A fear of the past: the place of the prehistoric burial mound in the ideology of middle and later Anglo-Saxon England', *World Archaeology* 30:1, 109–26.

Simpson, J., 1979: 'The King's whetstone', *Antiquity* 53, 96–101.

Stead, I.M., 1956: 'An Anglian cemetery on the Mount, York', *Yorkshire Archaeological Journal* 39, 427–35.

Stenton, F., 1971: *Anglo-Saxon England*. Oxford.

Stoodley, N., 1999: *The spindle and the spear*. Oxford.

Thäte, E., 1996: 'Alte Denkmäler und frühgeschichtliche Bestattungen: Ein sächsisch-angelsächsischer Totenbrauch und seine Kontinuität', *Archäologische Informationen* 19/1–2, 105–16.

Theuws, F., 1999: 'Changing settlement patterns, burial grounds and the symbolic construction of ancestors and communities in the late Merovingian Southern Netherlands', in C. Fabech and J. Ringtved (eds), *Settlement and landscape*. Moesgård. 337–50.

Tilley, C., 1994: *A phenomenology of landscape*. Oxford.

Timby, J., 1993: 'Sancton I Anglo-Saxon cemetery. Excavations carried out between 1976 and 1980', *Archaeological Journal* **150**, 243–365.

Toynbee, J.M.C., 1971: *Death and burial in the Roman world*. Baltimore.

Ulmschneider, K., 2000: 'Settlement, economy and the "productive" site: Middle Anglo-Saxon Lincolnshire AD 650–780', *Medieval Archaeology* **44**, 53–80.

Van Gennep, A., 1960: *Rites of passage*. London.

Vince, A., 2001: *A resource assessment and research agenda for the early and middle Anglo-Saxon period (5th to 9th centuries AD) in the East Midlands*. Unpublished Consultation Manuscript, Leicester University, East Midlands Archaeological Research Framework.

Vitebsky, P., 1993: *Dialogues with the dead: the discussion of mortality among the Sora of Eastern India*. Cambridge.

Wales, H.G.Q., 1931: *Siamese state ceremonies; their history and function*. London.

Webster, L., 1973: 'Loveden Hill, Medieval Britain in 1972', *Medieval Archaeology* **17**, 146.

Welch, M., 1992: *Anglo-Saxon England*. London.

Whitelock, D., 1952: *The beginnings of English society*. London.

Wilkinson, L., 1980: 'Problems of analysis and interpretation of skeletal remains', in P. Rahtz, T. Dickinson and L. Watts (eds), *Anglo-Saxon cemeteries 1979*. Oxford, 221–31.

Williams, D. and Vince, A., 1997: 'The characterization and interpretation of early to middle Saxon granitic tempered pottery in England', *Medieval Archaeology* **41**, 214–19.

Williams, H.M.R., 1997: 'Ancient landscapes and the dead: the reuse of prehistoric and Roman monuments as early Anglo-Saxon burial sites', *Medieval Archaeology* **41**, 1–31.

Williams, H.M.R., 1998: 'Monuments and the past in early Anglo-Saxon England', *World Archaeology* **30:1**, 90–108.

Williams, H.M.R., 1999a: 'Identities and cemeteries in Roman and early medieval archaeology', in P. Baker, C. Forcey, S.Jundi and R. Witcher (eds), *TRAC 98 Proceedings of the Eighth Annual Theoretical Roman Archaeology Conference*. Oxford. 96–108.

Williams, H.M.R., 1999b: 'Placing the dead: investigating the location of wealthy barrow burials in seventh century England', in M. Rundkvist (ed.), *Grave matters: eight studies of first millennium AD burials in Crimea, England and southern Scandinavia*. Oxford. 57–86.

Williams, H.M.R., 2000: '"The Burnt Germans of the Age of Iron", Early Anglo-Saxon mortuary practices and the study of cremation in past societies'. Unpublished PhD thesis, University of Reading.

Williams, H.M.R., 2001: 'An ideology of transformation: cremation rites and animal sacrifice in early Anglo-Saxon England', in N. Price (ed.), *The archaeology of shamanism*. London. 193–212

Williams, H.M.R., 2002a: '"The remains of pagan Saxondom"? The study of Anglo-Saxon cremation rites', in S. Lucy and A. Reynolds (eds), *Burial in early medieval England and Wales*. Leeds. 47–71.

Williams, H.M.R., 2002b: 'Cemeteries as central places – place and identity in Migration Period eastern England', in B. Hårdh and L. Larsson (eds), *Central places in the migration and Merovingian periods: papers from the 52nd Sachsensymposium, Lund, August 2001*. Uppåkrastudier 6. Lund. 341–62.

Williams, P., 1983: *An Anglo-Saxon cremation cemetery at Thurmaston, Leicestershire*. Leicester.

Williamson, T., 1993: *The origins of Norfolk*. Manchester.

Wilson, D. 1992: *Anglo-Saxon paganism*. London.

Wilson, D.M., 1959: 'Loveden Hill, Medieval Britain in 1958', *Medieval Archaeology* 3, 297.

Wylie, W.M., 1855: 'The burning and burial of the dead', *Archaeologia* 37/2, 455–78.

Locations of assembly in early
Anglo-Saxon England

SARAH SEMPLE

The hundredal system is first described in sources of the tenth century,[1] but the earliest detailed account of the Anglo-Saxon administrative framework is to be found in Domesday Book, a snap-shot of the eleventh-century system of governance. Although the corpus of surviving hundred and wapentake place-names provides a resource for identifying the locations of assemblies, again these are usually from late Anglo-Saxon and post-Conquest documentary sources. Scholars have argued that this late system could in part represent an earlier geography,[2] but it is questionable whether late Anglo-Saxon sources can be used to examine the social systems of the fifth to early eighth centuries.[3] Audrey Meaney has established a tentative developmental scheme based on the hundred-names of Cambridgeshire, in which she argues that the earliest types of assembly-site are those represented by hundred-names that indicate meeting locations at natural gathering points such as crossroads and fords.[4] Without being able to place this scheme within a chronological framework, however, questions of how early Anglo-Saxon political arrangements functioned, whether assembly was part of the process of governance, and if so where it took place, remain open to debate.

The English material provides a strong contrast to the evidence for assembly from pre-Christian societies in Ireland and Scandinavia. In early historic sources for Ireland, five 'royal' sites are mentioned as regional centres of kingship: ancient sacral seats of power.[5] It is argued from their coherent morphology, scale and siting, that the written sources are not purely invention, but that sacral aspects of medieval kingship, representing genuine artefacts of pagan prehistoric kingship,[6] were rooted in these sites.[7] Tara in particular was

---

1 Loyn 1974; Loyn 1984; Meaney 1997, 195. 2 Warner 1988; Hooke 1985, 75–116; Loyn 1984, 140–8; Sawyer 1978, 197–200. 3 Pantos, this volume. 4 Meaney 1995 and 1997. 5 Teamhair (Tara, Co. Meath), Emain Macha (Navan, Co. Armargh), Dún Ailinne (Knockaulin, Co. Kildare), Crúachain (Rathcroghan, Co. Roscommon) and Caisel (Cashel, Co. Tipperary). Newman 1998, 129. 6 Such as taboos, rites of passage, assembly and inauguration. 7 Newman 1998, 130–2.

a place of sacral pre-eminence and continued to have regional, royal and ritual status throughout the first millennium AD.[8] At such centres of prehistoric, pagan, sacral kingship,[9] the mound in particular is thought to have represented a central place sacred to the gods and a platform on which a divine king could 'communicate' with the 'otherworld'. Landscapes of ancient monuments, developed and elaborated in the late Iron Age, were thus the interface between the real world and the 'otherworld'.[10]

In the later and more developed societies of Scandinavia, between AD 800–1100, unity between royal power, assembly and religious/cult practice is strongly evident at ceremonial complexes such as Gamla Uppsala, Sweden. Here, in the eleventh century, Adam of Bremen described an elaborate and lavish temple,[11] a sacred well and tree and sacrificial acts such as the hanging of men and animals.[12] These various focal points of ritual, and the activities described, occurred within an enceinte of ancient royal burial mounds dating from the Migration Period.[13] The late sources for the Scandinavian world include tales and motifs in which burial mounds were seats of power from which a king or man might be acknowledged as a legitimate inheritor or heir.[14] In some cases the kings may even have been believed to reside in the burial mound after death.[15] These concepts are similar to Irish beliefs that the *síd* mound, a physical feature of the great royal sites such as Tara, was a seat of kingship *and* a conduit to the 'otherworld'.[16] In Scandinavia, the existence of assembly-sites conjoined with locations of pagan religious practice, and with royal connections, indicates a strong unity between administration, royalty and ritual.[17] As at early Irish royal/ritual sites, administration and cult practice were, 'two sides of the same coin',[18] and monuments from the ancient past, elaborated by the addition of contemporary monuments, formed a stage for both religious and political events. The mound, ancient or contemporary, sepulchral or non-sepulchral, seems to have been an integral component of the location and the rituals enacted.

---

8 Warner, this volume. 9 Newman 1998, 130–2. 10 Warner, this volume. 11 *Gesta Hammaburgensis Ecclasiæ Pontificum.* Book IV, XXVI. Schmeidler, 1917, IV, XXVI. 12 The description of sacrifices is found in ibid. ch. XXVIII whereas reference to the sacred well and tree is made in the later marginal note 138. 13 Roesdahl 1980, 157–8. 14 A summary of the source material is given by Ellis 1943, 106–11, and an example can be found in *Flateyjarbok: Oláfs saga helga,* II 9. 15 In *Friðólfs saga I,* 'My howe shall stand beside the forth. And there shall be but a short distance between mine and Þorsteinn's, for it is well that we should call to one another': Ellis 1943, 90–6. 16 Doherty 1985, 52; Warner this volume. 17 See Brink, this volume. In his discussion of Lytisberg, the name of the *thing* site is shown to contain the term *lytrr,* used for a pagan cult leader. 18 Brink, this volume.

AN ENGLISH MODEL?

Although parallels for Irish royal/ritual centres have been suggested in Scotland, both groups of sites have been attributed to a Celtic milieu: according to this view, comparable sites would not have existed in Anglo-Saxon England.[19] It can be suggested, however, that two excavated sixth-/seventh-century English sites provide a rare insight into the possible existence of similar arrangements in Anglo-Saxon England. Yeavering, Northumberland, provides evidence for the conjunction of a royal residence, an assembly structure and a pagan temple. Attested from historical sources as a place of assembly[20] – a function supported by the remarkable discovery of structure E[21] – it was within the British kingdom of *Goddodin* until *c*.605–16, and has been argued to follow the Celtic pattern of constituting royal centres around notable prehistoric sites.[22] Yeavering is, however, an extensive complex that developed spatially over time, and it is best regarded as a hybrid site combining both British and Anglo-Saxon building and ritual traditions from the earliest phases.[23] A palimpsest of ancient prehistoric remains is used as a background to a highly structured arrangement of buildings. Here, by the reign of Eadwine (AD 616–32) or his immediate predecessors, a centralized set of functions was in place; kingship seems to have gone hand in hand with cult, and assembly, as evidenced by structure E, clearly played a highly visible and important role within the organization of the settlement.[24]

In contrast, the burial ground at Sutton Hoo, Suffolk, does not exhibit clear evidence for assembly. The extensive, monumental burial ground contains burials elaborate enough to be described as royal,[25] and evidence for the killing and display of human victims.[26] It is similar in form to the royal/ritual centre at Gamla Uppsala, Sweden, in that burial mounds (in this case contemporary rather than ancient) formed a setting for activities such as sacrificial/judicial killing. Sutton Hoo differs from the Irish and Scandinavian ritual complexes and Yeavering, in that, although sited over an Iron Age field system, only marginal reference to these earlier remains is suggested.[27] Neither has the site produced evidence for either a settlement or a royal residence in close

---

19 Driscoll 1998, 143; Aitchson 1994, 310–11. **20** Bede records that people gathered at *Ad Gefrin* to hear Paulinus preach: *HE* II 14. **21** Hope Taylor 1977, fig. 57. **22** Driscoll 1998, 143; O'Brien 1999, 63. **23** Scull 1991. Some of the major ritual spatial arrangements and changes could be suggested to reflect Anglo-Saxon practice as much as British traditions particularly burial in relation to prehistoric monuments and the presence of standing posts and a square shrine type. See Blair 1995. **24** John Blair suggests that initial Anglian activity involved religious cult and meetings, but not necessarily a high-status residence, and that only with the planning and building of the major halls, did the site emerge as the *villa regia* referred to by Bede, Blair forthcoming, chapter 1. **25** Carver 1998, 134. **26** Ibid., 137–43. **27** Carver and Hummler 1990, 12–17; Hummler 1993, 21–3.

proximity. A key element that suggests Sutton Hoo perhaps functioned as more than just a place of disposal for the wealthy dead, is the complexity and ostentation of the burial assemblages. These are used to signal the perceived power and strength of the East Anglian kingdom, its continental ties and affiliations,[28] and, perhaps, through the use of certain objects, some burial deposits evoked *romanitas* as a way of legitimizing kingship.[29] In conjunction with elaborate grave display, the deviant burials suggest that people were killed and buried at the site as a further enactment of royal power.[30] It is clear from both the great funerary mounds and the deviant burials that both aspects of funerary practice were intended for an audience;[31] perhaps at certain times both rites took place simultaneously in a complex funerary display.[32]

Beyond suggesting that large gatherings may have occurred at these events, Sutton Hoo cannot be shown to be a site of assembly that functioned in the regularized manner of a late Anglo-Saxon hundred meeting-place; neither can Yeavering. These sites are remarkable as individual and unique entities, and they should rather be considered as evidence of the experimentation underway in emerging kingdoms. They are prototypes from a period when society was moving from tribal organization towards state formation, and only beginning to develop political and administrative organization. These sites were in operation in the same period that kings first began to issue laws, and at a time when the burial record is suggestive of experimentation, with communities, as well as emerging elite or aristocratic groups, trying extremely varied forms of funerary practice.[33] Direct parallels with either site are thus unlikely to be found. Between them, however, they present a core group of signifiers or functions that could be used as diagnostics – the use of prehistoric monuments, particularly complexes of monuments, and the creation of new contemporary monuments; the presence of buildings or indications of a royal residence; evidence of religious or ritual activity such as standing posts, building alignments, ox skulls or unusual burials; and some evidence of kingship, either in the form of elaborate or impressive burials, objects that could be symbols of authority such as the whetstone from Sutton Hoo, or perhaps through evidence of deliberate killing and deviant burial.

The most significant shared diagnostic, however, is the centrality of burial. At Yeavering complex and extended funerary activity continues throughout the life of the site in the context of rapidly changing ritual foci and spatial

---

28 Carver 1998, 107. 29 The burial rites at Sutton Hoo show a distinct leaning towards the funerary practice of contemporary Scandinavia: Carver 1998, 107, 134–6. 30 Carver 1998, 140. 31 The Mound 1 grave goods and the manner of their deposition are suggested to be a type of constructed assemblage, the purpose of which was to engender myths and legends surrounding the great burial deposit and the person buried within: Williams 2001. 32 Carver 1998, 137–44, describes the site as a 'ceremonial centre'. 33 Geake 2002.

arrangements.[34] Sutton Hoo is a large multi-focal cemetery now known to have been in use from the sixth century, with late sixth- to seventh-century elements that indicate it may have been a place of events which required and drew audiences. This shared characteristic suggests that the early Anglo-Saxon funerary record should perhaps be re-examined for complex cemeteries which include the various features and diagnostic elements discussed above.

BURIAL AS A FORM OF COMMUNAL RITUAL

Recent social theory sees mourners as active participants in burial practice.[35] The participation of the living in the burial of the dead must have made cemeteries locations of periodic gathering and, by the nature of repeated practice, important focal places for the living. Hines defines religion as 'a human response to a perceived but intangible spirit world that coexists with the real and concrete human world'.[36] In prehistory the funerary monument is commonly identified as an interface for that response. The monument is a 'locale of discourse', a place where communication was facilitated between the living and the dead, its use and reuse acting as a legitimate route to the past.[37] This view has a particular resonance for early Anglo-Saxon England. Just as Bullough has suggested that cemeteries were more than foci for funerary ritual, Williams has argued that burial at ancient monuments could have facilitated contexts for social interaction.[38]

In pre-Christian Ireland and Scandinavia, cult, kingship and assembly are known to coincide with ancient monuments. Relict remains legitimated the assembly, the past being used to confirm the authority of the present. The use of ancient remains was arguably more than just a political tool. The mound or barrow was a pre-requisite, a point of contact with the 'otherworld', a place where the dead might reside: its use as a location and platform for assembly or inauguration ensured that the kingship was accepted as divinely tolerated and inspired.

Similarly, in England, places where burials are made in relation to prehistoric monuments, particularly barrows, could be a starting-point from which to examine places of early assembly. In Anglo-Saxon England there is no shortage of evidence for funerary activity associated with prehistoric remains; it accounts for approximately 17% of the burial record.[39] Whilst many examples comprise single, centrally-placed, secondary interments in prehis-

---

34 Hope Taylor 1977, 244–5. **35** Lucy 1998, 23–4. **36** Hines 1997, 377. **37** Barrett 1994, 50–1, 72. **38** Bullough 1983; Williams 1997; Williams 1998; Williams, this volume. **39** Williams 1997; O'Brien 1999; Semple 2002.

toric barrows, sites such as Uncleby, East Yorkshire are evidence of the use of ancient barrows as foci for more extensive burial grounds.

Mortimer's excavations at Uncleby revealed the repeated funerary use of a prehistoric barrow during the sixth to seventh centuries. This aspect has specific implications (fig. 6.1a).[40] As the cemetery grew, the monument may have become emblematic of the cumulative ancestral presence, and thus developed into a suitable point of interface with ancestors. It is plausible to suggest that for an early ritual/assembly site to develop solely from a funerary context, monumentality would be a pre-requisite.

Although Uncleby may demonstrate how an ancient monument becomes a centre for funerary ritual, however, a greater degree of complexity is needed to provide any kind of analogy to the centres at Yeavering and Sutton Hoo. A site with extensive multi-focal burial, using a range of prehistoric remains, with evidence of contemporary monument construction such as primary barrow burials or standing posts, would seem more comparable. It is interesting that Uncleby, like many other cemeteries of the sixth and seventh centuries, lies not in isolation but in a landscape marked by contemporaneous and successive burials spanning the sixth and seventh centuries.[41] The idea of multi-focal burial in relation to monuments is accepted in more restricted spatial relationships as at Winklebury Hill, Wiltshire (fig. 6.1b).[42] At Uncleby, although the burial sites are more widely spaced, is difficult not to see these sites as associated, describing a landscape significant for funerary practice and religious belief. This kind of extensive complexity is much more evocative of the type of 'central place' evident at Yeavering or Sutton Hoo.

Not far from Uncleby, Garton Station in East Yorkshire is well known for the rare occurrence of Anglo-Saxon secondary burials positioned in relation to an Iron Age square barrow cemetery.[43] The area is perhaps even more remarkable because a number of cemeteries of early medieval date occur in close proximity, using a variety of ancient earthworks (fig. 6.2).[44] These cemeteries are usually viewed in isolation, but it is not implausible to see them as related by their use of prehistoric monuments: a series of cemeteries set among a palimpsest of ancient remains marking an area of landscape of significant ritual status. The most significant difficulty with such an interpretation is the lack of absolute dates for such sites. In the Uncleby area the dating is too poor to suggest whether the various cemeteries were contemporaneous or successive, but they seem to cover the sixth to seventh centuries with increased activity in the seventh century. Garton Station and Garton II are both seventh-

---

40 Smith 1912. **41** Uncleby lies within an area of landscape with evidence of three further cemeteries: Painsthorpe Wold I, Barrow 4, Painsthorpe Wold 102 and Painsthorpe Wold 200: Mortimer 1905, 113–118, 120–1, 123–4. **42** Pitt Rivers 1898. **43** Stead 1991, 17–24. **44** Garton Station lies north of Garton II. Mortimer 1905, 247–57.

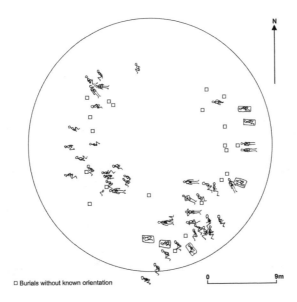

Figure 6.1a The cemetery at Uncleby, East Yorkshire (after Smith 1912, fig. 1).

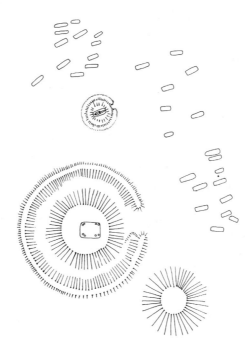

Figure 6.1b Multi-focal burial at Winklebury, Wiltshire (after Pitt Rivers 1898).

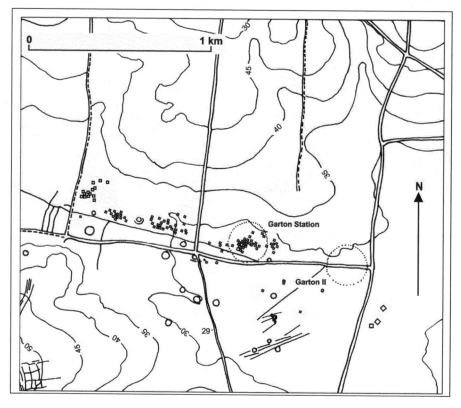

Figure 6.2 Garton Station and Garton II.

century,[45] although an explicit chronological relationship cannot be ascertained. It is difficult to imagine, however, that these broadly contemporary cemeteries, lying in close proximity, and distinctive in their use of visible monuments, existed in isolation from each other.

Two further locations of interest are Harford Farm, Norfolk and Dorchester-on-Thames, Oxfordshire. At Harford Farm, a series of five prehistoric barrows formed a backdrop for a cemetery of late seventh- to eighth-century date (fig. 6.3).[46] The spatial arrangement of the graves suggests multi-focal activity, and evidence for a square structure may indicate the presence of a Romano-British or early medieval shrine or religious building.[47] Dorchester-on-Thames shares these characteristics. An extensive complex of prehistoric remains forms a setting for five cemeteries of fifth- to

45 Lucy 1999, 12–43.   46 Penn 2000, fig. 3.   47 Blair 1995, 14–15.

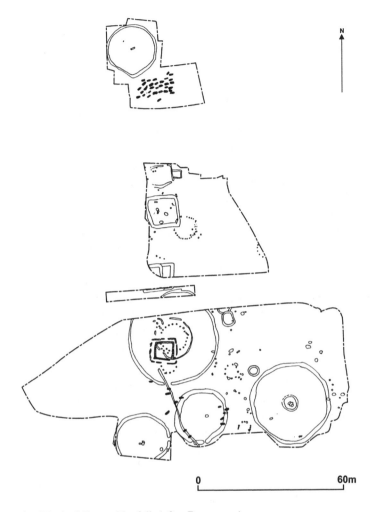

Figure 6.3 Harford Farm, Norfolk (after Penn 2000).

seventh-century date, three of which use prominent prehistoric remains.[48] A square structure, again suggested as a form of shrine,[49] lies north-west of the Roman town in close proximity to a group of barrows with secondary burials.

In both cases possible ritual structures/shrines are positioned in relation to complexes of prehistoric monuments also used for early Anglo-Saxon multi-focal funerary activity. By looking at the wider landscape rather than individual

48 Atkinson et al. 1951; Benson and Miles 1974, 66–8; Cook and Rowley 1985, 8–15. 49 Blair 1995, 13–15.

points, an integrated picture emerges of extensive ritual landscapes where the background of prehistoric remains is marked by both small and large funerary sites and ritual structures. The cemeteries of Ports Down and Portsdown III, Hampshire, usually discussed separately, can be considered in the same light. The dating is imprecise but at least two of the burial groups can be placed in the seventh century.[50] The evidence strongly indicates a funerary complex, rather than a series of separate and unrelated funerary events. A group of seventeen east-west burials (Ports Down), with few objects and a date range within the conversion period, are grouped around grave 6, which occupies a central position.[51] This burial truncated a Bronze Age interment, suggesting that it may have been secondary in a prehistoric barrow with focal burial occurring around the re-used mound. Some distance from the Ports Down cemetery (*c.*1km east), twelve skeletons were found in the nineteenth century, positioned around a long barrow at a crossroads (Portsdown III).[52] A spearhead indicated an Anglo-Saxon date for the group. Later excavations on the presumed site failed to re-locate either the long barrow or the cemetery. Instead, a prestigious male grave was discovered. This large grave, 2.44m (8ft) by 0.91m (3ft), contained a burial in a nailed coffin with a small bronze buckle, three iron knives and a bronze bound bucket of unusual form, with four small hanging-bowl-like escutcheons holding rings for suspension. Twenty-one metres (70ft) to the east, an east-west grave was discovered containing the body of an immature adult, possibly male, decapitated at the third cervical vertebra with the head replaced on the shoulders sideways, facing south. The long barrow is now thought to have been west of the crossroads. Here, varied use of prehistoric remains is very much in evidence, with multi-focal, extensive and complex funerary practice including an elaborate high-status burial. As at Sutton Hoo, the deviant or decapitate could suggest the presence of judicial killing. This range of funerary evidence, although quite disparate, overlaps in date, is placed in relation to a series of ancient monuments, and is marked by both elaborate wealthy burial and deviant burial. This is the type of eclectic mix of high-status and ritual behaviour that might parallel sites such as Yeavering or Sutton Hoo. Andrew Reynolds has suggested that the presence of deviant burials or killings is an important indication of a site of royal functions, and as at Sutton Hoo, the killings, sacrificial or judicial, were presumably intended for an audience.[53]

---

50 Geake 1997, 154. 51 Corney et al. 1967. 52 Bradley and Lewis 1968. 53 Reynolds 1998; Carver 1998.

BURIALS, MONUMENTS AND STRUCTURES

The structures found at some cemeteries, such as square enclosures, buildings and standing posts, may have provided focal points for forms of ritual practice. Simple square structures were identified at both Harford Farm and Dorchester-on-Thames placed in relation to monument groups that had provided a focus for extensive funerary activity. At Bishopstone, Sussex, an unusual trapezoidal timber building was positioned away from the main area of fifth- to sixth-century settlement and lay in immediate proximity to both the Anglo-Saxon cemetery and the prehistoric barrow that acted as a focus for the burials (fig. 6.4).[54] It has been suggested that the square structures at Dorchester-on-Thames and Harford Farm were shrines or religious structures of possibly late Roman or early Anglo-Saxon date. The building at Bishopstone is contemporary with the early Anglo-Saxon settlement. In all three examples, the structures could represent foci for ceremony and gathering.

A different form of ritual structure is found at Roche Court Down, Wiltshire, where a single prehistoric barrow and a possible Iron Age enclosure provided a focus for Anglo-Saxon funerary practice (fig. 6.5).[55] A small cemetery lies west of three barrows. The south-eastern barrow (3) was of prehistoric date, with evidence of a central secondary burial. Barrows 1 and 2 comprised a burial mound containing a primary, Anglo-Saxon, male inhumation (2) and a non-sepulchral mound (1). Although not wealthy in material terms, the large grave chamber (2) demonstrates that the east-south-east – west-north-west burial was perhaps of some prestige. Excavation of the non-sepulchral mound (1) revealed a central post-hole and internal concentric ditch. The monument was identical in proportion to the Anglo-Saxon grave mound and the orientation of the male grave in Barrow 2 was in alignment with the central post in Barrow 1. The two are therefore related and possibly contemporary. Once again multi-focal funerary practice is evident, and elite burial and secondary burial are also features. What is interesting here is the perhaps contemporary construction of a new non-funerary mound marked with a standing post, which seemingly performed a ritual function, perhaps as a marker for funerary and non-funerary ceremony. Standing posts and enclosures are both features of pre-Christian ritual practice evidenced by archaeological and written sources of the period.[56] John Blair has highlighted a group of examples where posts and enclosures make reference to prehistoric monuments.[57] A central standing post and a square enclosure replaced the stone circle within the western ring-ditch at Yeavering.[58] These structures

54 Bell 1977, fig. 86. 55 Stone 1932. 56 Meaney 1995; Blair 1995. 57 Blair 1995.
58 Hope Taylor 1977.

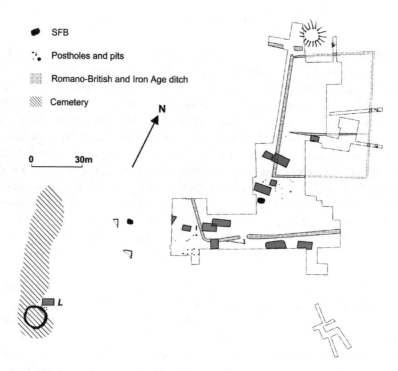

● SFB

∴ Postholes and pits

▦ Romano-British and Iron Age ditch

▨ Cemetery

N

0 ____ 30m

Figure 6.4 The Anglo-Saxon settlement and cemetery at Bishopstone, Sussex (after Bell 1977).

formed an important part of the ritual alignments of the site, and acted as a focus for early medieval burial. The alignments and structures at Yeavering were significant for religious ritual, and potentially for rituals witnessed by large groups of people. Harford Farm, Dorchester-on-Thames, Bishopstone and Roche Court Down all represent sites with a combination of contemporary and ancient monuments and multi-focal funerary practice. These various structures, whether enclosures, buildings or posts, can be used as evidence of developed ritual practice. Moreover, deviant burial also occurs at Roche Court Down, focused on a portion of the ditch characterized by a large mound. The burials in question are not dated but probably fall between the eighth and eleventh centuries, when deviant cemeteries and execution sites developed as part of the late Anglo-Saxon administrative and judicial system.[59]

A site with more complex structural evidence is Kemp Howe, East Yorkshire, a long barrow modified into a Bronze Age round barrow.[60] Both

59 Reynolds 1998. 60 Mortimer 1905, 336–8.

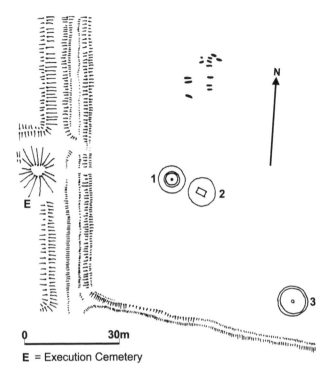

Figure 6.5 Roche Court Down, Wiltshire (after Stone 1932).

nineteenth-century and more recent excavations revealed Anglo-Saxon burials around the monument.[61] Radio-carbon dates place the cemetery within the eighth century.[62] As well as burial, groupings of posts are evident, along with a putative platform on the barrow and at least two sunken-featured buildings.[63] Here, at a relatively late period, a ritual complex based around a prehistoric monument may be evident. The barrow is one of three large and impressive monuments at a junction of potentially ancient routes. The late date of the burials at Kemp Howe is interesting and could be a further 'signifier'. The sites discussed so far, including Yeavering and Sutton Hoo, are marked by the extended complexity of burial. It could be argued that longevity of practice, or as in the case of Kemp Howe or Harford Farm, particularly late examples of funerary practice in relation to prehistoric monuments, are both suggestive of sites of long term, ritual significance.[64] Sites with a significant role in political and religious consciousness might have been relinquished only with great

61 Geake 1997, 158.   62 Geake 1997.   63 Dr Helen Geake pers comm.   64 Geake 1997, 154.

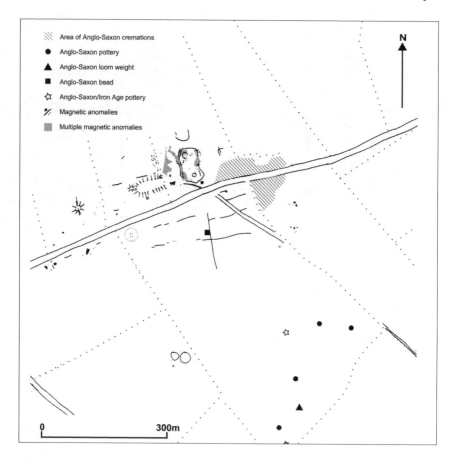

Figure 6.6 Rollright, Oxfordshire (after Lambrick 1988).

reluctance during the Conversion period, both due to their status as ancient and aristocratic burial grounds and perhaps because they had taken on further roles as prototype assembly-places.

A final cemetery for consideration is the cremation/inhumation cemetery at Little Rollright, Oxfordshire. The evidence for burial is very limited.[65] Cremations were discovered to the northeast of the extensive prehistoric

---

65 Prior to 1897, 200 yards east of the Kings Stone, a north – south bank incorporating stonework was revealed, overlying darker soil with 'many bones of men and horses. Burnt stones, and a very few fragments of pottery are scattered about.' East of this twelve skeletons were found and in 1836 an Anglo-Saxon cremation urn with a knife, circular bronze ring, disc or saucer brooch and beads was located, although the precise position is unknown. See Beesley 1855, Dryden 1897 and Lambrick 1988, 17 and fig. 2.

complex (fig. 6.6). This comprises an apparent long barrow (now known to be a natural mound), an array of round barrows, a stone circle, a single standing stone, a small group of standing stones (the Whispering Knights) to the southeast, and the remains of an Iron Age enclosure.[66] Two further features have recently been identified: a route leading to the complex and a circular mound, without a ring-ditch or evidence of burial, built in alignment with the long mound and surmounted by either a previously standing or recumbent stone slab (fig. 6.6).[67] The trackway is of late Bronze Age or early Iron Age origin and the mound is undated, but probably prehistoric. These features give the site the degree of complexity found at the prehistoric ceremonial complexes in Ireland such as Tara, a complexity which prompted their continuation into the early medieval period as locations of ceremony and gathering. The Anglo-Saxon archaeology at Rollright is almost certainly more complex than previously surmised. The find of a glass bead south of the long mound (fig. 6.6) may suggest that the cremations are more extensive than previously thought, and 300–400m to the south west, fragments of Anglo-Saxon pottery and a loom weight may indicate an area of settlement activity (fig. 6.6).[68]

What sets Rollright apart from the sites already discussed is its folklore.[69] Poems and stories collected locally in the nineteenth century encapsulate a motif which is virtually unique in the English folklore concerning prehistoric monuments, but similar to themes in the Irish *dinschendas*.[70] The story, romanticized in verse,[71] relates how a claim for kingship relied on seeing the village of Long Compton from Little Rollright. The king in the tale was, however, thwarted by a long mound that rose before him and blocked his view. In Irish law tracts of the sixth to seventh centuries, riding over a burial mound was used to establish a person's hereditary right to land.[72] It is suggested that it would be considered dangerous for an impostor to undertake this task because those buried in the mound (the ancestors or spirits) would repel outsiders.[73] The Rollright legend may reflect a similar concept. The long mound (probably the focus of the Anglo-Saxon cremation cemetery), representing the ancestral place, defies the claim for kingship by rising and blocking both the king's path and his view. To propose such an interpretation may be to stretch nineteenth-century local tales rather too far, although one of the few similar pieces of English folklore relating to another ancient monument should also be consid-

---

66 Lambrick 1988, 27–48. 67 For the small mound or Gough's Barrow see Lambrick 1988, fig. 11, and 68–70. For the trackway see Lambrick 1988, 80–2. 68 Lambrick 1988, fig. 46. 69 Evans 1895; Grinsell 1976, 146–49. 70 Driscoll 1998, 143. 71 'Seven long strides shalt thou take, and / If Long Compton thou canst see, / King of England shalt thou be.' / (the long mound rises before the king, preventing him from seeing Long Compton) / As Long Compton thou canst not see, / King of England thou shalt not be. / Rise up, mound, and stand still, stone, / For King of England thou shalt be none, / Thou and thy men hoar stones shall be, / And I myself an eldern tree. (Evans 1895, 18–19). 72 Charles-Edwards 1976. 73 Ibid., 86.

ered. The Anglo-Saxon Chronicle entry for the year 1006 records a very unusual tale regarding Scutchamer Knob or Cwichelm's Barrow, Berkshire. This large and undated barrow was a late Anglo-Saxon shire meeting-place. It is suggested that its association by name with the West Saxon king Cwichelm indicates its earlier importance.[74] Although no burial evidence has yet been forthcoming at the site, prehistoric activity is apparent and evidence of Roman activity too.[75] In 1006, as a show of bravado, a raiding Viking army camped at *Cwicchelmes hlæwe*, '... and there awaited the boasted threats, because it had often been said that if they sought out Cwichelm's Barrow they would never get to the sea'.[76] This challenge was important, perhaps not just because the monument was a shire moot, but also because it was regarded as a very significant and symbolic location. The folk-myth or aphorism in the Chronicle suggests that if unworthy parties took hold of or defiled the mound, it would result in their downfall. Once again an ancient monument, a mound, is symbolically linked to the authorization of legitimate kingship or political control.

CONCLUSIONS

The sites discussed above are cemeteries that share complex multi-focal, spatially extensive funerary practice, but which are varied in terms of components or layout. The basis of the argument that such sites may have been more than mere cemeteries is their common shared attribute: that funerary practice took place in relation to an array of prehistoric monuments of varying form. These funerary landscapes are special because of the additional presence of structures or standing posts, elaborate elite burial and, sometimes, deviant burials. Such places are suggested as microcosms, places where perhaps all the ritual functions and concerns of a pre-Christian tribal society were played out: religious belief and practice, displays of aristocratic power, enactment of justice and forms of assembly. There is no common model, and this is exactly to be expected in a period of great social change and experimentation by emerging power structures.

The central theme of using ancient monuments can be explained as relating to the need to associate the dead, and thus the ceremonies of the living, with monuments representative of an 'otherworld'. The monument may be the point of interface between ancestors and the living. The addition of elite or prestigious primary and secondary barrow burials to already extensive burial

74 Gelling 1973–6, 481–2.   75 Field-walking conducted in 1999 produced Bronze Age and Roman pottery, a hammer stone and a fragment of Cu alloy bracelet of probable Roman date: Semple forthcoming.   76 *ASC* s.a. 1006, MS E.

grounds (e.g. Sutton Hoo or Portsdown III) parallels the contemporary exploitation of prehistoric monuments for single, isolated, high-status burials (e.g. Laverstock, Wiltshire or Boars Low, Derbyshire). Both practices can be suggested as methods of lending credence to newly emergent elite groups. Association with a burial ground of extensive ancestral significance might signal acceptance of the new by the old (once again a concept strongly reminiscent of the use of the mound in Irish and Scandinavian pre-Christian societies as a kingly seat).

Certain sites discussed in this paper are localized while others cover considerable areas. It is possible that conservative approaches in Anglo-Saxon archaeology and history have overlooked the significance of the large-scale ritual landscape arrangements evident in other prehistoric or proto-historic societies and have not taken account of the very varied and experimental character of these groups.

In Ireland, sacral seats of kingship or complex ceremonial sites such as Emain Macha and Dun Ailine were eventually abandoned and their functions dispersed. Tara continued as a symbolic location of inauguration, and similarly we might expect a few of the English sites to continue as central places and emerge as late assembly-sites. However, it was in the interest of the Church to separate people from places of burial if these represented locations of pre-Christian belief and practice. Although the Church may have assimilated some sites, it may be more productive to take Roche Court Down as a significant model and see locations of execution and deviant interment as places that once functioned as early centres of funerary practice and tribal ritual (e.g. Guildown, Surrey). The majority of royal/ritual sites or complex ceremonial sites, however, would have ceased, and remain in the archaeological record as cemeteries, the surviving physical evidence only a vestige of their former significance and role as central places.

ACKNOWLEDGMENTS

I would like to thank John Blair, Howard Williams and Aliki Pantos for their helpful comments during the preparation of this paper.

ABBREVIATIONS

ASC Anglo-Saxon Chronicle
HE *Historia Ecclesiastica Gentis Anglorum*

REFERENCES

Aitchson, N.B., 1994: *Armagh and the royal centres in early medieval Ireland.* Woodbridge.

Akerman, J., 1855: *Remains of pagan Saxondom.*

Atkinson, R.J.C., Piggott, C. M. and Sandars, N.K., 1951: *Excavations at Dorchester, Oxon.* Oxford.

Barrett, J., 1994: *Fragments from antiquity.* Oxford.

Beesley, T., 1855: 'The Rollright Stones', *Transactions of the North Oxfordshire Archaeology Society* 1, 61–73.

Bell, M., 1977: 'Excavations at Bishopstone', *Sussex Archaeological Collections* **115**, 192–242.

Benson, D. and Miles, D., 1974: *The Upper Thames Valley: an archaeological survey of the river gravels.* Oxford.

Blair, W.J., 1994: *Anglo-Saxon Oxfordshire.* Stroud.

Blair, W.J., 1995: 'Anglo-Saxon pagan shrines and their prototypes', *Anglo-Saxon Studies in Archaeology and History* **8**, 1–28.

Blair, W.J., forthcoming: *The church in Anglo-Saxon society.* Oxford.

Bradley, R. and Lewis, E., 1968: 'Excavations at the George Inn, Portsdown', *Proceedings of the Hampshire Field Club and Archaeology Society* **25**, 27–50.

Bullough, D., 1983: 'Burial, community and belief in the early medieval West', in P. Wormald and R. Collins (eds), *Ideal and reality in Frankish and Anglo-Saxon society: studies presented to J. M. Wallace-Hadrill.* Oxford. 177–201.

Carver, M., 1998: *Sutton Hoo: burial ground of kings?* Philadelphia.

Carver, M. and Hummler, M., 1990: 'Excavations in Sector 4 (INT 48)', *Bulletin of the Sutton Hoo Research Committee* 7, April. 13–17.

Charles-Edwards, T.M., 1976: 'Boundaries in Irish law', in P.H. Sawyer (ed.), *Medieval settlement: continuity and change.* London. 83–7.

Cook, J. and Rowley, R.T. (eds), 1985: *Dorchester through the ages.* Oxford.

Corney, A., Ashbee, P., Evison, V. and Brothwell, D., 1967: 'A prehistoric and Anglo-Saxon burial ground, Ports Down, Portsmouth', *Proceedings of the Hampshire Field Club and Archaeology Society* **24**, 20–41.

Doherty, C., 1985: 'The monastic town in early medieval Ireland', in H. Clarke and A. Simms (eds), *The comparative history of urban origins in non-Roman Europe.* Oxford. 45–75.

Driscoll, S., 1998: 'Picts and prehistory: cultural resource management in early medieval Scotland', *World Archaeology* **30**:1, 142–58.

Dryden, H.E.L., 1897: 'The dolmens at Rollright and Enstone', *Oxfordshire Archaeological Society Report,* 40–51.

Ellis, H.R., 1943: *The road to Hel.* Cambridge.

Evans, A., 1895: *The Rollright Stones and their folklore.* London (reprinted from *Folklore* 6, vol. 1 (1895)).

Geake, H., 1997: *The use of grave-goods in Conversion-Period England, c.600–c.850.* Oxford.

Geake, H., 2002: 'Persistent problems in the study of conversion period burials in

England', in S. Lucy and A.J. Reynolds (eds), *Burial in early medieval England and Wales*. London.

Gelling, M., 1973–6: *The place-names of Berkshire*. English Place-Name Society 49–51. Cambridge.

Grinsell, L.V., 1976: *Folklore of prehistoric sites in Britain*. London.

Hines, J., 1997: 'Religion: the limits of knowledge', in J. Hines (ed.), *The Anglo-Saxons from the migration to the eighth century: an ethnographic perspective*. Woodbridge.

Hooke, D., 1985: *The Anglo-Saxon landscape: the kingdom of the Hwicce*. Manchester.

Hope Taylor, B., 1977: *Yeavering: an Anglo-British centre of early Northumbria*. London.

Hummler, M., 1993: 'The prehistoric settlement: an interim report', *Bulletin of the Sutton Hoo Research Committee* 8, 21–3.

Lambrick, G., 1988: *The Rollright Stones*. London.

Loyn, H.R., 1974: 'The hundred in the tenth and early eleventh centuries', in H. Hearder and H.R., Loyn (eds), *British government and administration*. Cardiff.

Loyn, H.R., 1984: *The governance of Anglo-Saxon England 500–1087*. London.

Lucy, S., 1998: *The early Anglo-Saxon cemeteries of East Yorkshire*. Oxford.

Lucy, S., 1999: 'Changing burial rites in Northumbria AD 500–750', in J. Hawkes and S. Mills (eds), *Northumbria's golden age*. Stroud.

Lucy, S. and Reynolds, A.J., 2002: 'Burial in early medieval England and Wales: past, present and future', in S. Lucy and A.J. Reynolds (eds), *Burial in early medieval England and Wales*, Society for Medieval Archaeology Monograph 17. London. 1–23.

Meaney, A.L., 1995: 'Pagan English sanctuaries, place-names and hundred meeting places', *Anglo-Saxon Studies in Archaeology and History* 8, 29–42.

Meaney, A.L., 1997: 'Hundred meeting-places in the Cambridge region', in A.R. Rumble and A.D. Mills (eds), *Names, places and people: an onomastic miscellany in memory of John McNeal Dodgson*. Stamford. 195–240.

Mortimer, J.R., 1905: *Forty years' researches in British and Saxon burial mounds of East Yorkshire*. London.

Newman, C., 1998: 'Reflections on the making of a "royal site" in early Ireland', *World Archaeology* 30:1, 127–41.

O'Brien, E., 1999: *Post-Roman Britain to Anglo-Saxon England: burial practices reviewed*. Oxford.

Penn, K., 2000: *Excavations on the Norwich southern bypass, 1989–91 Part II: The Anglo-Saxon cemetery at Harford Farm, Caistor St Edmund, Norfolk*, East Anglian Archaeology 92. Dereham.

Pitt Rivers, A.H.L.F., 1898: *Excavations on Cranbourne Chase near Rusholme on the Borders of Dorset and Wiltshire 1893–1896*, vol. IV. London.

Reynolds, A.J., 1998: *Anglo-Saxon law in the landscape*. Unpublished Ph.D. thesis, University of London.

Roesdahl, E., 1980: 'The Scandinavians at home', in D. Wilson (ed.), *The northern world*. London. 129–58.

Sawyer, P.H., 1978: *From Roman Britain to Norman England*. London.

Schmeidler, B., (ed.), 1917: *Gesta Hammaburgensis Ecclasiæ Pontificum*. Hanover.

Scull, C., 1991: 'Post-Roman phase I at Yeavering: a re-consideration', *Medieval Archaeology* **35**, 51–63.

Semple, S., 2002: *Anglo-Saxon attitudes to the past: a landscape perspective.* Unpublished DPhil thesis, University of Oxford.

Semple, S., forthcoming: 'Survey results from Cuckhamsley, Berkshire'.

Smith, R.A., 1912: 'The excavation by Canon Greenwell, FSA, in 1868, of an Anglo-Saxon cemetery at Uncleby, East Riding of Yorkshire', *Proceedings of the Society of Antiquaries of London* **24**, 146–58.

Stead, I.M., 1991: *Iron Age cemeteries in East Yorkshire.* London.

Stone, J.F.S., 1932: 'Saxon interments on Roche Court Down, Winterslow', *Wiltshire Archaeological and Natural History Magazine* **45**, 568–82.

Warner, P., 1988: 'Pre-Conquest territorial and administrative organization in East Suffolk', in D. Hooke (ed.), *Anglo-Saxon settlements.* Oxford. 9–34.

Williams, H.M.R., 1997: 'Ancient landscapes and the dead: the reuse of prehistoric monuments as early Anglo-Saxon burial sites', *Medieval Archaeology* **41**, 1–32.

Williams, H.M.R., 1998: 'Monuments and the past in early Anglo-Saxon England', *World Archaeology* **30**:1, 90–108.

Williams, H.M.R., 2001: 'Death, memory and time: a consideration of the mortuary practices at Sutton Hoo', in C. Humphrey and W.M. Ormrod (eds), *Time in the medieval world.* York.

The location and form of Anglo-Saxon assembly-places: some 'moot points'

ALIKI PANTOS

In 1898 Pollock and Maitland wrote concerning the Anglo-Saxon legal system:

> it suffices to know that, in its general features, Anglo-Saxon law is not only archaic, but offers an especially pure type of Germanic archaism.[1]

In the century or so since this statement was made, the accepted view of the Anglo-Saxon legal system, and the government and administration through which it was implemented, has altered considerably. Far from regarding it as archaic, more recent scholars have emphasized the remarkable sophistication of the late Anglo-Saxon state, including the crown's effective regulation of justice and taxation through a network of royal officials and regional courts, and the extensive use of written documentation.[2] The role of the administrative units through which this control was implemented – shires, hundreds and wapentakes – and the nature of their associated assemblies has likewise been re-evaluated. Rather than being characterized as the descendants of the primitive 'folk-moots' described by Tacitus, hundredal assemblies have come to be regarded as agents of royal power functioning within a tightly managed, hierarchical and remarkably modern system of government.[3]

There is, however, one aspect of late Anglo-Saxon administrative organization which is still regularly characterized as archaic or 'primitive'. In spite of the apparently complex nature of pre-Conquest government, place-name and other evidence suggests that hundred, and to some extent shire courts, continued to meet outdoors at locations removed from the main concentrations of habitation, but often connected with natural features or man-made monuments. This fact is frequently remarked upon in order to stress the potential antiquity of the territorial divisions served by such meeting-places,

---

1 Pollock and Maitland 1898, 44. 2 Wormald 1988; Keynes 1990. 3 E.g. Pollock and Maitland 1898, 40–1; Liebermann 1913, 3; Loyn 1974; Wormald 1986; 1999a; 1999b; Keynes 1990; 1991.

since it is considered that their 'primitive nature' suggests they 'served units older than the hundreds'.[4] Nevertheless, comparatively little attention has been paid to the moot-sites themselves and in the absence of substantial documentary evidence, most identifications and discussions of assembly-places rely to a great extent on place-names. Moreover, though many sites have been located, very few have undergone any detailed archaeological investigation.

This paper seeks to assess the current state of knowledge concerning Anglo-Saxon assembly-places and to evaluate the efficacy of traditional approaches to them. Its main contention is that the techniques of place-name study have had a fundamental, and to some extent detrimental, effect on consideration of this topic, leading to the widespread acceptance of assumptions which are not always supported by the evidence of the sites themselves. Most important of these is the perception that assemblies were associated with individual, isolated features. The consequences of this approach can be seen as threefold. Firstly, methodological difficulties have been created in attempts to classify and study sites at a general level. Secondly, detailed and extensive investigation of sites has been discouraged. Finally, the interpretative possibilities of many individual sites, and of assembly-places in general, have been insufficiently explored. The ultimate suggestion of this paper is that established approaches to the study of assembly-places are insufficient substantially to further our understanding of their form, operation and role in late Saxon government. It seeks to demonstrate not only that a case can be made for more intensive and wide-ranging investigation of individual assembly-places, but that our understanding of moot-sites in general may benefit from a less functional approach, which draws more on recent trends in archaeological interpretation and relies less on the evidence of place-names.

ASSEMBLY-PLACES AND PLACE-NAMES: 'TREES, STONES AND THE LIKE'

The major role played by place-name evidence in identifying Anglo-Saxon assembly-places is reflected in the fact that for sixty years or more the standard text on the subject, and the only comprehensive study of assembly-places in England, has remained O.S. Anderson's *English hundred names*.[5] This work outlines the morphology of the administrative units in each county as well as giving details of many assembly sites, making it a significant resource for archaeologists, historians and place-name scholars alike. Nevertheless, its main aim is onomastic – to give an etymological explanation for the name of every hundred – and this fact is reflected in Anderson's methodology.

4 Gelling 1978, 210; Gelling 1992, 142; Reynolds 1999, 77; cp. Warner, 1988.   5 Anderson 1934; 1939a; 1939b.

In order to facilitate comparison of hundred names which refer to assembly-places, Anderson groups them into categories. The division is ostensibly made on practical grounds, distinguishing names denoting 'mere physical features' reflecting the location of the meeting in general, those apparently referring to structures purposely erected for the meeting, and those which contain references to 'particular objects, natural or artificial, such as barrows, trees, stones or posts, at which the hundred would meet'.[6] This classification emphasizes a characteristic of assembly-places that is evident from the most cursory examination either of their names or their sites, namely that assemblies appear to be particularly associated with certain features and topographical locations. Among the most common are sites at mounds, trees, stones, earthworks and at points of communication such as at crossroads, fords, bridges and along important routeways. It should be noted however, that though Anderson's division is apparently a functional one, it is adopted on purely onomastic grounds. His intention is to illuminate the names of the hundredal units, not the sites at which they met; he therefore groups hundreds according to the elements that occur in their names without considering the physical evidence of the sites.

This methodology does not reveal the extent to which these categories overlap when the actual assembly-sites themselves are taken into account. For a significant number of sites appear to be associated with more than one of the features listed above, although this is not immediately apparent from their names. For example, the Hundred Stone in Yeovil Parish, Somerset, from which Stone Hundred was named, stands on a flat-topped mound.[7] The name of Guthlaxton Hundred (Guthlac's Stone*)*, Leicestershire likewise seems to reflect a meeting-place at a stone. The name persists in Guthlaxton Gap and the adjacent Guthlaxton Bridge where the Roman Fosse Way crosses a stream, and the meeting-place is likely to have been in the vicinity. Barry Cox has suggested that the stone may have been a milestone on the Roman road. However, eighteenth-century accounts connect the holding of the hundred court with a lost tumulus which lay on land known as Guthlaxton Meadow in the same parish.[8] The Northamptonshire double hundred of Nassaborough is thought to have met at a site known as Langdyke Bush in Ailsworth parish.[9] The name of the meeting-place ('long-earthwork') reflects its position on the Roman road known as King Street.[10] The feature identified as the meeting-place, however, is a flat-topped mound, and the site is also associated with a crossroads, being only *c*.650m south of the junction of King Street and a ridge-

6 Anderson 1939b, 157.   7 Ibid., 58; Aston 1986, 68–9.   8 Anderson 1934, 44–5; Cox 1971–2, 14–21; Nichols 1795–1815, 140.   9 The hundred is referred to as the hundred of Langdyke in 1305 and may be the *twegera hundreda ... æt Dicon* recorded in BCS 1130 (AD 972–92). 10 Margary 1973, no. 26.

road from Peterborough to Ermine St.[11] The name of Copthorne Hundred, Surrey means 'pollarded thorn-tree', but Dorothy Nail's work on the location of the moot-site revealed not only a group of fields in Ashtead Parish still bearing the name Copthorn, but a linear earthwork known as Nutshambles. This name apparently derives from OE *(ge)mot-sceamol* – 'assembly-bench' – and may refer to a structure built specifically to accommodate assemblies (fig. 7.1).[12] These examples demonstrate the partial character of the information that can be extracted about a meeting-place from its name alone, since in each of these instances examination of the assembly-place reveals an association with an earthwork or other feature which is not indicated by the hundred or site name.

Moreover, although Anderson's categories are distinguished on a broadly functional basis, he makes no attempt to establish that the purposes served by the features he identifies are truly distinct. This is not significant in a discussion of the names of assembly-places, but it is important if conclusions are to be drawn about the similarities between physical sites. This fact has not, however, been adequately recognized: some work on the topic continues to group meeting-places by *name*, while claiming to distinguish different types of *place*.[13] The assumption made is that all meeting-places connected by name with a particular sort of feature or location had comparable venues with analogous properties. This need not necessarily be the case. Although many hundreds are named from fords, for example, their situation and character may differ considerably. An assembly-place at an important crossing-place on a major navigable river must have been very different from one lying at a minor ford on an unimportant stream. The former can be seen as a natural meeting-point where traffic from several directions (both down the river and over the ford) would meet, and in this respect could most easily be compared to one at a major crossroads or road intersection.[14] The latter site has no such obvious importance as a communication node, and may simply function as a convenient marker for meetings. A site of this second type can more appropriately be compared with one where a tree, stone or other feature marks the meeting-place.

Failure to distinguish between the sites of assemblies and their names in attempts to classify and interpret assembly-places can thus have problematic consequences, keeping together examples which, though similar in name, are physically very different, while also obscuring useful comparisons between sites which differ in 'name-type'.

11 Meaney 1993, 89; *SMRPeterb* 786; Margary 1973, no. 25.   12 Nail 1965.   13 E.g. Meaney 1997.

ASSEMBLY-PLACES AND ARCHAEOLOGY: FORM, EXTENT AND FUNCTION

Place-name based methods of classifying assembly-places may also have affected archaeological approaches to the topic, since by emphasizing the association of a given site with a particular sort of object or location, they have encouraged a perception that assemblies were associated with single, solitary

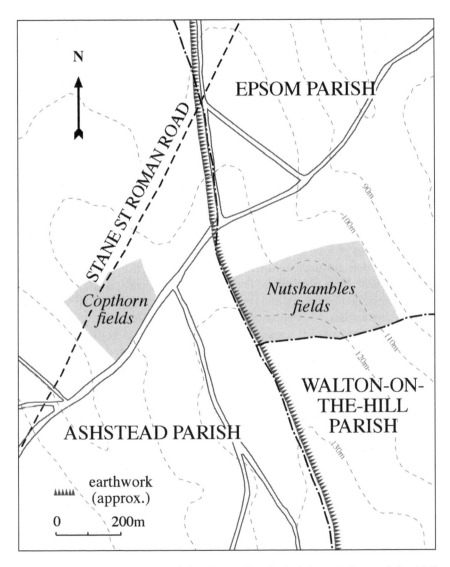

Figure 7.1 The meeting-place of Copthorne Hundred, Ashstead, Surrey (after Nail 1965).

features. Consequently, wider investigation of sites has been seen as unneces-
sary and consideration of other features in the vicinity of assembly-places is
rare. Moreover, the idea that the character of a site can largely be determined
by its association with a certain type of feature or topographical situation has
tended to discourage detailed archaeological investigation. Often mere identification of the feature referred to in the site-name is seen as constituting a
satisfactory study of a meeting-place, and though many have been noted, very
few have undergone any detailed investigation in modern times. Where excavation has taken place it has generally been confined to a small area, usually a
proposed 'moot-mound'.

Adkins and Petchey's rescue excavation of the moot-mound of Secklow
Hundred, Buckinghamshire is probably the most important study of an
assembly-site to have been undertaken in the last thirty years. The project
proved particularly influential because it raised the possibility that Anglo-
Saxon 'moot-mounds' may have been purpose-built, since the Secklow
'barrow' was found to be both non-sepulchral and of post-Roman date.[15]
However, the investigation concentrated solely on the mound identified as the
'-*hlaw*' of the hundred-name, and no attempt was made to investigate the
surrounding area. This restricted focus may be understandable in the context
of a rescue excavation. Nevertheless, precisely because of its remarkable
findings, the dig has concentrated attention even more sharply upon the
central features at such sites, to some extent reinforcing the idea that investigation of such features constitutes the most effective way to study an
assembly-place. This need not be the case. On the contrary, it could be argued
that by focusing on moot-mounds to the complete exclusion of their surroundings, archaeologists are concentrating on the areas least likely to provide
substantial information about assemblies. For, if the interpretation usually put
forward to explain these features is correct – that they served as platforms for
speakers – such mounds would have been the part of the site used by the
smallest number of people and hence the least likely to produce substantial
numbers of finds. Illuminating though the investigation of such features may
be at one level, then, they may have less to tell us about the actual operation of
the site than less intensive, less invasive exploration.

The existence of sites like Guthlaxton and Copthorne, described above,
may indicate that many assembly-places were fact more complex than has
generally been appreciated. It may be worthwhile considering more fully the
relationship between the various features associated with such meeting-places,
and the potential for this to alter our interpretation of them. Working from the
evidence of the hundred names alone it would be presumed that meetings of

14 Meaney 1997, 204.   15 Adkins and Petchey 1984.

Copthorne Hundred were held at the tree from which the name is taken. In the light of Nail's research, however, it seems more likely that these took place at the Nutshambles earthwork or on some purpose-built structure in its vicinity. If this is the case, how can we interpret the fact that the meeting-place took its name from a tree?

A number of possible scenarios can be envisaged. It may be that the tree acted as a marker for the site – hence giving its name to the unit – but played no further part in the assembly. Alternatively, the two parts of the site may not be contemporary. Perhaps the earthwork with its purpose-built benches replaced an older assembly at the thorn-tree, but the traditional name had already become attached to the unit it served. The transfer might even have taken place the other way around, although this seems less likely. A third possibility is that the assembly-place comprised two features, both of which had parts to play in the activity of the assembly. For support for this suggestion we might look to better-documented medieval assemblies abroad. At the Icelandic Althing, for example, the business of the court appears to have been divided, with different activities taking place in different areas of the site. At the *Lögberg* or 'Lawrock', the notional centre of the site, laws were promulgated, summonses and public announcements made and the assembly formally initiated and prorogued. The legislative court or *lögretta* met elsewhere, however, and the judicial Quarter Courts had no fixed site but were convened at points designated for them by the Lawspeaker on the plain of Thingvellir.[16] It is possible that a similar division took place at some hundred meeting-places and that the multiplication of features reflects this.

While, in the absence of documentary evidence for the use of meeting-places, we cannot prove that such polyfocal assemblies existed in England, the archaeological and place-name evidence from some sites might be interpreted in this way. Until the eighteenth century, meetings of the court for Bingham Hundred, Nottinghamshire took place at Moothouse Pit, a large, shallow, bowl-shaped depression alongside the Foss Way near the boundary of Cropwell Butler and Bingham parishes.[17] This feature is characterized by *Place-Names of Nottinghamshire* as 'a shallow depression, like a miniature amphitheatre'. Presumably it is this quality which led to its use for meetings of the hundred (fig. 7.2; fig 7.3). Though its acoustic properties cannot have been those of an amphitheatre, the feature would have provided a demarcated space in which a large number of people could gather to debate or listen to speeches. Similar locations may have been in use for assemblies elsewhere.[18]

16 Foote and Wilson 1970, 57; Jóhannesson 1974, 42–3; Magerøy 1981, lvi. 17 Anderson 1934, 42; *PNNotts* 219; Thoroton 1797, 139. 18 The name of Odsey Hundred in Hertfordshire potentially refers to such a feature, although it has not been located (Anderson 1939b, 25–7; *VCHHert* iii 193; *PNHert* 150–1; Meaney 1993, 82). Likewise, the hundred of Younsmere,

Figure 7.2 Moothouse Pit, Bingham, Nottinghamshire from the Fosse Way.

However, the name of the site (*Motehowes* 1375) and the Domesday Book name of the hundred (*Bingehamhou*, *Bingameshou*) both have as their second element the ON word *haugr* – 'mound/barrow', suggesting that the assembly was originally associated with a mound. The feature referred to appears to have lain approximately 100m further north, on the crest of the hill over which the Roman road passes. A farm at this point was known as Moothill Farm in the nineteenth century and the tumulus itself is shown in an engraving in Stukeley's *Itinerarium Curiosum*.[19] It lay directly on the line of the Roman road, a fact which no doubt accounts for its eventual destruction (fig. 7.3). The relationship between the two features at an early date cannot be known. However, in the light of their close physical proximity it seems possible that both originally played a part in meetings of the hundred. The differences between them would make them appropriate for different activities; the pit

Sussex is thought to have met at Younsmere Pit, a shallow boat–shaped depression in Rottingdean parish (*PNSx* 290; Anderson 1939b, 87; Macleod 1932–3, 154–5). The meeting–place of the late joint hundred of Copthorne and Effingham, Surrey appears to have been held at Leith Pit on the boundary of Fetcham and Great Bookham parishes and the sheriff's tourn was later known as the Leith Pit Court (*PNSr* 99; *VCHSr* iii 320; Anderson 1939b, 60; Harvey 1953, 157–161). **19** Stukeley 1724, plate 90 'a prospect of Ad Pontem upon the eminence a mile south on the Fosse'.

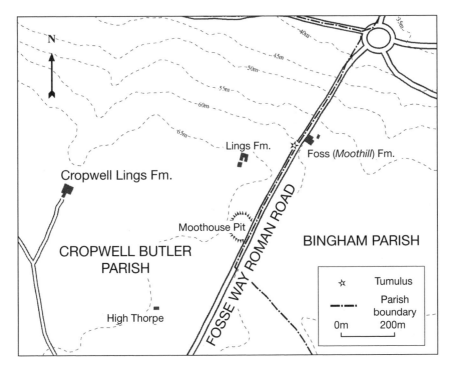

Figure 7.3 Plan of Moothouse Pit, Bingham, Nottinghamshire.

could accommodate a large number of people, perhaps for the purposes of discussion, whereas a mound might be more appropriate for announcements or speech-making.

In the absence of detailed evidence for the organization and operation of Anglo-Saxon hundred assemblies, such notions must remain speculative. Nevertheless, other evidence can be cited to support the possibility that some sites may have been associated with more than one feature. Even a cursory examination of the archaeological evidence indicates that many sites lie in close proximity to other ancient features, and it is possible that this is significant. Of particular interest is a group of sites where a potential meeting-place is associated with an enclosure of some kind. The name *Motelowe* recorded in a fourteenth-century document relating to the Derbyshire parish of Edensor suggests there was a meeting-place in the area. The site has been identified with Moatless Plantation, on the end of the high ridge known as Carlton Pastures.[20] It is likely that the original *hlaw* was one of a string of prehistoric

20 *PNDb* 91.

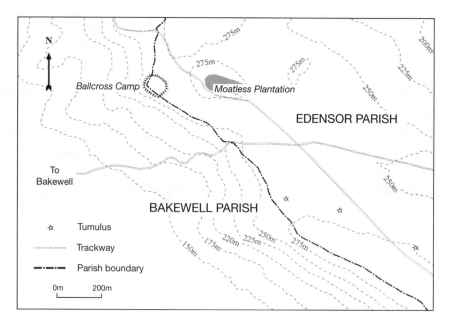

Figure 7.4 Plan of Moatless Plantation and Ballcross Camp, Edensor, Derbyshire.

barrows running along this ridge.[21] Immediately below the site, approximately 300m due west, lies a prehistoric promontory fort known as Ball Cross Camp. The earthwork is still clearly visible and would presumably have been a distinctive landscape feature in the early medieval period (fig. 7.4, 7.5). Barry Cox proposes that the name Shericles Farm in Leicestershire (*Sherakehilles* 1553) represents OE *scir-ac* – 'shire-oak' and thus reflects the location of an assembly-place.[22] The name suggests meetings were associated with a tree, but a large, sub-rectangular enclosure has been identified in the vicinity of the farm. This was visible on the ground until the 1940s.[23] A smaller enclosure of possible Roman date is known to have existed approximately 100m north of a round barrow in Swinfen parish, Staffordshire which is believed to mark the meeting-place of Offlow Hundred, although it is not clear how long this feature remained visible.[24]

The association of hillforts and enclosures with assembly-places is not is itself surprising: many such features are thought to have served as hundred meeting-places. Blewbury Hundred, Berkshire is believed to have centred on Blewburton hillfort,[25] while Badbury Rings, Dorset seems to have given its

21 Marsden 1977, 32–3; Bateman 1844, 22; Bateman 1861, 64.   22 Cox 1971–2.   23 Hartley and Pickering 1985, 74–5.   24 *SMRStaffs* 01093, 01102; Gould 1971–2, 7; Gunstone 1965, 48. 25 Anderson 1939a, 217.

Figure 7.5 Moatless Plantation, Edensor, Derbyshire from the south-east.

name to Badbury Hundred,[26] and Yarborough Camp was the assembly-place of Yarborough Wapentake, Lincolnshire.[27] What is potentially significant about the sites discussed above, however, is the repeated appearance of enclosures in combination with other features thought to be associated with assembly. It seems at least worth considering the possibility that this relationship is not entirely fortuitous, but reflects the fact that some sites were of greater extent than is usually presumed and combined a number of features.[28]

26 *PNDo*, 133, 177–8; Anderson 1939a, 129–30. **27** Anderson 1934, 50; *PNSLincs*, 8,100. A number of other examples are possible. The occurrence of the names *Spelborw*, *Spello*, and *Spelwell* (< OE *spel* – 'speech') within Borough Hill hillfort, Northamptonshire suggests that the eastern end of this enormous earthwork may also have served as a venue for assemblies (*PNNp*, 131–2; Pantos 2002, 376). Likewise, in the twelfth century the hundred of Thurgarton in Nottinghamshire is known to have met at a site called *Iverishaghe* a prehistoric camp approximately one mile north of Oxton. (*PNNotts* 154) The Iron Age hillfort of Wandlebury in Cambridgeshire was the location of at least two judicial meetings. The settlement of a land dispute is recorded as having taken place there *c*.990, while an assembly of nine shires is mentioned in writ of Edward the Confessor (Wormald 1988, no.143; Harmer 1989, no. 79; Wormald 1988, no. 87). **28** It may be worth noting that the enclosure at *Iverishaghe* (now known as Oldox) itself closely associated with a prominent mound which, although natural, closely resembles a tumulus (*SMRNotts* 02769, 05490, 02772, 02771). A number of ring–ditches,

Other evidence may support this proposition. Names such as *Plaistow*, from Old English *plegestow* – 'gaming/play place', are occasionally found in association with assembly-places, as at Seisdon, Staffordshire, and may indicate that activities other than speech-making such as sports, wrestling or horse racing took place at assemblies.[29] This is known to have been the case in Ireland and Scandinavia.[30] The name of the Berkshire hundred of Ganfield, which is derived from OE *gama-feld* – 'open land of games', provides an important parallel. It has been suggested that the phrase *eal gama feld*, which refers to the place in a charter of 957, indicates that the name referred to a considerable area, including the whole of 'the projecting corner of Buckland parish' in which Gainfield Farm is now situated (fig. 7.6).[31] It may be that the whole of this area was at one time set aside for hundredal assemblies and/or sporting activities associated with them.[32]

Several scholars have also noted the potential for hundredal and shire assemblies to have acted as opportunities for trade and exchange.[33] Again the absence of investigation at assembly-places means that there is little archaeological evidence for this.[34] However, comparison with assemblies elsewhere in Britain and in Scandinavia would suggest that such functions are not unlikely. A substantial fair is associated with the holding of the Manx Tynwald, for example, taking place on a field adjoining the assembly-site (fig. 7.7). The Anglo-Saxon law-codes reflect the important role played by the hundred in regulating trade, and the hundred court would have been an ideal place for transactions to take place, providing not only an opportunity for large numbers of people to come together and exchange goods, but also the requisite witnesses.[35] We may note that the law-code II Æthelstan 12, issued in the 920s, forbids people to buy goods worth more than twenty pence unless it is done in the presence of the port-reeve or *on þara gerefena gewitnesse on folcgemote*.[36]

Activities more directly associated with the judicial duties of the hundred courts may also have taken place at or near assemblies – for example the execution of criminals. The majority of the evidence is currently against this proposition.[37] Although place-name evidence from number of assembly-sites

possibly representing a Bronze Age barrow cemetery, have also been identified in the immediate vicinity of Yarborough Camp, Lincolnshire (*SMRLincs* 2273, 11344). **29** *VCHStaffs* xx, 185; Pantos 2002, 439; Pantos 2003. **30** Raftery 1994, 81–3; Grettisaga, Ch 72: trans. Palsson and Fox 1974, 148–52. **31** S 639; Gelling 1974, 385. **32** Pantos 2002, 89. **33** Britnell 1978; Sawyer 1981; Aston 1986, 68. **34** At Bloodmoor Hill, Suffolk a concentration of metal-detector finds in the neighbourhood of a possible high-status barrow burial and Anglo–Saxon cemetery have been connected with the use of the area for hundred courts (Newman 1996). The location – known as Mootway Common – is tentatively identified with the meeting-place of Mutford Hundred. But the finds in question date from the seventh/eighth century, rather earlier then might be expected if they were associated with the use of the site for late Anglo-Saxon hundred courts. **35** IV Edgar 6; I Æthelred 3. **36** In the witness of the reeves at the 'folk-moot'. **37** See Pantos 2002, 90–4.

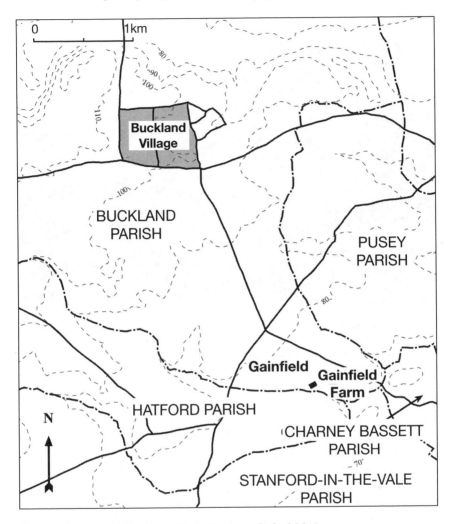

Figure 7.6 Gainfield, Buckland, Berkshire (now Oxfordshire).

suggests that places of execution existed in their vicinity at some date, often this cannot be carried back to the Anglo-Saxon period with certainty.[38] Moreover, a major new study of the location of Anglo-Saxon execution cemeteries suggests that they had a strong correlation with the boundaries of

38 Though 'gallows' place–names occur in the vicinity of many sites, these may be derived either from OE *galga* or ME/ModE *gallow* and it is very unusual to find forms early enough to allow a distinction to be made. Particularly where meeting-places continued to be used into the later medieval and even modern period, such names may reflect later practices. Similarly, the meeting-

Figure 7.7 Tynwald, Isle of Man and the associated fair, July 2000. Tynwald Hill is on the right of the picture linked to St John's Chapel (far left) by the processional way. The original fair-field lies between the professional way and the road, although the modern fair occupies a still larger area.

hundredal units, rather than with the hundred meeting-places at which criminals were presumably sentenced.[39]

Nevertheless, the name of Gallows Hundred, Norfolk (< OE *galga*) suggests that such functions may have been concentrated at a few such sites, and a small amount of archaeological evidence exists to support this. A possible Anglo-Saxon execution cemetery has been located at Wandlebury, Cambridgeshire, the site of at least two major tenth- or eleventh-century judicial meetings.[40] Whether this should be seen as a typical site is uncertain, however. The second meeting to take place at Wandlebury was a joint assembly of nine shires, and hence of a much greater magnitude than any regular hundred-court. It may be that, although executions were not habitually carried out at hundredal assemblies, extraordinary meetings of this size did serve as

place of Wixamtree Hundred, Bedfordshire has been identified with Deadman's Oak in Willington parish. This suggestion is supported by the proximity of the site to Sheerhatch Wood (< OE *scīr-āc* – 'shire-oak'). While the name Deadman's Oak may indicate that this was the traditional site of a gallows, however, the name itself is too modern to be accepted as evidence for the existence of such a feature in the pre-Conquest period (*PNBH*, 87–8; Anderson 1939b, 20–1; Meaney 1993, 82, 91; Marsom 1943. **39** Reynolds 1997; 1999, 105–110; forthcoming. **40** Taylor and Denton 1977, 3; Reynolds forthcoming.

venues for the high-profile dispatch of felons.[41] Some support for this may come from a slightly later date. The Anglo-Saxon Chronicle entry for AD 1124 describes an extraordinary meeting of 'all the king's thanes' held by Ralph Basset at *Hundehoge* in Leicestershire. Here he hanged forty-four thieves – 'more than ever before' – and mutilated six others.[42] Two secondary burials in the Shipton Barrow, Oxfordshire have been explained as possible execution victims.[43] The barrow is thought to be the *Cheneward'berge* of the early hundred-name and may have been its meeting-place.[44] Several burials are also recorded from the vicinity of the Copthorne assembly-place identified by Dorothy Nail, and it has been suggested that these also represent the victims of executions associated with the court.[45] Unfortunately, published details regarding the discovery of the skeletons are too vague to be conclusive.[46] The same is true of a group of inhumations discovered in the nineteenth century close to the site of the Gartree Bush, the assembly-place of Gartree Hundred, Leicestershire. One of these was buried with the skull on the breast, while another lacked the skull altogether.[47]

There is, then, evidence to suggest that some Anglo-Saxon assemblies at least were the venue for activities other than the hearing of judicial cases. This in turn raises the possibility that they did not take place at isolated points but extended over substantial areas, and it is conceivable we should see the multiplication of features at some sites as indicative of this. We might speculate for instance that some of the earthworks and enclosures identified in the vicinity of assembly-places functioned as pens for livestock brought to market or venues for trading activity.[48] Other features may have acted as places of execution or marked locations for sporting activities. Alternatively, the several features associated with a site may have served to mark the outer limits of a large space given over to the court and its associated activities.

There is considerable potential for the archaeological exploration of such possibilities. Controlled field-walking and metal-detecting of the area around an assembly-place could be used to test for concentrations of stray finds such as one might expect to find in an area habitually used for large gatherings and trading. Work of this sort, combined with wider excavation of sites, has the

41 Reynolds forthcoming. **42** *Anglo-Saxon Chronicle* 1124: trans. Garmonsway 1972. **43** Chambers 1978; Reynolds forthcoming. **44** Cam 1936, 117; Anderson 1939a, 227–8; *PNOx*, 335. Nevertheless, the insertion of the corpses into the proposed assembly–mound may indicate their burial here was exceptional. **45** Nail 1965, 50, 53. **46** Carpenter 1949, 151 n.1. **47** A disarticulated arm–bone and part of a skull were also discovered and it was noted that another skeleton had been found nearby some years before (*SMRLei* 79NWBA; Richard Knox, *SMRLei* pers. comm.). **48** The occurrence of the name *Stotfald* (stud–fold) in association with hillforts and enclosures, as at Borough Hill, Northamptonshire, suggests that some such features may have been used in this way (Brown, Key and Orr 1977). Elsewhere, finds of sceattas from hillforts have been interpreted as indicating they functioned as trading places (Rigold and Metcalf 1977).

capacity considerably to increase our understanding of the form, extent and operation of assembly-places and might enable firmer conclusions to be drawn about, for instance, the prevalence of execution at assemblies. Nevertheless, because of the continued perception that assemblies were associated with isolated features, little effort has been made to study the wider area of any meeting-place. Indeed, it is relatively unusual even for the existence of other archaeological features in the vicinity to be noted. Until this attitude is overcome and an attempt is made to study assembly-places more thoroughly in their archaeological and landscape context, it is difficult to see how our understanding of such matters can advance beyond the purely speculative.

ASSEMBLY-PLACES AND IDEOLOGY: 'SOME TRIFLING OBJECT'

It has been argued above that the physical extent and practical operation of Anglo–Saxon assemblies has been insufficiently explored. At the same time, principally functional explanations have dominated recent work on these sites and their associated features, to the exclusion of more conceptual interpretations. Yet the ideology of assembly and the assembly-place is surely a topic worthy of consideration. Public assembly-places were intimately connected both with the exercise of royal power and with the expression of community through collective activity. It is highly likely, therefore, that the venues at which they were convened held ideological associations for the people who used them. Such associations may have developed gradually through the use of a meeting–place over many generations, or even have influenced the choice of location in the first place.

This aspect of assembly-places has been infrequently discussed. Usually the features and locations chosen for assemblies are explained in purely practical terms. Mounds are characterized as platforms or 'soap-boxes': trees, stones and posts as 'landmarks'.[49] Some scholars have remarked with surprise on the naming of hundredal units from their meeting-places, dismissing the possibility that a 'trifling object' such as a barrow or tree could have been viewed as important.[50] Others have rejected outright the need to consider anything other than practical reasons for the choice of court-sites. Thus in one standard textbook we are told

> The choice of a burial-mound, as of a natural hill, for a hundred meeting-place should be ascribed to no deeper motive than the desire for a site which would be prominent to all concerned.[51]

49 Anderson 1939a, 157; Nail 1965, 46; Meaney 1997, 206, 212–13; Anderson 1934, xxxiii; Gelling 1978, 134; Cameron 1996, 63; Hooke 1998, 21. 50 Duigan 1912, 20. 51 Hunter–Blair

This attitude is perhaps particularly marked in relation to the widespread use of mounds for assembly. In the past, hundred names of the 'personal-name + barrow' type were often taken as indicating that assemblies met at the graves of kings, leaders or heroes.[52] More recently, however, interpretations of this sort have fallen out of favour, since it is now recognized that the appearance of a personal-name as the first element of a barrow name need not reflect the individual buried there.[53] Instead, greater emphasis has come to be placed on utilitarian explanations, particularly since the publication of Adkins and Petchey's work on Secklow raised the possibility that some, perhaps many, moot-mounds may have been purpose-built platforms. Such an unromantic, practical approach perhaps appears more in keeping with the revised idea of the late Anglo-Saxon state as highly developed, modern and efficient, but it may be argued that it has contributed to the lack of detailed research into assembly-places. Just as identification of a single feature is thought to constitute examination of an assembly-site, so the assigning of a practical function to that feature is considered to be sufficient interpretation of it. The possibility that deeper motivations may have been operating in the choice of an assembly-place is largely dismissed.

As platforms for speakers it is clear that mounds have a number of practical advantages. They are relatively easy to construct, and do not require special building materials. Moreover, unlike the presumably wooden structures represented by place-names like Nutshambles, they would not be subject to decay after prolonged exposure to the elements. Nevertheless, while such factors may have played a part, they need not be seen as the sole explanation for the popularity of mounds as venues for assembly. It may be that mounds had particular ideological associations which made them particularly appropriate for this purpose.

A recent discussion of Anglo-Saxon attitudes to barrows and burial mounds in the eighth to eleventh centuries by Sarah Semple has suggested that these features were widely treated with mistrust and envisaged as the home of evil spirits and supernatural beings.[54] According to this interpretation, the superstitious beliefs surrounding the barrow in late Anglo-Saxon England can be traced to the 'remembrance of early Anglo-Saxon pagan activity which took place at barrows'. During this period barrows may have been viewed as 'the home of spirits, ancestors or gods' and as places of contact with the otherworld.[55] Beliefs of this kind may be invoked to explain the frequent insertion of early and middle Saxon burials into prehistoric earthworks, and the location of substantial cemeteries in close proximity to, or focusing upon, earlier monuments.[56] It is clearly apparent from place-names and literary works such

1978, 237. **52** E.g. *VCHBerks* iv 294; Anderson 1939, 158. **53** See Meaney 1997, 212. **54** Semple 1998. **55** Ibid. **56** Ibid.

as Beowulf that in the later period such features were the haunts of evil spirits and supernatural creatures. Semple contends that this was actively encouraged by the Church in a concerted attempt to place such vestiges of pagan belief firmly within the context of a Christian worldview. Thus barrows became the burial-places of executed criminals and the socially and morally untouchable.[57]

Regardless of this, however, mounds continued to be used as places of assembly throughout the late Anglo-Saxon period and beyond. Indeed, there is some suggestion that the prevalence of such monuments at assembly-places actually increased.[58] Moreover, in spite of Adkins and Petchey's findings at Secklow, it is clear that some moots did reuse earlier monuments; Audrey Meaney lists several possible examples including Mettle Hill and Thriplow in Cambridgeshire, Thingoe, Suffolk and Mutlow in Uttlesford Hundred, Essex.[59] Elsewhere the name Spellow Hills (< OE *spel-hlaw* – 'speech mound') in Lincolnshire is associated with a Neolithic long-barrow,[60] while a mound known as Moat Low (*Motlawe* 1243 < OE *(ge)mot* + *hlaw* – 'assembly-mound') in Newton Grange, Derbyshire, was excavated by Thomas Bateman in the nineteenth century and found to be of Bronze Age date (fig. 7.8).[61]

There are a number of possible ways of reconciling the apparent contradiction between the late Saxon attitudes to the barrow identified by Semple and the continued use of these features for assembly. At an early date a burial mound, being a place of ancestral or divine influence, might very well be seen as an appropriate place for judicial or legislative business to be carried out. Not only would the site have been a focal point for the community, there may even have been a sense in which the supernatural power was seen as focused through the mound to inspire or reinforce the judgments given.[62] Recent work has drawn attention to the similarities between hundred meeting-places and pagan shrines both in terms of location and the features with which they were associated. This may well reflect the fact that, in their earliest forms, such sites were identical.[63] In some cases, then, the enduring use of barrows as assembly-places may be explained in terms of continuity. Some sites may have originated as early religious or communal centres and continued in use for many centuries, gradually altering their function after the introduction of Christianity. No fear would attach to such sites which had continuously been regarded in a positive light as traditional assembly-places.[64] Conversely, the construction of purpose-built assembly-mounds at other sites may indicate the

---

57 Semple 1998, 113.   58 Meaney 1997, 214.   59 Meaney 1993, 70, 86, 89.   60 *SMRLincs* 43619; Cameron unpublished preparatory notes for *PNLincs*, English Place–Name Society, Nottingham University; White 1842, 346; Jones 1998, no.11; Phillips 1933, 176, 193–6. 61 *PNDb*, 399; Marsden 1977, 78; Bateman 1844, 68; Barnatt and Collis 1996, no. 13. In fact, many of the examples given by Adkins and Petchey as indicative of purpose-built moot mounds can be questioned (Pantos 2002, 104–10).   62 Semple, Warner, this volume.   63 Meaney 1995. 64 Semple 1998, 11; this volume.

Figure 7.8 Moat Law,
Newton Grange,
Derbyshire.

creation of a 'clean mound' in order that a new meeting-place should be preserved from any sinister associations.

Nevertheless, it is not necessary to see every late Saxon assembly-place which reuses an earlier feature as having been in continuous use since the pagan period. Many hundreds which seem to have been of later origin arc also named from, and presumably met at, mounds. Though lack of excavation makes it impossible to tell whether these were re-used barrows or purpose-built, their occurrence at least suggests a continued perception that mounds were appropriate venues for assembly.[65] It should be borne in mind that the

---

65 For instance, Steven Bassett has argued that the Warwickshire hundred of Pathlow was created out of the area which originally comprised Ferncombe Hundred. The meeting–place is thought to have been at a mound in Aston Cantlow parish, but unfortunately the feature, which was never excavated, no longer survives (Bassett 1996; *SMRWa* 6082, 1579; Anderson 1934, 132–3; *PNWa*, 95). The post–Conquest hundred of Knightlow, which comprised three earlier hundreds, likewise met at a mound recorded by the SMR as a possible Bronze Age round barrow (*PNWa*, 179; Anderson 1934, 134; *SMRWa* 4273).

associations held by comparable features in the popular imagination need not always be identical, and even within the same area, features of the same type may be interpreted in different ways. Recent anthropological work by David Shankland has demonstrated this in a modern context.[66] Shankland focused upon the folklore and popular beliefs associated with the archaeological remains around the major Neolithic site of Çatalhöyük. His study reveals that although there is a general perception among the local inhabitants that these features are associated with the supernatural, this is not applied uniformly to every site, neither is the supernatural force necessarily envisaged as 'evil'. It may be that a similar situation existed in Anglo-Saxon England with regard to mounds and barrows.

While the burial mound as the dwelling-place of restless heathen ancestors may have had negative associations in a Christian context, its association with the communal past may have taken on a very different aspect when used as a site for assembly. The idea that in some circumstances the reuse of earlier monuments may have been a conscious 'appropriation of the past' designed to reinforce claims of territorial and political power is increasingly being applied to Anglo-Saxon studies. Richard Bradley has suggested that the positioning of the Anglo-Saxon royal vill at Yeavering, Northumbria in relation to a concentration of prehistoric monuments represents the intentional 'creation of continuity' by an Anglo-Saxon elite, analogous to the incorporation of pagan gods and heroes into royal genealogies.[67] Others have applied similar explanations to the re-use of earlier monuments for high-status burial during the early Anglo-Saxon period.[68] It is easy to see how comparable arguments might be put forward for Anglo-Saxon assembly-places which were, after all, sites intimately connected with the control and cohesion of the community.

Elsewhere I have argued that the location of many assemblies on territorial boundaries may be linked not so much to the desire for 'neutrality' (a place which belonged to no-one), as to 'community' (a place which belonged to everyone). In the same way, it can be argued that the location of a late assembly-place at a site of earlier importance (or perceived earlier importance) was an exercise in communality, serving to reinforce the authority of the court. In many ways, the function of such assemblies was to cement the social links which played an important part in the operation of late Anglo-Saxon justice and administration. The members of a hundred court were bound together through the organization and responsibilities of the hundred and tithing, and justice in part relied upon the accountability of members of these units for one another. The choice to site an assembly at a location which had a long-standing significance for the community, or to continue to use such a site in spite of its 'pagan' connotations, may have been closely linked to this ideology.

66 Shankland 1999.   67 Bradley 1987.   68 Williams 1998.

This suggestion presents another possible angle from which to view the multiplication of features at assembly-places and their location close to sites of importance in earlier periods. The location of hundredal assemblies at hillforts, barrows and other ancient features might be interpreted as intentional archaism. For it may be that by choosing sites similar to the traditional venues of early assemblies, later hundredal courts sought to claim for themselves a degree of authority and precedent. The use of the large early Saxon cemetery at Loveden Hill as a venue for wapentake assemblies in the tenth and eleventh centuries may well indicate continuity of use and the preservation of an important community focus for several centuries.[69] Another Lincolnshire wapentake, Winnibriggs, seems to have met in the vicinity of a complex of prehistoric monuments including a longbarrow and henge. This is thought to have been an important ritual, inter-regional contact point in the Neolithic.[70] In this instance continuity is less likely. As at Yeavering, however, what it may signal is the appropriation of a complex of early monuments in order to lend authority to a new place of regional and communal significance.

CONCLUSION

The above discussion does not seek to present new interpretations of any individual assembly-place, neither does it hope to address many of the questions raised by the location of such sites. Rather, the aim of this paper has been to draw attention to the scope for investigation which remains. It has been argued that the study of assemblies and assembly-places has been hampered by overly simplistic approaches largely governed by a reliance on place-name material. The perception that assemblies took place at single features has restricted the archaeological investigation of sites and led to excessively functional discussions which constrain interpretation. At the same time the absence of detailed archaeological work makes even the most general conclusions uncertain. Many alternative interpretations of Anglo-Saxon assembly-places and their role in the late Saxon state are possible. Without substantial reassessment of the way the subject is approached, however, little progress is likely to be made.

ABBREVIATIONS

BCS   *Cartularium Saxonicum*, ed. W. de G. Birch.
OE   Old English

69 Williams, this volume. 70 *SMRLincs* 33382; Jones 1998.

ON	Old Norse
PNBH	*The place-names of Bedfordshire and Huntingdonshire*, ed. A. Mawer.
PNDb	*The place-names of Derbyshire*, ed. K. Cameron.
PNDo	*The place-names of Dorset*, ed. A.D. Mills.
PNHert	*The place-names of Hertfordshire*, ed. J.E.B. Gover.
PNLincs	*The place-names of Lincolnshire*, ed. K. Cameron.
PNNotts	*The place-names of Nottinghamshire*, ed. J.E.B. Gover.
PNNp	*The place-names of Northamptonshire*, ed. J.E.B. Gover.
PNOx	*The place-names of Oxfordshire*, ed. M. Gelling.
PNSr	*The place-names of Surrey*, J.E.B. Gover, A. Mawer, F.M. Bonner and A. Bonner.
PNSx	*The place-names of Sussex*, A. Mawer and F.M. Stenton.
PNWa	*The place-names of Warwickshire*, J.E.B. Gover.
S	Sawyer, *Anglo-Saxon charters*
SMRLei	Leicestershire sites and monuments record
SMRLincs	Lincolnshire sites and monuments record
SMRNotts	Nottinghamshire sites and monuments record
SMRPeterb	Peterborough sites and monuments record
SMRStaffs	Staffordshire sites and monuments record
SMRWa	Warwickshire sites and monuments record
VCHBerks	*Victoria county history of Berkshire*, ed. W. Page with P.H. Ditchfield, and J.H. Cope.
VCHHert	*Victoria county history of Hertfordshire*, ed. W. Page.
VCHSr	*Victoria county history of Surrey*, ed. H.E. Malden.
VCHStaffs	*Victoria county history of Staffordshire*, ed. M.W. Greenslade.

REFERENCES

Adkins, R.A. and Petchey, M.R., 1984: 'Secklow hundred mound and other meeting-place mounds in England', *Archaeological Journal* 141, 243–51.

Anderson, O.S., 1934: *The English hundred names*. Lund.

Anderson, O.S., 1939a: *The English hundred names: the south-western counties*. Lund.

Anderson, O.S., 1939b: *The English hundred names: the south-eastern counties*. Lund.

Aston, M., 1986: 'Post Roman central places in Somerset', in E. Grant (ed.), *Central places: archaeology and history*. Sheffield.

Barnatt, J. and Collis, J., 1996: *Barrows in the Peak District: recent research*. Sheffield.

Bassett, S., 1996: 'The administrative landscape of the diocese of Worcester in the tenth century', in N. Brooks and C. Cubitt (eds), *St Oswald of Worcester: life and influences*. London.

Bateman, T., 1848: *Vestiges of the antiquities of Derbyshire*. London.

Bateman, T., 1861: *Ten years' diggings in Celtic and Saxon grave hills in the counties of Derby, Stafford, and York*. London.

Birch, W. de G., 1885–1893: *Cartularium saxonicum*. London.

Bradley, R., 1987: 'Time regained: the creation of continuity', *Journal of the British Archaeological Association* **140**, 1–17.

Britnell, R.H., 1978: 'English markets and royal administration before 1200', *Economic History Review* (2nd series) **31** (part 2), 183–96.

Brown, A.E., Key, T.R. and Orr C., 1977: 'Some Anglo-Saxon estates and their boundaries in south-west Northamptonshire', *Northamptonshire Archaeology* **12**, 155–76.

Cam, H. M., 1936: 'The hundred outside the north gate of Oxford', *Oxoniensia* **1**, 113–28.

Cameron, K., 1959: *The place-names of Derbyshire*, English Place-Name Society **27–9**. Cambridge.

Cameron, K., 1985–: *The place-names of Lincolnshire* (Part 2), English Place-Name Society **64**. Nottingham.

Cameron, K., 1996: *English place-names* (revised edn.). London.

Carpenter, L.W., 1949: 'Saxon spearhead from Cheam', *Surrey Archaeological Collection* **51**, 151–2.

Chambers, R.A., 1978: 'A secondary burial on Shipton Barrow, Oxon, 1976', *Oxoniensia* **43**, 253–5,

Cox, B.H., 1971–2: 'Leicestershire moot-sites: the place-name evidence', *Transactions of the Leicestershire Archaeological and Historical Society* **47**, 14–21.

Duigan, W.H., 1912: *Warwickshire place-names*. Oxford.

Foote, P. and Wilson, D.M., 1970: *The Viking achievement*. London.

Garmonsway, G.N. (trans), 1972: *The Anglo-Saxon Chronicle* (2nd edn.). London.

Gelling, M., 1953–4: *The place-names of Oxfordshire*, English Place-Name Society **23–4**. Cambridge.

Gelling, M., 1973–6: *The place-names of Berkshire*, English Place-Name Society **49–51**. Cambridge.

Gelling, M., 1978: *Signposts to the past*. London.

Gelling, M., 1992: *The West Midlands in the early Middle Ages*. London.

Gould, J., 1971–2: 'Romano-British farming near Letocetum (Wall, Staffs.)', *South Staffordshire Archaeology and History Society Transactions* **13**, 1–8.

Gover, J.E.B., 1933: *The place-names of Northamptonshire*, English Place-Name Society **10**. Cambridge.

Gover, J.E.B., 1936: *The place-names of Warwickshire*, English Place-Name Society **13**. Cambridge.

Gover, J.E.B., 1938: *The place-names of Hertfordshire*, English Place-Name Society **15**. Cambridge.

Gover, J.E.B., 1940: *The place-names of Nottinghamshire*, English Place-Name Society **17**. Cambridge.

Gover, J.E.B., Mawer, A., Stenton, F.M. and Bonner, A., 1934: *The place-names of Surrey*, English Place-Name Society **11**. Cambridge.

Greenslade, M.W., 1984: *The Victoria history of the county of Stafford*, vol. 20. London.

Gunstone, A.J.H., 1965: 'An archaeological gazetteer of Staffordshire. Part 2: the barrows', *North Staffordshire Journal of Field Studies* **5**, 20–63.

Harmer, F.E., 1989: *Anglo-Saxon writs*. Stamford.

Hartley, R.F. and Pickering, J., 1985: *Past worlds in a landscape: archaeological crop marks in Leicestershire*. Leicester.

Harvey, J., 1946–7: 'The hundred of Copthorne and Effingham', *Surrey Archaeological Collections* **50**, 157–61.

Hooke, D., 1998: *The landscape of Anglo-Saxon England.* London.

Hope-Taylor, B., 1977: *Yeavering: an Anglo-British centre of early Northumbria.* London.

Hunter-Blair, P., 1978: *An introduction to Anglo-Saxon England* (2nd edn.). Cambridge.

Jóhannesson, J. (trans H. Bessarson), 1974: *A history of the Old Icelandic commonwealth: Islendinga saga*, University of Manitoba Icelandic Studies. Winnipeg.

Jones, D., 1998: 'Long barrows and Neolithic elongated enclosures in Lincolnshire: an analysis of the air photographic evidence', *Proceedings of the Prehistoric Society* **64**, 83–114.

Keynes, S., 1990: 'Royal government and the written word in late Anglo-Saxon England', in R. McKitterick (ed.), *The uses of literacy in early Medieval Europe.* Cambridge. 226–57.

Keynes, S., 1991: 'Crime and punishment in the reign of Æthelred the Unready', in I. Wood and N. Lund (eds), *People and places in northern Europe 500–1600.* Woodbridge. 67–81.

Liebermann, F., 1913: *The national assembly in the Anglo-Saxon period.* London.

Loyn, H.R., 1974: 'The hundred in England in the tenth and eleventh centuries', in H. Hearder and H.R. Loyn (eds), *British government and administration.* Cardiff. 1–15.

Loyn, H.R., 1984: *The governance of Anglo-Saxon England 500–1087.* Stanford.

Macleod, D., 1932–3: 'Yonesmere pit', *Sussex Notes and Queries* **4**, 154–5.

Magerøy, H., (ed.), 1981: *Bandamanna Saga.* Oslo.

Malden, H.E., 1902–: *The Victoria history of the county of Surrey*, vol. 3. London.

Margary, I.D., 1973: *Roman roads in Britain* (3rd edn.). London.

Marsden, B.M., 1977: *The burial mounds of Derbyshire.* Privately printed.

Mawer, A., 1926: *The place-names of Bedfordshire and Huntingdonshire*, English Place-Name Society 3. Cambridge.

Mawer, A., 1929–30: *The place-names of Sussex*, English Place-Name Society **6–7**. Cambridge.

Marsom, F.W., 1943: 'The meeting-place of Wixamtree Hundred', *Transactions of the Bedfordshire Historical Record Society* **25**, 1–3.

Meaney, A.L., 1993: 'Gazetteer of hundred and wapentake meeting-places of the Cambridge Region', *Proceedings of the Cambridge Antiquarian Society* **82**, 67–92.

Meaney, A.L., 1995: 'Pagan English sanctuaries, place-names and hundred meeting-places', *Anglo-Saxon Studies in Archaeology and History* 8, 29–42.

Meaney, A.L., 1997: 'Hundred meeting-places in the Cambridge region', in A.R. Rumble and A.D. Mills (eds), *Names, places and people: an onomastic miscellany in memory of John McNeal Dodgson.* Stamford. 195–240.

Mills, A.D., 1977–89: *The place-names of Dorset* (Part 2), English Place-Name Society 53. Nottingham.

Nail, D., 1965: 'The meeting-place of Copthorne Hundred', *Surrey Archaeological Collections* **62**, 44–53.

Newman, J., 1996: 'New light on old finds: Bloodmoor Hill, Gisleham, Suffolk', *Anglo-Saxon Studies in Archaeology and History* **9**, 75–9.

Nichols, J., 1795–1815: *The history and antiquities of the county of Leicester*, vol. 4, part 1. London.

Page, W., 1912: *The Victoria history of the county of Hertford*, vol. 3. London.

Page, W. with Ditchfield, P.H. and Cope, J.H., 1927: *The Victoria history of Berkshire*, vol. 4. London.

Palsson, H. and Fox. D. (trans), 1974: *Grettir's Saga*. Toronto.

Pantos, A., 2002: 'Assembly-places in the Anglo-Saxon period: aspects of form and location'. Unpublished DPhil thesis, University of Oxford.

Pantos, A., 2003: 'On the edge of things: the boundary location of Anglo-Saxon Assembly-Sites', *Anglo-Saxon Studies in Archaeology and History* 12.

Phillips, C.W., 1933: 'The present state of archaeology in Lincolnshire: Part I', *Archaeological Journal* 90, 193–6.

Pollock, F. and Maitland, W., 1898: *The history of English law before the time of Edward I*. Cambridge.

Raftery, B., 1994: *Pagan Celtic Ireland*. London.

Reynolds, A.J., 1997: 'The definition and ideology of Anglo-Saxon execution sites and cemeteries', in G. De Boe and F. Verhaeghe (eds), *Death and burial in medieval Europe: papers of the 'Medieval Europe Brugge 1997' Conference*, vol. 2. Brügge. 33–41.

Reynolds, A.J., 1999: *Later Anglo-Saxon England: life and landscape*. Stroud.

Reynolds, A.J., forthcoming: *Anglo-Saxon law in the landscape*. Oxford.

Rigold, S.E. and Metcalf, D.M., 1977: 'A check-list of English finds of sceattas', *British Numismatic Journal* 47, 31–52.

Sawyer, P.H., 1968: *Anglo-Saxon charters: an annotated list and bibliography*. London.

Sawyer, P.H., 1981: 'Fairs and markets in early Medieval England', in N. Skyum Nielsen and N. Lund (eds), *Danish medieval history: new currents*. Copenhagen. 153–68.

Semple, S., 1998: 'A fear of the past: the place of the prehistoric burial mound in the ideology of middle and later Anglo-Saxon England', *World Archaeology* 30:1, 109–26.

Shankland, D., 1999: 'Integrating the past: folklore, mounds and people at Çatalhöyük', in A. Gazin-Schwartz and C. Holtorf (eds), *Archaeology and folklore*. London. 139–57.

Stukeley, W., 1724: *Itinerarium Curiosum*.

Taylor, A. and Denton, B., 1977: 'Skeletons on Wandlebury Hill-fort. TL 495533', *Cambridge Antiquarian Society Proceedings* 67, 3.

Thoroton, R. with Throsby, J., 1790–6: *Thoroton's history of Nottinghamshire*, vol.1. Nottinghamshire.

Warner, P., 1988: 'Pre-Conquest territorial and administrative organization in East Suffolk', in D. Hooke (ed.), *Anglo-Saxon settlements*. Oxford. 9–34.

White, W. 1842: *History, gazetteer, and directory of Lincolnshire, and the city and diocese of Lincoln*. Sheffield.

Williams, H.M.R., 1998: 'Monuments and the past in early Anglo-Saxon England', *World Archaeology* 30:1, 90–109.

Wormald, P., 1986: 'Charters, law and the settlement of disputes in Anglo-Saxon

England', in W. Davies and P. Fouracre (eds), *The settlement of disputes in early medieval Europe*. Cambridge.

Wormald, P, 1988: 'A hand-list of Anglo-Saxon lawsuits', *Anglo-Saxon England* **17**, 247–81.

Wormald, P., 1999a: 'Lordship and justice in the early English kingdom: Oswaldslow Revisited', in P. Wormald, *Legal culture in the early medieval West: law as text, image and experience.* London. 114–36.

Wormald, P., 1999b: *The making of English law: King Alfred to the twelfth century.* Oxford.

"*In medle oððe an þinge*": the Old English vocabulary of assembly

ALIKI PANTOS

The surviving Anglo-Saxon law-codes and other pre-Conquest texts contain many references to assemblies of various kinds and the terms for 'meeting' used in these sources also occur as elements in place-names across England. Other papers in this volume have noted the extent to which the identification of early places of assembly relies on the interpretation of these names. The purpose of the present essay is to consider the most common of these 'assembly' elements in their literary, onomastic and geographical contexts.[1] By surveying their use in written Old English it attempts to shed some light on the precise use and meaning of these words and seeks to glean an incite into the operation of the assembly-places themselves. At the same time it endeavours to highlight potential problems surrounding their identification and interpretation in place-names.

WORDS FOR ASSEMBLY

Gemōt or *mōt* is by far the most frequent word for assembly in written Old English. It occurs regularly in law-codes from the late seventh or early eighth-century onwards,[2] and is applied to a variety of formal assemblies including meetings of the *witan*, shire and borough courts, and hundred moots.[3] It can also refer to ecclesiastical assemblies.[4] In glosses *(ge)mōt* renders Latin *consessum, conuentio* while *to gemōte* translates *ad forum*.[5] The occurrence of *(ge)mōt* is not restricted to legal and historical texts, however. Neither does it always refer to a legal assembly. Perhaps unsurprisingly, in religious works, the

---

1 The words discussed include OE *(ge)mōt*, OE/ON *þing*, OE *mæðel*, OE *spell* and OE *sp(r)æc*. Other terms which are sometimes taken to indicate assembly-places, such as OE *stōw* and *scīr*, are discussed in Pantos 2002.   2 Wihtred 5.   3 e.g. VI Æthelstan 10; III Edgar 5.1; S. 1454, 1460; II Cnut 17.1.   4 *The Old English Bede*: Miller 1890–98, 276 l. 4.   5 MS Cotton Cleopatra A. III. Reference from *COE*; Meritt 1959, 96.

image of the Last Judgment as an assembly is a common one.[6] More interestingly, the word is relatively frequent in poetry, where it often occurs in
references to physical combat, seemingly with the general sense of 'meeting' or
'encounter'.[7]

The wide range of contexts in which *(ge)mōt* occurs suggest it was the usual
word for any sort of meeting or gathering, regardless of size, purpose or
importance. Thus in itself, the occurrence of the term imparts little information about the event it describes. Unusually large, formal councils are, however,
regularly distinguished by the use of the phrase *micel gemōt* ('great assembly').[8]
It is therefore interesting that the same expression is used in the Vercelli
Homilies to refer to the census announced by Caesar Augustus in chapter two
of St Luke's gospel.[9] Presumably a major assembly was the only thing the
Anglo-Saxon homilist could conceive of which would result in large numbers
of people travelling to the same place. The size of the gathering may not have
been the only thing distinguishing a *micel gemōt*, however. The 'greatness' of
the occasion might also reflect the importance of the business discussed and
the status of the participants. It may be for this reason that the Anglo-Saxon
translator of St Matthew's gospel uses *micel gemōt* to refer to the meeting of
the chief priests and elders prior to the arrest of Jesus. Like a major Anglo-
Saxon assembly, this was a gathering of both ecclesiastical and secular leaders:
þa ealdras þæra sacerda & hlafordas þæs folces.[10]

The existence of an early assembly-place may also be indicated by the
element *thing*. Often this is derived from the usual ON word for 'assembly' –
þing[11] – and, as one might expect, it is most common in place-names in those
parts of Britain where Scandinavian influence was strongest. Peter Foote has
studied the word's occurrence in some of the earliest extant Norse verse,
thought to date from the Viking Age (*c.*900–1100), and thus broadly contemporary with its widespread introduction into England by Scandinavian settlers.
The spread of meanings he identifies suggests that the use and semantic range
of *þing* in ON was very similar to *(ge)mōt* in OE.[12] Although ON *þing* is
probably the most frequent source of the element in English place-names,
however, particularly in areas away from the main concentration of
Scandinavian settlement, some place-names in *thing-* may derive from the
identical, cognate OE *þing* – 'assembly'. This word is rare in written OE and,
with one significant exception, is found only in poetry. It does appear, however,

---

6 E.g. Vercelli Homily X: Scragg 1992, 200 l. 74. cp. *Judgement Day I* l. 36–7. Unless otherwise
stated, all line references given for citations in OE poetry correspond to the *Anglo-Saxon Poetic
Records* series. 7 E.g. *Maldon*, l. 301; *Beowulf*, ll. 1140, 2355; *Guthlac*, l. 236; *Riddle* V,
l. 10. 8 E.g. *ASC* 1020, 1065. cp. Latin *grande placitum* in the *Liber Eliensis* ii, 24: Blake
1962, 97. 9 Scragg 1992, 111, l. 11. 10 Grünberg 1967, 126, ll. 1528–30. 11 Cleasby and
Vigfusson 1874, 1060–1. 12 Foote 1984.

in the late seventh-century laws of Hlothere and Eadric.[13] The article concerned refers to the procedure when one man brings a charge against another *in medle oððe an þinge*. It is unclear whether the two words *mæðel* and *þing* are synonymous here. Nevertheless, this reference indicates that OE *þing* was at one time used in a legal context, although it seems subsequently to have been supplanted by *(ge)mōt*.

The history of *þing* in OE is touched on by Eric Stanley in his consideration of the phrase *þing gehēgan* in Beowulf.[14] Stanley notes that this expression is not infrequent in poetry where it seems usually to have the meaning 'hold a meeting'.[15] The idiom does not occur outside poetry, however. In contrast the cognate phrase *heia thing* occurs frequently in the early Frisian law-codes. Likewise, Old Icelandic *heyja þing* is well-attested. Stanley argues that this suggests the antiquity of the phrase in a legal sense, indicating that it 'goes back to the inherited diction of the Germanic tribes and was not in origin poetic'.[16] In OE, however, *þing gehēgan* seems to have become obsolete in formal legal terminology, surviving only in poetic vocabulary. On this evidence it seems likely that OE *þing* also went out of general use as a word for 'assembly' at an early period, and names derived from OE *þing* may therefore be particularly early. Nevertheless, its use in poetry and appearance in compounds suggests that *þing* was still understood by speakers of late OE and it is thus possible that it remained an active name-forming element, despite being absent from the prose vocabulary. It may even have been borrowed back into late OE from ON.

Interestingly, the distribution of OE *mæþel* is almost identical to that of OE *þing*. With the meaning 'assembly' this word occurs only twice in a legal context, both times in early law-codes. It is coupled with *þing* in the Laws of Hlothere and Eadric mentioned above, while the compound *mæðelfrið*, presumably referring to the peace given in such a meeting, appears in the even earlier Laws of Æthelbert.[17] Otherwise, in the sense of 'assembly' *mæðel* occurs almost exclusively in poetry.[18] It does gloss *in curia* in the Corpus and Epinal-Erfurt glossaries,[19] but we may be justified in wondering how representative the language of these texts is of normal spoken Old English, since glossators may have drawn on several registers of speech in order to find words which most fittingly encapsulated the Latin terms they wished to render. Like *þing*, the early Germanic origin of OE *mæðel* is indicated by the existence of cognates in a number of other languages.[20] By analogy with the arguments put forward for OE *þing*, therefore, it seems possible that the absence of OE *mæðel*

---

13 Hlothere and Eadric 8.   14 Stanley 1979.   15 Ibid., 78; Foote 1984, 81.   16 Stanley 1979, 87.   17 The word was restored by Liebermann from a transcription of MS Cotton Julius C II made in 1589: Liebermann 1898–1916, i 3.   18 Barney 1977, 51.   19 Hessels 1890, 9.223; Pheifer 1974, 30 no. 549.   20 *BTD*, 664; Holthausen 1934, 213.

in prose and later law-codes indicates that it fell out of general use at a relatively early date.

The evidence therefore suggests that a shift took place in the vocabulary of assembly in the course of the Anglo-Saxon period. Except in the poetic register, the older words for meeting – *þing* and *mæðel* – seem to have been abandoned in favour of *(ge)mōt* and in the law-codes at least, this change appears to have taken place around the end of the seventh century.

WORDS FOR SPEECH

Place-names including an element meaning 'speech' can also be taken as indicative of assembly-places, and in poetry OE *mæðel* also occurs with this meaning.[21] Moreover, like *þing*, in this sense the word appears in combination with *gehēgan* giving the meaning 'to hold speech, converse', while the related compound *mæðel-hegende* occurs in both Andreas and in Elene.[22]

Close examination of the contexts in which *mæþel* appears when used in this way may suggest that it was more than a general word for 'talking', however. Firstly, it occurs in compounds in combination with other terms for 'speech', which might suggest that *mæðel* itself had some quality that rendered it distinct.[23] Moreover, *mæðel* is particularly associated with the speech of wise men or heroes. Of especial interest is the formulaic use in poetry of the related expression *X maðelode* to introduce formalized speeches such as the heroic '*bēot*'. This phrase occurs no fewer than twenty-six times in Beowulf and is also common elsewhere.[24] Although the situations in which *mæðel* and its derivatives are used vary, therefore, a detailed study seems to suggest that they all share a common thread of formality or importance.[25] The speech acts concerned often impart significant wisdom or are declarations of heroic intent, and thus *mæðel* seems belong to a register of speech above that of general communication. The associated verbs *maðelian, (ge)mælan* and (in poetry) *maðlan* demonstrate similar connotations: all mean 'to speak' or more specifically, 'to make a formal speech'. Other related words are likewise particularly linked with formal discourse, rhetoric and educational speech.[26]

The relationship between the two meanings of *mæðel* – 'assembly' and 'speech' – is unclear, but it is tempting to see them as closely linked and to

---

21 E.g. *Elene*, ll. 592–3; *Exodus*, l. 255. 22 *Andreas*,ll. 262, 609, 1096, 1496; *Elene*, l. 279. See also Stanley 1979, 78. 23 E.g. *mæðelword: Beowulf*, l. 236; *mæðelcwida: Guthlac*, l. 1007, 1015, 1219; *Solomon and Saturn*, l. 434. 24 E.g. *Widsith*, l. 1; *Elene*, l. 332, 642, 685; *Maldon*, l. 42, 309. Similar use is made of the comparable phrase *wordum mælde* – 'he spoke in words' e.g. *Maldon*, l. 26. 25 Pantos 2002, 43–4. 26 See for example the following glosses: Goosens 1974, nos. 2279, 2282, 2850; Napier 1900, nos. 2947, 2323, 2321.

conclude that, in the latter sense, the word describes the sort of speech which might be expected at an assembly. It is therefore interesting that similar suggestions can be put forward regarding the semantic range of the OE word *spell* which is also usually translated 'speech'. *Spell* is relatively common in place-names and occurs as the first element of two hundred names – Spelhoe, Northamptonshire, and Spelthorne, Middlesex – a fact which indicates its association with assembly-places beyond question.[27]

In both OE prose and in poetry *spell* appears fairly frequently. Smith explains its meaning in general terms as 'speech, discourse',[28] however, Bosworth-Toller's Anglo-Saxon dictionary gives more attention to the nuances of the word in different contexts, listing four main definitions and a variety of subsidiary ones. The first of these is 'A story, narrative, account, relation'. Many instances of *spell* used in this sense can be identified[29] and in similar contexts it also corresponds to Bosworth-Toller's secondary definition 1a: 'a historical narrative, history'. From the point of view of this study, the most significant example is that in the so-called Fonthill Letter.[30] Here the word is applied to a narrative account given as evidence in a court of law. The letter tells how men were appointed to bring about an agreement between the opposing parties in the lawsuit and *ða reahte heora ægðer his spell* – 'then each gave his own account'. This source not only gives an unusual insight into the actual operation of a late Anglo-Saxon court, but the use of *spell* in the context of a formal legal assembly strengthens the case for identifying place-names including the element as the sites of such meetings.[31]

It is significant, however, that several different types of story can be designated by the word *spell*. The term is frequently used of instructive speeches, particularly holy ones. Ælfric's homily for Palm Sunday notes that Church customs forbid any sermon (*ænig spell*) to be said on the three days on which silence was observed.[32] One eleventh-century homily is entitled *Sunnandæges spell*, and the compound *spell-boc* is used to refer to collections of such homilies, such as those given to Exeter by Bishop Leofric.[33] Similarly, in the poem Genesis, God's speech to Abraham is described as a *spell*.[34] In these instances, *spell* clearly refers to 'good' narratives which impart wisdom or holy teaching. The word is also used of less edifying stories, however, particularly what might be described as 'fables'; in the phrase *ealdra cwena spell*, for example, it is applied, quite literally to 'old wives' tales', glossing Latin *Anilis fabula*.[35]

---

27 *PNNp*, 131–2; Anderson 1934, 122. **28** Smith 1956, ii 136. **29** E.g. *Widsith*, l. 54–6: *Forþon ic mæg singan ond secgan spell* – 'therefore I can sing and tell a tale'. cp. *Beowulf*, ll. 2109–10; *Andreas*, ll. 814–7. **30** S 1445. **31** The significance of the document is discussed in Keynes 1992. **32** Clemoes 1997, 298, l. 220. **33** Napier 1883, no. 43; Robertson 1956, 228. **34** *Genesis*, ll. 2406–7. **35** Kindschi, 'The Latin Old-English Glossaries in Plantin-Moretus

The use of the same word to describe such different types of narrative suggests that as a term for a tale or spoken account the word *spell* itself was a neutral one which derived specific meaning from its context. Nevertheless, although Christian sermons may appear diametrically opposed to fables and old wives' tales, they have one element in common: they all purport to be informative, whether or not this is actually the case. It may be, then, that the sort of speech act implied by the word *spell* is one which sets out to impart knowledge, be that knowledge divinely inspired, regrettably misguided or intentionally false. This interpretation of the word would be in keeping with its occurrence in certain contexts with the sense 'tidings, news, announcement' and the use of the compound *spell-boda* meaning 'messenger, tale-teller, someone who brings intelligence'.[36]

Spell occurs in several compounds the meanings of which support the word's association with imparting information. In a religious context it is, of course, very common in the word *gōdspell* – 'gospel', and also in *lārspel* – 'a discourse, sermon, homily, treatise' (OE *lār* – 'lore, teaching, instruction'), while *bi(g)spel* means 'parable'.[37] In contrast, an *inwitspell* – 'wicked speech/ story' – appears in Genesis.[38] As Brodeur notes, the meaning 'tidings' is particularly frequent in compounds of *spell*.[39] In both Juliana and Exodus we find *færspel* – 'a sudden message, sudden news, horrible message' (OE *fær* – 'sudden, intense, terrible, horrid'), and Exodus includes the compound *bealospella* – 'a baleful message or tale'.[40] It is perhaps also worth noting, as Bonser does, that in other Germanic languages the equivalent word is used in exactly parallel contexts, with Gothic *spilla* used to mean 'old wives' tales' and its OHG counterpart rendering *sermo, parabola* and *fabula*.[41]

It is also interesting that OE *spell* differs from related words such as the verb *spellian* and noun *spellung* in that it only refers to a speech act performed by an individual, for instance an oration, narrative or announcement, rather than a reciprocal one such as a conversation or discussion. *Spellian* can be either transitive, meaning 'to announce, proclaim, tell, utter', or intransitive, with the sense 'to talk, converse, discourse'. Similarly, *spellung* means both 'narrative, tale' and 'talking, conversation'.[42] Although Bosworth and Toller's dictionary gives the general meaning 'speech, language of prose' as one of the definitions of OE *spell*, in practice this sense appears to be very rare. It does occur once in the preface to the Old English translation of the Consolation of Philosophy

---

MS 32 and British Museum MS Additional 32246', (Stanford dissertation, 1955), no. 417, reference from *COE*. **36** E.g. *Maldon*, l. 50; *Daniel*, l. 478, l. 742; *Christ*, l. 336; *Exodus*, l. 514. **37** *BTD*, 622; Godden 1979, 183, l. 120–1; 306, l. 66–7; 213, l. 3. **38** *Genesis*, l. 2024. **39** Brodeur 1959, 266. **40** *BTD*, 266; *Juliana*, l. 277, *Exodus*, l. 135; *BTD*, 71; *Exodus*, l. 511. cp. *BTD*, 1230, 632, 697; *Elene*, l. 983, l. 1016, l. 969. **41** Bonser 1963, 146. **42** *Spellung* occurs particularly frequently in combination with adjectives like *idele* – 'idle' and *bysmorlice* – 'opprobrious', and Stanley has suggested that it has pejorative overtones: Stanley 1971, 414.

where Alfred states his intention to translate the book *'of Lædenum to Engliscum spelle'*.[43] However, the more general word *sp(r)æc* occurs far more frequently in this sort of context. There is, then, no sense of 'discussion' in the use of the word *spell*. In place-names, therefore, OE *spell* seems more likely to refer to the making of announcements and formal speeches at assemblies, than to deliberation. It should perhaps be noted that the compound *spelboda* not only means 'messenger' but also 'public speaker', occurring in glosses rendering Latin *causidicus .i. legator . disertus .facundus* and *oratores*.[44]

The usual OE word for 'speech' in a general sense was *spæc* (Angl./Nthb. *spēc*), derived from earlier OE *spræc*. This also occurs in some place-names and has been taken to indicate a place of assembly.[45] Bosworth-Toller gives citations which reflect the word's use with all of the following meanings: 'speech, talking', 'the faculty of speaking', 'skilful speech, eloquence', 'a speech, a saying, what is said', 'talk, discourse, words', 'speech, language', 'conversation, discussion', 'a question, case which needs explanation', 'a sentence, decision, agreement, terms', 'a case, cause, suit, claim', 'talk about a person or thing, report, fame'.[46] It is clear from this that *spæc* had a much less specific range of meanings than OE *spell* or *mæðel* seem to, referring to many different types of speech both formal and casual. The verb *sprecan, specan* likewise is widely used, having the general sense 'to speak, to exercise the faculty of speech, converse, discuss'.[47]

Of particular interest to this study is the sense 'a case, cause, suit, claim'. The word is used with this specifically legal meaning in several charters and law-codes. For example, S 1460 records *þa ferde se bisceop to sciregemote to Wigeranceastre & draf þær his spræce* – 'then the bishop went to the shire-court at Worcester and pursued his case there', while II Cnut 28.1 states that no one shall dismiss one of his men from his service until he has been cleared of every accusation (*ælcere spræce*) made against him.[48] The verb *sp(r)æcan* appears in a similar sense in the Fonthill Letter in which we are told *ongan Higa him specan sone on mid oðran onspecendan* – 'Higa at once began to bring a charge against him along with other claimants'.[49]

It may be that in place-names OE *spæc* refers to locations in which cases of this nature were heard. Alternatively, the word may indicate places at which speeches were made or discussions held: Bosworth-Toller notes that 'in the Northern Gospels *sprēc* translates words denoting places where there is speaking', namely *synagoga* and *forum*.[50] It is noteworthy that both these terms are elsewhere glossed by *(ge)mōt* and other words for assembly, and that in

---

43 Sedgefield 1899, Proem, p. 1 l. 9.   44 Oliphant 1966, 64; Hessels 1890, 86.   45 Smith 1956, ii 136.   46 *BTD*, 903–4.   47 *BTD*, 904.   48 Cf. S 1211, 1503; Laws of Alfred and Guthrum 3.   49 Keynes 1992, 64.   50 Skeat 1871–87, Mark 6:2 p. 43; Luke 11:43 p. 125.

both of the above instances *in sprece* is accompanied by *in somnunga* (OE *(ge)samnung* – 'assembly, council').[51]

PEOPLE AND PLACES

Two OE words appear to refer to individuals associated with assemblies: *mōtere* derived from OE *gemōt* and *maðelere* from *mæþel*. These terms appear together in the Harley Glossary where the Latin *contionator .i. locutor* is rendered *motere uel maðelere*, and they are thus both usually translated 'speaker'.[52] The refer- ence to a *motera ford* in the bounds of South Cerney, Gloucestershire suggests that the first word at least was in general use in OE, and the allusion here is presumably to a meeting-place.[53] OE *mōtere* has also been suggested as the source of Mottistone, Isle of Wight and Mottisfont, Hampshire.[54]

Whether it is appropriate to translate these words 'speaker' is unclear, however. It may be that locations known as the 'speaker's ford' or the 'speaker's stone' were designated spots from which any participant in the assembly was expected to speak, serving a purpose similar to that of the witness-box in a modern court-room. On the other hand, at documented assemblies outside England, features such as assembly-mounds usually seem to have functioned seats of authority for an individual or group, rather than as general 'soap- boxes'.[55] It may be, therefore, that the people in question were officials in charge of the assembly. Although there is little evidence for professional 'judges' in Anglo-Saxon England, several sources indicate that an individual (often the reeve, ealdorman or a bishop) was responsible for directing proceed- ings and bringing cases to a satisfactory resolution, and this person undoubtedly wielded considerable power.[56] It may have been this 'assembly president' who was known as the *motere*.

Though related to OE *þing* and similar in form to *motere* and *maðelere* OE *þingere* seems to have had a different meaning, however. It is linked to the verb *þingian* – 'to intercede, ask favour, supplicate, plead'[57] frequently appearing in a Christian context with reference to saints or intercessors. In the Corpus and Cleopatra glossaries *þingere* renders Latin *advocatus*,[58] but it seems unlikely that the secular sense of the word generally referred to trained lawyers. Instead

---

51 *BTD*, 814.   **52** Oliphant 1966, C1715.   **53** S 896.   **54** Cameron 1996, 140; Gelling 1978, 86.   **55** Pantos 2002, 75; cp. FitzPatrick, Charles-Edwards, Darvill this volume.   **56** See Keynes 1992, 80 n.107; Kennedy 1995, 173–4; Wormald 1986, 164.   **57** *BTD* associates *þingian* with OSax. *thingón*, OFris. *thingia* – *placitare*, OHG *dingón* – *concionare, judicare, disceptare, pascisci*, German *dingen* 'to bargain for, agree on' and O.Icel. *þinga* 'to hold a meeting, consult about, discuss'. Cp. Holthausen 1934, 365–6.   **58** Hessels 1890, 12; J.J. Quinn, 'The Minor Latin-Old English Glossaries in MS. Cotton Cleopatra A III' (Stanford dissertation, 1956), 716, reference from *COE*.

it may have been applied to those who, like Ealdorman Ordlaf in the Fonthill Letter, agreed to exercise their influence on another's behalf.[59] Unlike *motere þingere* does not appear in place-names.

Compounds of 'assembly/speech words' referring specifically to locations of assembly also appear in a number of OE texts. Frequently these combine an 'assembly' element with one of two words for 'place' – OE *stōw* or *stede*. Thus we find both *gemōtstōw* and *gemōtstede* ('assembly-place'),[60] although the former is the most common and is the only one found in place-names.[61] *Spell-stōw* – 'speech-place' – occurs only twice in pre-Conquest documents. Both examples come from charters relating to neighbouring estates in Gloucestershire and it seems likely that both references are to a single site.[62] Nevertheless, these documents confirm the existence of the word in OE. It is probably also the source of a lost name *Spelestowe* in Marton, Warwickshire.[63]

Þing-stede also occurs twice, on both occasions in poetry, and in both instances referring to a place where a group of people are assembled.[64] It seems to be the root of the name *Thingstede* recorded in a twelfth-century document in Authorpe, Lincolnshire.[65] Interestingly, direct parallels to this compound can be found in a number of cognate languages.[66] In contrast OE *þing-stōw* does not appear in poetry, but only in glosses or translations of Latin texts. In the Harley Glossary it renders Latin *competum*, a word originally meaning 'crossroads' which, in Medieval Latin had taken on the additional senses 'boundary, limit' and 'meeting-place'.[67] Elsewhere, in the OE versions of the gospels, it repeatedly glosses Latin *forum*.[68] *Mæðel-stede*, appears fairly frequently[69] and again has cognates in other Germanic languages.[70] Its literal meaning is 'a place of assembly or speech', although metaphorically, it may also be used of a place of battle.[71]

---

59 Keynes 1992, 66–7; cp. S 1462. **60** See for example Bazire and Cross 1982, 73, l. 131; *Soul and Body I*, l. 150. In religious texts such as the Paris Psalter, *on gemōtstōw* glosses Latin *synagoga* in the sense of 'congregation'. **61** E.g. *Motslow Hill* (earlier *Mostowe*), the meeting-place of Stoneleigh Hundred, Warwickshire: *PNWa*, 152, 184. A field-name *Muster* in Seisdon parish, Staffordshire may indicate the meeting-place of Seisdon Hundred: Greenslade 1984, 185; Pantos 2002, 437–8. **62** S 99; S 550. **63** *PNWa*, 123. **64** *Andreas*, l. 1098; *Christ*, l. 497. **65** Pantos 2002, 361; Stenton 1920, 408. **66** E.g. ON *þingstaþr*, OHG *dingstat*, OLG *thingstedi*, MDu *dincstat* – 'meeting-place, judgment-place': Carr 1939, 52. **67** Latham 1975–, 407. This word is also rendered by OE *ceorla samnung ł gemotstōw* in the Antwerp Glossaries: L. Kindschi, 'The Latin Old-English glossaries in Plantin-Moretus MS 32 and British Museum MS Additional 32246', (Stanford dissertation, 1955) no.463, reference from *COE*. **68** E.g. Skeat 1871–87, Mark 7.4 p. 53; Matthew 20.3 p. 159. **69** *Andreas*, l. 658, 697; *Maldon*, l. 199; *Exodus*, l. 397, 543; *Daniel*, l. 145; *Elene*, l. 554; *Beowulf*, l. 1082. **70** Carr 1939, 101. **71** E.g. *Beowulf*, l. 1082. It is interesting that in poetry words for assembly are repeatedly used to refer to battle. Although Foote considers that the use of ON *þing* in this way simply reflects its generalized meaning 'meeting', it is tempting to see the application of these words to descriptions of warfare – the antithesis of organized dispute resolution – as ironic.

In none of these instances is a meeting-place specifically described. Nevertheless, certain occurrences of these words may perhaps reflect the way that such sites were perceived. In the glosses to Aldhelm's De Laudibus Virginitatis, MS Brussels Royal Library 1650, the Latin *pro rostris* is glossed by *muris* and OE *for heahseldum ł gemotstowum*.[72] The gloss comes in a passage describing the practices of skilled orators *qui pro rostris in edito stantes, popularibus catervis concionantur*. Clearly the glosses refer to the speaker's elevated position in relation to his audience: Latin *rostrum* usually refers to a platform in the forum from which a speaker addresses the people, while OE *heahseld* is translated by Bosworth and Toller as 'throne', the literal meaning being 'high-seat'.[73] The glossator's use of *gemōtstōw* may have been inspired simply by the need for a word describing a location from which a speaker might address a large group of people. However, given the context, it might be suspected that the *gemōtstōw* was envisaged as an elevated place.[74] This would be in keeping with the frequency with which words for hills and mounds occur in the names of Anglo-Saxon assembly-places. As many of the other papers in this volume demonstrate, the presence of such features at assembly-places is well evidenced throughout northern Europe and it is highly likely that they acted as platforms on which a speaker could stand to address his audience in exactly the way described above.

Although infrequent, references to 'moot-hills' do appear in the documentary record: the compound *(ge)mōtbeorg* (assembly hill/mound) is recorded in several sets of charter-bounds.[75] A comparable formation *(ge)mōthlāw* (< OE *hlāw* – 'mound/hill') is generally accepted as the source of place-names such as *Motlow* and *Mutlow* although it is not otherwise documented.[76] Charter-bounds also mention a *gemotleage* (assembly wood/clearing) in connection with land at Taunton and Bishops Lydeard in Somerset, while an 'old assembly-spring' – *ealdan gemotewil(l)e* – occurs in the bounds of Baverstock, Wiltshire.[77] Again these rare entries in the documentary record support much more plentiful onomastic evidence (particularly from hundred-names) indicating the sort of locations chosen for assemblies.

Two compounds of *(ge)mōt* which may have greater significance, however, are *gemōtǣrn* and *gemōthūs*, both of which include words for buildings (OE *ǣrn* – 'building, house, habitation'; OE *hūs* – 'house, building').[78] These can be paralleled by *mǣðel-ǣrn*, *sp(r)ǣc-ǣrn* and *sp(r)ǣc-hūs*. There is little evidence that buildings of any sort were used as places of assembly in the Anglo-Saxon

72 Goossens 1974, 295 no.2280.   73 *BTD*, 516.   74 In the same text *on gemotstowe* glosses *in edito, in alto; in fastigio*, but Goossens considers this is an error: Goosens 1974, 296 no.2281. 75 S 425, S 766, S 1581.   76 Smith 1956, ii 44.   77 S 311, S 380; S 766.   78 Neither of these words has been certainly identified in place-names although *gemōtǣrn* has been suggested for Mottram, Cheshire: *PNCh*, i 202–3.

period. Even ecclesiastical councils appear to have been held in the open, although the Chronicle's account of St Dunstan's miraculous escape at Calne suggests that the *witan* sometimes met indoors.[79] Words for buildings are scarce in hundred-names. Although OE *sele* ('hall') has been proposed as the second element of Odsey Hundred, Hertfordshire, *seað* – 'pit', is as likely.[80] OE *hlōse* appears in Clacklose, Norfolk and Loes, Suffolk[81] and the Wiltshire hundred of *Scipe* might derive its name from OE *scypen*,[82] but both these words usually refer to animal shelters, and in the hundred-names they may designate partial or temporary structures rather than buildings as such.

The existence in documentary sources of these compounds combining OE *ærn* and *hūs* with words for assembly or speech thus provides virtually the only support for the existence of permanent moot-halls in the pre-Conquest period. Nevertheless, this evidence is not conclusive. *Gemōtærn* occurs twice in the written sources, but on neither occasion does it refer to an Anglo-Saxon building; the first instance being in the Old English *Orosius*, the second in the Lindisfarne Gospels, where it glosses Latin *praetorium*.[83] Its occurrence cannot, therefore, be taken as proof that such buildings existed in Anglo-Saxon England, or that the term was in general use in late Old English.

The same is true of *mæðel-ærn* which is only used to gloss the Latin *in preterium*.[84] *Sp(r)æc-ærn* and *sp(r)æc-hūs* similarly occur almost without exception as translations of Latin terms such as *pretorium*, *auditorium*, *curia* and *senatus*.[85] *Spræchūs* is used by Ælfric in his Lives of Saints, but in this instance refers to a particular room in a monastery and not to a meeting-place as such.[86]

Gemōthūs, however, does appear to have been applied to a contemporary Anglo-Saxon structure: it occurs in the OE bounds of the Micheldever charter (S 360). The exact character and date of the feature are not altogether clear, since the charter, which is dated AD 900, is almost certainly an eleventh-century forgery.[87] Despite the dubious character of the document, however, there is good reason to believe that the estate bounds it includes were based on authentic texts. The *gemōthūs* may well, therefore, refer to a genuine meeting-place: according to Nicholas Brooks's solution of the charter-bounds, the site

79 Cubitt 1995, 34; *ASC* 978. **80** *PNHert*, 150–1; *PNCam*, 62–3; Meaney 1997, 212; Anderson 1939b, 25–7. **81** Anderson 1934, 74, 90. **82** Anderson 1939a, 160. **83** Bately 1980, 129; Skeat 1871–87, 27. **84** J.J. Quinn, 'The Minor Latin-Old English Glossaries in MS. Cotton Cleopatra A III' (Stanford dissertation, 1956), no. 293, reference from *COE*. **85** Skeat 1871–87, John 18.28 p. 161; Logeman 1891, 432, l. 965; Kindschi, 'The Latin-Old English Glossaries in Plantin-Moretus MS 32 and British Museum MS. Additional 32246' (Stanford dissertation, 1955) nos. 605. 607, reference from *COE*. **86** *Ælfric's Lives of Saints*: Skeat 1881–1900, 272, l. 847; 276, l. 907; 292, l. 1183; 336, l. 41. Nevertheless it is noteworthy that forms cognate with OE *spræchūs* occur in other Germanic languages: Carr 1939, 134. **87** Brooks 1982, 215.

lies in a typical position for a meeting-place, on an estate boundary at the junction of two important routes.[88] This single instance thus raises the possibility that some Anglo-Saxon assemblies did take place indoors, and that the compounds discussed above were more generally known than their use in the surviving texts suggests. The meetings in 'alehouses' referred to in Æthelred's Wantage Code might perhaps be relevant to this issue.[89] Although the translation 'alehouse' conjures up the image of a pub or tavern, it may be that the buildings intended acted more like local village halls, providing venues in which communal business, including both meeting and drinking, could take place.

ASSEMBLY-WORDS IN PLACE-NAMES

Thus far this paper has concentrated on the meaning and use of words related to assembly in OE seeking to demonstrate that, although references to assembly in written sources are infrequent, a study of the terms associated with it can usefully supplement and support conclusions drawn from other sources. However, as already stated, by far the most frequent use of these words by Anglo-Saxon scholars is as indicators of assembly-places when they appear in place-names. The remainder of this paper looks at the occurrence of 'assembly-terms' in English place-names and seeks to highlight some of the problems associated with the use of this evidence.

OE *gemōt* appears in a number of the names recorded by the English Place-Name Society county surveys. Forms such as *Motlow* and *Mutlow*, apparently from OE *gemōt-hlāw*, are particularly common and Motley/Mutley, potentially from *gemōt-lēah* (assembly-clearing), is also fairly frequent.[90] Other compounds represented in place-names include *gemōt-beorg* – 'assembly-mound/hill' (Modbury, Dorset); *gemōt-cumb* – 'assembly-valley' (Motcombe, Dorset);[91] and *gemōt*-ford – 'assembly-ford' (Mutford, Suffolk).[92] A minor name Nutshambles near to the meeting-place of Copthorn Hundred in Surrey has been interpreted as deriving from *gemōt* and the word *sceamol* meaning 'benches' or 'stalls'.[93] In Scandinavian areas, occasional name forms such as *Mootha* and *Mothow* may derive from compounds of OE *(ge)mōt* and the ON word for mound *haugr*, although OE *hōh* – 'spur' is also a potential source. The name Mottram, which appears twice in Cheshire, may also have *gemōt* as its first element but has yet to be fully explained.

Although relatively numerous, however, many *gemōt*-names are minor names or field-names, recorded only from the thirteenth century or later, and

88 Brooks 1982, 202–3. 89 III Æthelred 1.1–2. 90 E.g. Motley Heys, Cheshire: *PNCh*, ii 54. 91 Anderson 1939a, 116; Gelling 1978, 133. 92 Ekwall 1960, 319. 93 Nail 1965.

the absence of early forms can make their identification as early medieval assembly-places problematic.

It may, for instance, be difficult to ascertain the precise derivation of a name for which early forms are scarce. In the north of England long 'ō' was raised to 'u' about 1300. This change may account for the existence of forms such as Mutlow/Mutley. But *mut-* names appear even in the south of England, where such phonological changes do not seem to have taken place (e.g. Mutford, Suffolk).[94] Without early spellings the origins of these names cannot be known for certain and it may be that alternative sources should be sought in some cases; at least one example of Mutlow can be shown to have developed from an earlier *Mucklow* (OE *micel hlāw* – 'big hill/mound').[95]

It should also be borne in mind that the element *mōt* also occurs in place-names with the meaning 'confluence, junction', particularly in the compound *ēa-mōt* – 'a confluence of streams'. This sense is not recorded in OE and is considered to be a borrowing of ON *mót*.[96] Unlike OE *(ge)mōt* it occurs mainly as a second element in place-names, but the possibility of confusion should, nevertheless, be noted. The *Merce mot* which occurs in the Anglo-Saxon bounds of Barrow-upon-Humber was interpreted by Kemble as the site of a *Mark-moot* and appears as such in Bosworth and Toller's dictionary.[97] Later the name was interpreted as 'the Mercian's assembly-place'.[98] But a recent consideration of the charter-bounds has demonstrated that the name in fact refers to a 'meeting of boundaries' (OE *mearc* – boundary) and not an assembly of any kind.[99]

The *Motlow/Mutlow* names also present particular difficulties of dating. The accepted practice is for place-names to be traced to their earliest possible forms. Thus names with the first element *mot-* are usually derived from OE *gemōt*. However, this word survived into Middle English as *mōt* and OE *hlāw* likewise persisted, surviving until the present day as the dialect word *low/law* in some parts of the country.[100] Consequently, it is not always possible to be certain whether such sites originated as pre-Conquest assembly-places.[101] Audrey Meaney has suggested that the increasing number of recorded *Motlow* names from the thirteenth century may represent a growing tendency to use mounds as assembly-places at this time.[102] But other sources suggest that open-air assemblies became less frequent in the post-Conquest period, and it is possible that the high number of thirteenth-century *Motlows* simply reflects

94 Ekwall 1960, 319; cp. Anderson 1934, 86. **95** *PNWo*, 178. I am grateful to Dr Mark Griffith and Dr Margaret Gelling for their advice concerning the phonological development of these forms. **96** Smith 1956, ii 44. **97** S 782; Kemble 1847, 56; BTD, 674. **98** Brown 1906, 17. **99** Everson and Knowles 1992–3, 26. **100** Kurath, Kuhn et al. 1952–, 720; Smith 1956, i 249; Wright 1896–1905, iii 539–40. **101** The same is true of *mot*-names with some other second elements, e.g. *ford*. **102** Meaney 1997, 213–14.

more extensive documentation and better documentary survival. The late appearance of these names need not, therefore, preclude an early medieval origin, but equally their early date should not be assumed. Ultimately, however, it seems likely that many minor *Motlows* did originate as Anglo-Saxon meeting-places, and the comparative frequency of these names has interesting implications for our understanding of pre-Conquest local administration, suggesting that many more assemblies may have been in existence than previously thought.[103]

þing is less common than *gemōt* but still occurs in a considerable number of place-names, the majority of which are minor names and field-names in areas with substantial Scandinavian settlement. Forms such as *Thinghou* and *Thingoe* from ON *þing-haugr* ('assembly-mound') are especially common. *Þing-vǫllr* – 'assembly-field' also appears several times, for example in Thingwall, Cheshire.[104] Both these compounds are also found in place-names in Scandinavia. In Tingley, Yorkshire the second element may be OE *lēah* – 'clearing/wood',[105] while Finedon, Northamptonshire has OE *denu* – 'valley'.[106] *Þing* almost always appears as a first element, the one possible exception being Morthen, Yorkshire (*Mordinges* 1164–81) which has been interpreted as 'the moorland assembly'.[107] It occasionally seems to occur as a place-name forming element in areas where Scandinavian influence was not strong: it has been suggested, for instance, in Thinghill, Herefordshire; Tinhale Barn, Sussex; and Thingley and Tinkfield, Wiltshire.[108] As mentioned above, these names may derive from OE as opposed to ON *þing*. Generally speaking *þing* is not easily confused, although the change of initial *þ* to *t-*, *d-* or sometimes *f-* is fairly common. In ME field-names *þing* occurs very frequently in the alternative sense of 'possession' but always as a second element.

OE *mæðel* is rare in English place-names. It does not occur in hundred names and its distribution is suggestive given the possibility, discussed above, that the word went out of use in spoken OE at an early date. Of twelve identified names from OE *mæðel* (or the contracted form *mǣl*), seven are the names of parishes. It is relatively unusual for an assembly-place to give its name to a parish (only five of the ninety-two *(ge)mōt*-names collected have done so) and the comparatively large number of *mæðel* parish-names may indicate that they were established at a particularly early date, so that over time the name came to be applied to a substantial area around its original site. These names may, therefore, represent an early group of assembly-places. It is also striking that

---

103 Pantos 2002. 104 The occurrence of such names in the British Isles has been discussed by Gillian Fellows-Jensen: Fellows-Jensen 1993. 105 *PNWi*, 97; *PNWY*, ii 175–6. 106 *PNNp*, 181. 107 *PNWY*, i 101–2, 168–9. 108 Ekwall 1960, 466; Anderson 1939b, 75–6; *PNWi*, 97, 249.

of the twelve names in *mæðel*, five are combined with words for trees or groups of trees. Madehurst, Sussex and Malehurst, Shropshire have OE *hȳrst* – 'wooded hill' as a second element, whilst oak (OE *āc*) appears in Matlock, Derbyshire and ash (OE *æsc*) in Matlask, Norfolk and Molash, Kent. This pattern is interesting as it is sometimes suggested that the frequency with which hundreds are named from trees reflects an association with pre-Christian religious practices.[109]

OE *mæþel* is a difficult element to identify in place-names since its phonology allows for the possibility of confusion with a number of other words. Most significantly, a sound-change leading to loss of medial *ð* and the lengthening of *æ* to *ǣ* seems to have operated throughout the country under certain circumstances, resulting in a variant form *mǣl²*.[110] This cannot be differentiated from OE *mǣl¹* meaning 'sign' or 'cross'.[111] Additional confusion is possible with ON *meðal* – 'middle'.[112] A late OE *māl* – 'law-suit, bargaining' – derived from ON *mál*, also existed and may be present in some names.[113]

In contrast with *mæþel* OE *spell* is relatively common in place-names, although not as frequent as *(ge)mōt*. Like *(ge)mōt* and *þing* it most often appears in minor names in combination with a word for hill or mound, such as OE *beorg*, *hlāw*, *hōh* ('spur'), or ON *haugr*. However, where early forms are absent, distinguishing between the last three elements can be tricky, since all may produce forms such as *Spellow*, *Speller* and *Spella*. Furthermore, the word *spell* continued in use as late as the late sixteenth century.[114] As with *(ge)mōt*, then, it is possible that some of the place-names derived from OE *spell* in the English Place-Name Society volumes are actually later coinings. With the exception of the Gloucestershire *spell-stōw* mentioned above, only one *spell* place-name appears in a pre-Conquest document: *Spelbeorghe*, on the border of Cambridge and Essex.[115] Nevertheless, a significant number of *spell* place-names are recorded relatively early, with at least seventeen of the fifty-four identified appearing before the fourteenth century. Although not conclusive, this strongly suggests that the element was an active place-name forming element at an early date, and strengthens the likelihood that many of the names identified may have originated in the Anglo-Saxon period.

The distribution of *spell* is interesting when plotted in relation to OE *(ge)mōt* and *þing*. *(Ge)mōt* is found throughout England, while unsurprisingly *þing* is much more common in areas of strong Scandinavian settlement. Despite deriving from OE rather than ON, however, *spell* is also most common in the north and east of the country, though it is found as far south and west as

109 Anderson 1939b, 185; Meaney 1995, 35; Loyn 1984, 144.   110 Campbell 1959, §419, 421.   111 Smith 1956, ii 34.   112 E.g. Malton, Yorkshire: *PNNY*, 43.   113 Smith 1956, ii 34.   114 Kurath, Kuhn et al. 1952–, xi 420–1.   115 *PNCam*, 95–6; Meaney 1993, 82, 89.

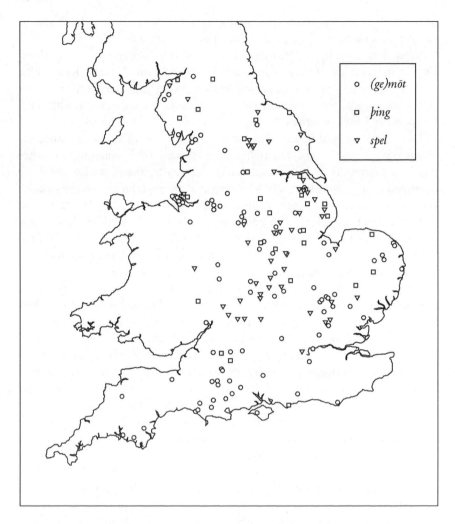

Figure 8.1 Distribution of OE *(ge)mōt*, OE/ON *þing* and OE *spell* in English place-names.

Wiltshire.[116] The extent to which this pattern results from the variable amount of place-name evidence available for each county cannot be known; the English Place-Name Society volumes for Lincolnshire and the West Riding of Yorkshire are some of the most detailed, whereas many of the southern counties were among the earliest in the series to be published. Nevertheless,

116 Spilsbury, Wardour (ST954276): *PNWi*, 183, 197–8.

the absence of *spell*-names from, for example, Dorset, where no fewer than ten possible *(ge)mōt*-names are found, may well reflect a dialect difference. Of particular interest also is a concentration of *spell*-names in north Oxfordshire, south Gloucestershire and Northamptonshire, in an area where *(ge)mōt*-names seem to be generally fewer (fig. 8.1).

The last remaining element to be discussed is *sp(r)ǣc*. Identifying this word in place-names is problematic, owing to the existence of a second OE word, identical in form (Angl./Kt. *spēc* WSax. *spǣc*), but meaning 'a small branch, twig, tendril'. A related word *sprǣc* meaning 'a shoot' also exists.[117] Telling these elements apart is extremely difficult, particularly in names where the second element is a word for 'wood/clearing', or a tree name, since in these instance either meaning might be appropriate.[118] Perhaps because of this *sp(r)ǣc* has been identified in comparatively few place-names. Unlike *gemōt*, *spell* and *þing* it does not appear in association with words for mound.

CONCLUSION

It has been argued above that the significance of words such as *þing* and *(ge)mōt* for the study of Anglo-Saxon assemblies goes beyond their appearance in place-names. Information gleaned from detailed investigation of their use in Old English can be used to support existing conclusions, for instance that assembly-places frequently included an elevated feature from which speeches could be made, while chronological differences in the use of terms for assembly in Old English texts raise the possibility that some 'assembly place-names' may be earlier coinings than others. Similarly, the appearance in written sources of compounds which are absent from the place-name record may indicate that meetings took place in a wider range of contexts than previously assumed.

Conversely, however, it has also been demonstrated that the identification of 'assembly' elements in place-names is, in many cases, more problematic than often assumed. This is particularly true of names including the elements *mot*, *spell* and *sp(r)ec*. Although place-names remain the main source for identifying early assembly-places, therefore, it is suggested that the onomastic evidence needs to be treated with more circumspection than has often been the case. Once again, this provides a powerful argument for combining place-name study, wherever possible, with both documentary and archaeological research.

117 Smith 1956, ii 136.   118 Cp. Spetchley, Worcestershire: *PNWo*, 165–6.

ABBREVIATIONS

ASC   *Anglo-Saxon Chronicle*
BTD   *An Anglo-Saxon dictionary*, ed. J. Bosworth and T.N. Toller
COE   *Corpus of Old English*, Institute of Medieval Studies, University of Toronto.
OE   Old English
ON   Old Norse
PNCam   *The place-names of Cambridgeshire*, ed. P.H. Reaney
PNCh   *The place-names of Cheshire*, ed. J.McN. Dodgson
PNHert   *The place-names of Hertfordshire*, ed. J.E.B. Gover
PNNp   *The place-names of Northamptonshire*, ed. J.E.B. Gover, A. Mawer and F.M. Stenton
PNNY   *The place-names of the North Riding of Yorkshire*, ed. A.H. Smith
PNWa   *The place-names of Warwickshire*, ed. J.E.B. Gover, A. Mawer, F.M. Stenton and A. Bonner.
PNWi   *The place-names of Wiltshire*, ed. J.E.B. Gover, A. Mawer and F.M. Stenton
PNWo   *The place-names of Worcestershire*, ed. A. Mawer, F.M. Stenton and F.T.S. Houghton.
PNWY   *The place-names of the West Riding of Yorkshire*, ed. A.H. Smith
S   Sawyer, *Anglo-Saxon Charters*

REFERENCES

Anderson, O.S., 1934: *The English hundred names.* Lund.
Anderson, O.S., 1939a: *The English hundred names: the south-western counties.* Lund.
Anderson, O.S., 1939b: *The English hundred names: the south-eastern counties.* Lund.
Barney, S.A., 1977: *Word-hoard: an introduction to Old English vocabulary.* London.
Bately, J. (ed.), 1980: *The Old English Orosius*, Early English Texts Society S.S. **6**. London.
Bazire, J. and Cross, J.E. (eds), 1982: *Eleven Old English rogationtide homilies.* Toronto.
Blake, E.O. (ed.), 1962: *Liber Eliensis.* London.
Bonser, W., 1963: *The medical background of Anglo-Saxon England.* London.
Bosworth, J. and Toller, T.N. (eds), 1898: *An Anglo-Saxon dictionary.* London.
Brodeur, A.G., 1959: *The art of Beowulf.* Berkeley.
Brooks, N.P., 1982: 'The oldest document in the college archives? The Micheldever forgery', in R. Custance (ed.), *Winchester College: sixth centenary essays.* Oxford.
Brown, R. 1906: *Notes on the earlier history of Barton-On-Humber.* Barton.
Campbell, A., 1959: *Old English grammar.* Oxford.
Carr, C.T., 1939: *Nominal compounds in Germanic.* St Andrews.
Cleasby, R. and Vigfusson, G. (eds), 1874: *An Icelandic-English dictionary.* Oxford.
Clemoes, P. (ed.), 1997: *Ælfric's Catholic homilies: the first series*, Early English Texts Society S.S. **17**. Oxford.

Cubitt, C., 1995: *Anglo-Saxon Church councils c.650–c.850*. London.

Dobbie, E.V.K. (ed.), 1942: *The Anglo-Saxon minor poems*, Anglo-Saxon Poetic Records 6. New York.

Dobbie, E.V.K. (ed.), 1953: *Beowulf and Judith*, Anglo-Saxon Poetic Records 4. New York.

Dodgson, J.McN. (ed.), 1970–97: *The place-names of Cheshire*, English Place-Name Society 44–8, 54, 74. London.

Ekwall, E. (ed.), 1960: *The concise Oxford dictionary of English place-names* (4th edn.). Oxford.

Everson, P., and Knowles, G.C., 1992–3: 'The Anglo-Saxon bounds of *Æt Bearuwe*', *Journal of the English Place-Name Society* 25, 19–37.

Fellows-Jensen, G., 1993: 'Tingwall, Dingwall and Thingwall', in *Twenty-eight papers presented to Hans Bekker-Nielsen on the occasion of his 60th birthday*. Odense. 53–67.

Foote, P., 1984: 'Things in early Norse verse', in *Festskrift til Ludvig Holm-Olsen*. Øvre. 74–83.

Gelling, M., 1978: *Signposts to the past*. London.

Godden, M. (ed.), 1979: *Ælfric's Catholic homilies: the second series*, Early English Texts Society S.S. 5. Oxford.

Goosens, L. (ed.), 1974: *The Old English glosses of MS Brussels, Royal Library, 1650*. Brussels.

Gover, J.E.B. (ed.), 1938: *The place-names of Hertfordshire*, English Place-Name Society 15. Cambridge.

Gover, J.E.B., Mawer, A. and Stenton, F.M. (eds), 1933: *The place-names of Northamptonshire*, English Place-Name Society 10. Cambridge.

Gover, J.E.B., Mawer, A. and Stenton, F.M. (eds), 1939: *The place-names of Wiltshire*, English Place-Name Society 16. Cambridge.

Gover, J.E.B., Mawer, A., Stenton, F.M. and Houghton, F.T.S. (eds), 1936: *The place-names of Warwickshire*, English Place-Name Society 8. Cambridge.

Greenslade, M.W., (ed.), 1984: *The Victoria history of the county of Stafford*, vol. 20. London.

Grünberg, M., 1967: *The West-Saxon gospels: a study of the gospel of St Matthew with the text of the four gospels*. Amsterdam.

Hessels, J.H. (ed.), 1890: *An eighth-century Latin-Anglo-Saxon Glossary*. Cambridge.

Holthausen, F. (ed.), 1934: *Altenglisches Etymologisches Wörterbuch*. Heidelberg.

Kemble, J.M., 1847: *The Saxons in England*. London.

Kennedy, A., 1995: 'Law and litigation in the Libellus Æthelwoldi', *Anglo-Saxon England* 24, 131–83.

Keynes, S., 1992: 'The Fonthill letter', in M. Korhammer (ed.), *Words, texts and manuscripts*. Cambridge. 53–97.

Krapp, G.P. (ed.), 1931: *The Junius manuscript*, Anglo-Saxon Poetic Records 2. New York.

Krapp, G.P. (ed.), 1932: *The Vercelli book*, Anglo-Saxon Poetic Records 1. New York.

Krapp, G.P. and Dobbie, E.V.K. (eds), 1936: *The Exeter book*, Anglo-Saxon Poetic Records 3. New York.

Kurath, H., Kuhn, S.M., et al. (eds), 1952–: *Middle English dictionary*. Ann Arbor.

Latham, R.E., et al. (ed.), 1975–: *Dictionary of medieval Latin from British sources.* London.

Liebermann, F. (ed.), 1898–1916: *Die Gesetze der Angelsachsen.* Halle.

Logeman, W.S., 1891: 'De Consuetudine Monachorum', *Anglia* 13, 365–454.

Loyn, H.R., 1984: *The governance of Anglo-Saxon England 500–1087.* Stanford.

Mawer, A., Stenton, F.M. and Houghton, F.T.S. (eds), 1927: *The place-names of Worcestershire*, English Place-Name Society 4. Cambridge.

Meaney, A.L., 1993: 'Gazetteer of hundred and wapentake meeting-places of the Cambridge Region', *Proceedings of the Cambridge Antiquarian Society* 82, 67–92.

Meaney, A.L., 1995: 'Pagan English sanctuaries, place-names and hundred meeting-places', *Anglo-Saxon Studies in Archaeology and History* 8, 29–42.

Meaney, A.L., 1997: 'Hundred meeting-places in the Cambridge region', in A.R. Rumble and A.D. Mills (eds), *Names, places and people: an onomastic miscellany in memory of John McNeal Dodgson.* Stamford. 195–240.

Meritt, H.D. (ed.), 1959: *The Old English Prudentius glosses at Boulogne-Sur-Mer.* Stanford.

Miller, T. (ed.), 1890–98: *The Old English version of Bede's Ecclesiastical History of the English people*, Early English Texts Society 95, 96, 110, 111. Oxford

Nail, D., 1965: 'The meeting-place of Copthorne Hundred', *Surrey Archaeological Collections* 62, 44–53.

Napier, A.S., 1883: *Wulfstan*, Sammlung englischer Denkmäler 4. Berlin.

Napier, A.S. (ed.), 1900: *Old English glosses.* Oxford (reprint Hildesheim, 1969).

Oliphant, R.T. (ed.), 1966: *The Harley Latin/Old English glossary.* The Hague.

Pantos, A., 2002: *Assembly-places in the Anglo-Saxon period: aspects of form and location.* Unpublished DPhil thesis, University of Oxford.

Pheifer, J.D., 1974: *Old English glosses in the Epinal-Erfurt glossary.* Oxford.

Reaney, P.H. (ed.), 1943: 'The place-names of Cambridge and the Isle of Ely', English Place-Name Society 19. Cambridge.

Robertson, A.J. (ed.), 1956: *Anglo-Saxon charters* (2nd edn.) Cambridge.

Scragg, D. (ed.), 1992: *The Vercelli homilies and related texts*, Early English Texts Society O.S. 300. Oxford.

Sedgefield, W.J. (ed.), 1899: *King Alfred's Old English version of Boethius' De Consolatione Philosophiae.* Oxford (reprint Darmstadt 1968).

Skeat, W.W. (ed.), 1871–87: *The four gospels in Anglo-Saxon, Northumbrian and Old Mercian versions.* Cambridge.

Skeat, W.W. (ed.), 1881–1900: *Ælfric's Lives of Saints*, Early English Texts Society 76, 82, 94, 114. London.

Smith, A.H. (ed.), 1928: *The place-names of the North Riding of Yorkshire*, English Place-Name Society 5. Cambridge.

Smith, A.H. (ed.), 1961–3: *The place-names of the West Riding of Yorkshire*, English Place-Name Society 30–7. Cambridge.

Smith, A.H. (ed.), 1956: *English place-name elements*, English Place-Name Society 25, 26. Cambridge.

Stanley, E.G., 1979: 'Two Old English poetic phrases insufficiently understood for literary criticism: *þing gehegan* and *seono þ gehegan*', in D.G. Calder (ed.), *Old English poetry: essays in style.* London. 67–90.

Stanley, E.G., 1971: 'Studies in the prosaic vocabulary of Old English verse', *Neuphilologische Mitteilungen* **72**, 385–418.

Stenton, F.M., 1920: *Documents illustrative of the social and economic history of the Danelaw*. London.

Wormald, P., 1986: 'Charters, law and the settlement of disputes in Anglo-Saxon England', in W. Davies and P. Fouracre (eds), *The settlement of disputes in early Medieval Europe*. Cambridge.

Wright, J. (ed.), 1896–1905: *English dialect dictionary*. London.

PART III

*Isle of Man, Scandinavia
and Continental Europe*

Legal assembly sites in early Scandinavia

STEFAN BRINK

Önund carried on violently for a time. But once Egil could see that Önund wanted no fair solution of the case, he summoned him to the Thing, referring the suit to the Gulathing Law. [...]

The winter passed away and it grew time to go to the Gulathing. Arinbjörn took a crowd of men to the Thing, and Egil kept him company. King Eirík was there too, and had a big body of men. Bergönund was in the king's troop with his brothers, and they had a strong following. And when there should be decision in men's lawsuits, both sides proceeded to where the court was established, to set out their proofs. Önund was now all big talk. Where the court was established there was a level field (*vollr sléttr*), with hazel poles (*heslisteingr*) set down in the field in a ring, and ropes (*snæri*) in a circuit all around. These were called the hallowed bands (*vébond*). Inside the ring sat the judges, twelve out of Firthafylki, twelve out of Sognfylki, and twelve out of Hördafylki. It was for these three twelves to reach a verdict in men's lawsuits. Arinbjörn decided who were the judges from Firthafylki, and Thórd of Aurland those from Sogn. They were all in the one party. Arinbjörn had brought a powerful body of men to the Thing. He had a fully-manned snekkja, and had a lot of small ships, skútur and rowing-ferries of which his tenants had control. King Eirík had a big force there too, of six or seven longships. There was also a big gathering of farmers there. [...]

At that Askman and the men of his troop ran to the court, cut through the hallowed bands and broke down poles, scattering the judges abroad. A great uproar broke out at the Thing, but everyone was weaponless there.

'Can Bergönund hear my words?' asked Egil then.

'I hear', said he.

'Then I am challenging you to holmgang, that we fight here at the Thing. Let him have the property, land and movable goods, who wins the day. And be every man's dastard if you dare not.'[1]

---

1 *Egil's Saga* Ch. 56: trans. Jones 1960, 138 ff.

In this famous episode in the Saga of Egill Skallagrímsonar, we get a description of the assembly at Gula thing in western Norway. The thing site was a
level field, thus a *thingvǫllr*, with some hazel poles holding a length of rope
forming a circle. The rope was called the *vébǫnd* – the hallowed bands –
containing the word *vé* 'holy'. Inside the ring sat the judges, and consequently
the rest of the assembled thingsmen stood outside, around the ring.

Egil's Saga was written down in the fourteenth century, but the events
related in it took place in the tenth century. Of course, we may assume that the
story of Gula thing is pure fiction, invented by the author, but interestingly
enough, the words of the saga are in this case backed up by the actual law codes
of both Gula thing and Frosta thing.[2] The description in Egil's saga of the
assembly site may thus be accurate.

To begin with, I have to clarify that by 'early Scandinavia' I mean more or
less the Viking period, slipping into the late Iron Age as well as the early
Middle Ages, i.e. *c*.600–1300, with a focus on the period 800–1100. From the
Continental viewpoint, this period is interesting because we still had a pre-
Christian society and an indigenous legal system in Scandinavia, not based on
Roman or canon law. We thus have a pagan, legal society different from that
found in England and on the Continent. When the Provincial laws were
written down, in the twelfth, thirteenth and fourteenth centuries for
Scandinavia, we get lawbooks based on the Continental legal traditions, though
written in the vernacular. Also in Scandinavia we had a settlement with the old
Germanenrechtschule, which was rather late, though fierce,[3] leaving us with an
annoying and obtrusive silence regarding the study of our oldest laws. Today
practically no one discusses medieval law, not to mention possibly pre-
medieval, pagan law (horrible thought!). We do not have a Patrick Wormald in
Scandinavia, but we certainly need one. I shall not continue with this topic, but
instead turn to the physical remains of this pre-Christian, legal society in
Scandinavia, which will be my main subject in this paper. However, I cannot
refrain from interpolating some observations regarding the legal customs in
this pagan society.

The first mention that we have of things in Scandinavia is to be found in
Rimbert's *Vita Ansgarii*, and here we get a most vivid and interesting descrip-
tion of pre-Christian thing sites and thing rituals. It all takes place in the
ancient town of Birka in central Sweden in the ninth century. In Chapter 19
Rimbert describes a situation in which a thing is going to take place and the
Christian *praefectus* of Birka, Hergeir, is attending: 'Once he sat at a thing,
where a hut was erected on the ground or field for the session.' Later on,
Rimbert gives us the famous episode in which king Björn did not dare to take

---

2 *GuL* X, 19 (240); *FrL* I, 2.   3 Sjöholm 1988.

an independent decision as to whether Ansgar was going to be allowed to spread the Christian word in Birka; he submitted the question to the thing assembly. Before the actual thing took place, king Björn called together his chieftains and with them discussed Ansgar's case: 'They decided then to find out the attitude of the gods by casting lots'. Later, Rimbert writes: 'Then when the day for the thing came, a thing that was held in Birka, the king told his herald to shout out what was going to be decided'.[4] There are several very interesting points in this account that make it historically probable: the hut on a field, the thing on a field, and the casting of lots to communicate with the gods, showing that cult and law were intimately connected.

In discussing legal assembly sites in early Scandinavia, an illustrative start may be made with the Tynwald Hill in the Isle of Man. As is well known, the name *Tynwald* goes back to an Old Norse *þingvǫllr* 'assembly site'. This name is found in many places, such as *Dingwall* in northern Scotland, *Thingwall* on Orkney and *Tingvalla* in the city of Karlstad in the province of Värmland in Sweden. However, the best known example is, of course, *Thingvellir*, the site of the *althing* on Iceland. The centre of Thingvellir was the *Lögberg*, a hill on the thing site; at Tynwald Hill it is a mound. Many of the thing mounds presented below are large burial mounds, normally dating from the Roman Iron Age or the Migration Period, but in some cases it seems that special thing mounds were built with a noticeably flat top. We find examples of this at the royal seat of the Svear in Gamla Uppsala, as well as at Fornsigtuna, the ancient royal seat and predecessor of the town of Sigtuna.[5]

It is a well-known fact that large mounds have been used as foci for thing sites in Scandinavia. Several of the hundreds (*hundare*, *hærað*) held their assemblies at large mounds. I shall discuss some of the most prominent of these sites, the first being the thing site of the hundred or *hundare* of Österrekarne, Kjula ås, in the province of Södermanland in Sweden.

Österrekarne hundred was situated on a shallow bay, Kafjärden, of the large Lake Mälaren in central Sweden. Across the bay runs an esker, which, in the southern part, constitutes a high ridge, which is what the name *Kjula* actually means. Over this ridge, an ancient road passed, crossing a large burial ground with one prominent mound, called *Tingshögen* (fig. 9.1). At the foot of this mound a runestone is placed and from older paintings and maps we know that this stone was part of a long row of standing stones, on both sides of the road. This is the site of the Österrekarne-hundred thing assembly, where the mound, Tingshögen, must have been the focus. It is also notable that the site is situated on land belonging to, or next to, the hamlet of *Karlåker* 'the field of the comitatus (*karlar*)' and also near the hamlets of *Viby* and *Ällevi* (<

---

4 *Vita Ansgarii* Ch. 19: trans. Odelman 1986, 35–41. 5 Hedlund and Christiansson 1990–1; Christiansson and Nordal 1989; cf. Allerstav et al. 1991.

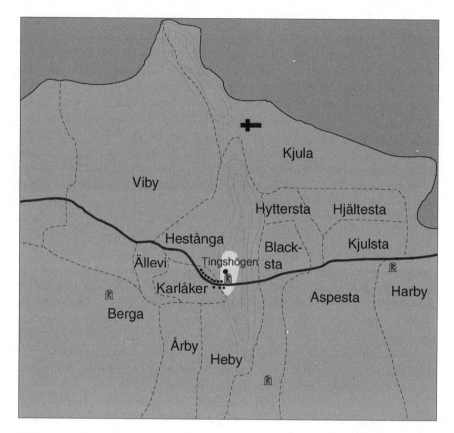

Figure 9.1 The old thing assembly site at Kjula ås for the hundred of Österrekarne, in the province of Södermanland, central Sweden. Note the thing mound, Tingshögen, an Iron Age burial mound, the runestone and the double row of standing stone slabs, leading up the road to the thing mound.

Hælghavi), both containing the word *vi, vé* 'holy'. The runestone is interesting in several respects. It is to be linked with the famous Ramsund runic inscription, some kilometres to the north. Both obviously commemorate an eleventh-century family, most probably the leading family in the district and presumably the one in charge of the thing site.[6] However, we do not know whether this thing was an *althing*, i.e. a thing for all assembled men led by an 'elected' law speaker, or a thing conducted by a chieftain, some leading men or a family.

I take my second example from the same province, but in the south, in the hundred of Rönö at *Aspa* or *Aspa löt*, as the assembly was called during the

6 Larsson 1997, 18 ff.

Middle Ages. At this site the ancient and famous *Eriksgata* (the road that a newly elected king in Svíþjóð had to travel to get acquainted with, and to be accepted by, the different peoples in his realm, i.e. the provinces of Södermanland, Östergötland, Västergötland, Närke and Västmanland) crossed a watercourse. There is also a large mound called *Tingshögen* here, and five runestones nearby (fig. 9.2). One of them (Sö 137), next to the mound, bears an inscription saying that *Sten sarsi standr at Öbbi a þingstaði*, i.e. 'this stone is standing after [to the memory of] Öbbi on the thing assembly site'. This is one of the very few runic inscriptions that mentions a thing. The thing assembly site was in use during the Middle Ages for the *hundare*, the hundred district, and thus according to the runic inscription also during the Viking Age (whether for the hundred or not, we do not know). We have here at Aspa löt the same elements that were found at the Kjula thing, namely, a large mound more than 30m in diameter called *Tingshögen* 'the thing mound'; a runestone immediately beside the mound (in the case of Aspa löt with an inscription saying that it is standing on the thing site); and then probably double rows of standing stone slabs running along an ancient road leading up to the thing site. Also at Aspa löt, the inscriptions on the runestones make it possible to conclude that there was an aristocratic family that in some respects was in charge of the assembly.

The same ingredients as mentioned above we also find at a third, famous, thing site, namely that of the hundred (*hundare*) of Seunda in the province of Västmanland. The actual thing site is situated on one of the most prominent archaeological sites in Sweden, with the famous boat-graves with gold finds from Tuna in Badelunda. The focal point here is, of course, the huge mound called *Anundshögen*, which was used as a thing mound during the Middle Ages (fig. 9.3). This is one of the largest burial mounds in Sweden. Only 45m south of the mound is a runestone, with a not very exciting inscription (*Folkviðr ræisti stæina þasi alla at sun sin Heðin, broður Anundar. Vræiðr hiogg runar* – 'Folkviðr erected all of these stones for his son, Heðin, the brother of Anund. Vræiðr cut the runes'). As the text on the runestone says, it stands together with several other stones in a row of fourteen stone slabs standing along an ancient road, again the old *Eriksgata*, and the stone row leads the road towards a ford or bridge. The construction has been called the most magnificent runestone bridge in Sweden. Thus, here we also have a thing mound, a runestone and several standing stone slabs along an old road.

These structural criteria cannot be a coincidence. We may assume that these ingredients constituted a Viking Age thing assembly site or – to be more circumspect – were essential elements that constituted a Viking Age thing assembly site.

It is interesting to note that the names of several ancient thing assembly sites around Lake Mälaren in central Sweden are compounds with the element

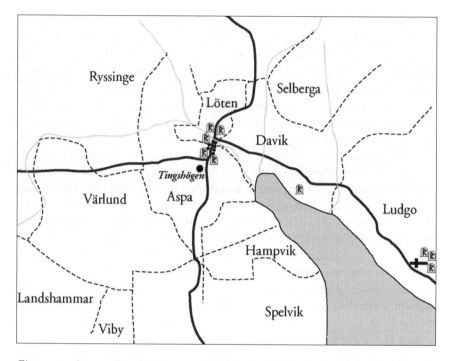

Figure 9.2 Aspa or *Aspa löt*, the assembly-place in the hundred of Rönö showing the large mound called *Tingshögen*, and runestones nearby beside the old road.

löt 'green, grass-ground, level field', as in the case of Aspa löt. The word *löt* is thus a direct synonym of *vall*, *vǫllr* 'green, grass-ground, level field', which is also found in many place-names of ancient thing assemblies, such as *Þingvellir*, *Tynwald Hill*, *Dingwall*, etc. Thing assembly names often denote level or dry land, suitable to assemble on, and beside *löt* and *vall*, *vǫllr*, we also find *ås* 'esker', *vång*, *vang* 'green, grass-ground, level field' and probably also *åker*, *aker* 'arable land'.

We find a thing assembly name in *-åker* in the province of Uppland in both Ulleråker and Torsåker hundreds. Per Vikstrand has made an important analysis of the latter, in which he has probably been able to identify the small area of arable land (*åker*) that the name of the district must have denoted. The name of the district is a compound of *åker* 'arable land' and the name of the god *Thor*; in other words, the arable land was a sacred cult site, where people assembled for ritual performances.[7] In prehistoric times, cult and law seem to have been intimately connected in Scandinavia.

7 Vikstrand 2001, 151ff.

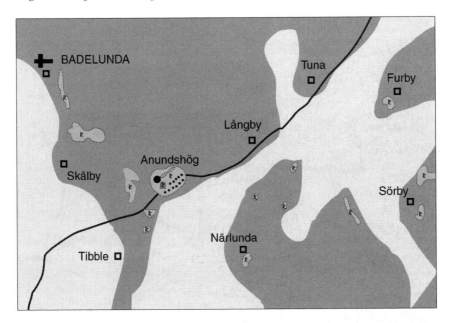

Figure 9.3 A third, famous, *thing* site, that of the hundred (*hundare*) of Seunda in the province of Västmanland. The focal point here is, of course, the huge mound called *Anundshögen*, which was used as a *thing* mound during the Middle Ages.

Apart from the sites mentioned above, the best-known thing site dating from the Viking Age is probably not an assembly site for a hundred or a large district, but more likely a private thing or a thing for a small congregation, namely the famous thing site of Bällsta, in the parish of Täby just north of Stockholm (fig. 9.4). On two runestones one can read [ulfkil] uk arkil uk kui þir kariþu iar þikstaþ – 'Ulvkel and Arnkel and Gye they made here a thing site (*þingstaðr*)'.[8] The runestones and some other stone slabs, placed in rows and in a square, are still *in situ*. Again we may assume that a prominent family or some leading men were in charge of the thing, and in this case it is clearly declared in one runic inscription that Ulvkel, Arnkel and Gye actually made the thing site.

In these four cases we are lucky that the thing sites have not been totally destroyed but can still be visited today. The normal case is that on other known thing sites we may find only one or two of the above-mentioned structures, normally the thing mound or a runestone. This is the case with the impressive thing site for the people called *Hälsingar* at Hög in the province and *land* of Hälsingland, in northern Sweden. From the Middle Ages we have documents

8 Jansson 1977, 121.

Figure 9.4 The famous *thing* site of Bällsta, in the parish of Täby just north of Stockholm.

that testify that this was the thing site for the *Hälsingar* (*ad placitum nostrum commune ... apud høgh* 1314). This is a very important site. It has a church and a medieval royal farm called an *Uppsala öd* in the old provincial law (the Hälsinge Law), i.e. part of the *bona regalia* belonging to the king of the *Svear* in Uppsala. Immediately behind the church is a large burial mound, the so-called *Kungshögen* 'the King's mound'. At the church, we also find two runestones, though they are obviously not in their original positions. The focal point of the thing of the *Hälsingar* was thus this large mound, which also gave its name to the parish, *Hög*. It is extremely interesting that it is possible to connect with this thing site a remarkable object, namely an iron ring with a runic inscription, containing the oldest law or legal prescription in Scandinavia. It should most likely be dated to the ninth century, and the text is probably concerned with the maintenance of a *vi*, i.e. a sacred place or an assembly and cult site.[9] The part of the text that runs: *svað liuðir aighu at liuðretti* 'that the people owns (or may claim) according to the law of the people', is extremely important, since here, *c*.AD 800, we become aware of the

9 Brink 1996.

term *liuðrettr*, i.e. the law of the people of the *land*, and this in a period with no traces of any Roman or canon law or Christian religion in this part of the world. We must therefore reckon with a pagan law or legal custom that was termed 'the law of the people' and was mentioned on a rune-ring (an oath ring?) as being connected with the actual thing assembly for the people, the *Hälsingar* in Hälsingland. This case is quite unique and extremely important for understanding early Scandinavian society.

I could go on and mention more or less certain assembly sites located on huge burial mounds, as is the case in some *fylki* districts in Trøndelag, Norway, where the focal points were mounds called *Haug*, *Sakshaug* and *Alstadhaug*. And in Trøndelag, one cannot exclude the actual assembly site for all of the Trøndelag, the *Frostatingslag*, the district of the Frosta thing law, i.e. the thing site of *Frosta*. Here, we still have the thing mound in the hamlet of *Logtu*, i.e. *Lǫgtún* 'the site or farm of the law'.

Another interesting example is Högsby in Handbörd hundred in the province of Småland. The name of the hundred, *Handbörd* < OSw *Andhbyrdh(e)*, is typical of an assembly place.[10] To understand the name, one has to analyse the central part of the hundred. The focal point of the district is where an esker crosses a river (fig. 9.5). At this place on the river, there is a stream that must have forced people in boats on the river to walk and carry the boats and cargo past the stream. This is in fact what the second element in the name *Andhbyrdh(e)* means. The first element says that the assembly is 'opposite' the site where one has to carry one's boat, i.e. where we find the hamlet of the parish church, *Högsby*, going back to an older †*Hög*. The neighbouring hamlet is *Huseby*. We thus here find a direct parallel to what was found in Hälsingland: a place-name *Hög*, denoting a thing mound, and a regal farm or hamlet, *husaby/kungsgården*. The thing assembly site for the district of Handbörd (and earlier most probably for the land of *Aspeland*) was most probably located on this mound, situated where the esker crosses the river.[11]

An especially interesting case is Tyrved, just south of Stockholm. In a district consisting of an ancient large island called *Tør*, we find the settlement called *Tyrved*, going back to a *Tøravi*, meaning 'the cult and assembly place for the inhabitants of *Tør*'. Here we have a unique example in which a place-name reveals the existence of an assembly and cult site for a whole *land*. Another extremely interesting fact is that the neighbouring settlement to Tyrved is called *Gudby*, going back to a *Gudhaby*, meaning 'the farm of the *gudhi*' (cf. Old Norse *goði*).

I will end with a most interesting case, the thing site of the hundred of Östkind in the province of Östergötland (fig. 9.6). During the Middle Ages we

10 See Andersson 1965.   11 Brink 1998.

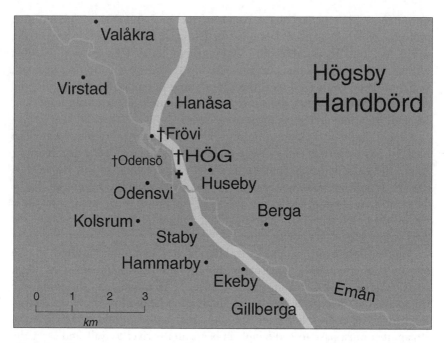

Figure 9.5 The location the assembly at Högsby in Handbörd hundred in the province of Småland.

know that the 'correct' assembly site for this hundred was a place called *Lytisberg*, situated close to the church in the parish of Östra Husby. This parish has a settlement structure that reveals the occurrence of an administrative organization and regal power in the Viking Age and the early Middle Ages. The district may be regarded as a model. A bay of the Baltic has found its way deep into this district, to the site of the church, which has the name *Husby*. This name goes back to an administrative term denoting a royal hamlet, *husaby*. Next to the Husby we have *Bosgård*, most probably denoting a 'manor' in the same period. In the vicinity we also had the thing assembly, †*Lytisberg*. At the mouth of the bay, we have the intrinsic *Tuna*, probably denoting some kind of aristocratic or administrative farm in prehistoric times.

The name of the actual thing site, *Lytisberg*, is a compound of *berg* 'hill, hillock' and a term †*lytir*, which was most probably a word for a pagan cult leader, derived from the word *hlut* 'lot'.[12] A *lytir* must have been some kind of divine interpreter in the noble art of casting lots and looking into the future, something that Rimbert so vividly described from the thing at Birka in the

---

12 Elmevik 1990.

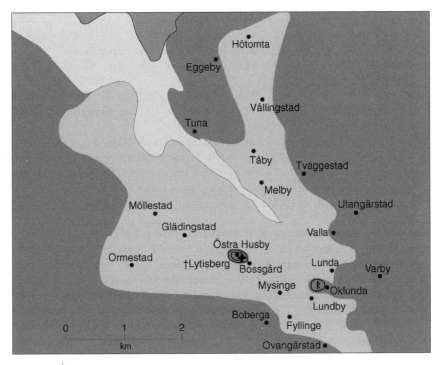

Figure 9.6 The *thing* site of the hundred of Östkind in the province of Östergötland.

ninth century, mentioned at the beginning of this article. We thus have here, as was also the case with *Tøravi*, the existence of a cult leader, a *lytir* or a *godhe*, attached to the thing assembly (probably) during the Viking Age.

To sum up, this confirms that in pagan, early-Scandinavian society, cultic and legal practices were more or less different sides of the same coin. Another interesting piece of evidence is that the actual thing site seems to have had certain elements in its structure that we have seen occurring at all the preserved thing sites, with a large thing mound, one or more runestones and a row of standing stone slabs. Very often the thing site was located by an important road. The communications aspect was, of course, most important. And, finally, although the character of law and legal procedure must have changed between pagan and Christian Scandinavia, i.e. between the Viking Age and the Middle Ages, we have seen that the physical assembly site showed continuity – people continued to assemble on the thing site. The structure survived, but the content changed.

REFERENCES

Allerstav, A. et al., 1991: *Fornsigtuna. En kungsgårds historia.* Upplands-Bro.

Andersson, Th., 1965: *Svenska häradsnamn*, Nomina Germanica 14. Uppsala–Stockholm.

Brink, S., 1996: 'Forsaringen – Nordens äldsta lagbud', in E. Roesdahl and P. Meulengracht Sørensen (eds), *Femtende tværfaglige Vikingesymposium: Aarhus Universitet 1996.* Århus.

Brink, S., 1998: 'Land, bygd, distrikt och centralort i Sydsverige. Några bebyggelse-historiska nedslag', in L. Larsson and B. Hårdh (eds), *Centrala platser Centrala frågor: Samhällsstrukturen under järnålder. En vänbok till Berta Stjernquist*, Uppåkrastudier 1; Acta Archaeologica Lundensia. Series in 8° 28. Lund.

Eithun, B., Rindal, M. and Ulset., T. (eds), 1994: *Den eldre Gulatingslova*, Norrøne tekster 6. Oslo.

Elmevik, L., 1990: 'Aschw. *Lytis*- in Ortsnamen. Ein kultisches Element oder ein profanes?', in T. Ahlbäck (ed.), *Old Norse and Finnish religions and cultic place-names*, Scripta Instituti Donneriani Aboensis 13. Stockholm.

Jansson, S.B.F., 1977: *Runinskrifter I Sverige*, 2nd edn. Stockholm.

Hagland, J.R. and Sandnes, J., 1994: *Frostatingslova*, Norröne bokverk, Oslo.

Jones, G. (trans), 1960: *Egil's Saga.* New York.

Jónsson, F., 1886–88: *Egils Saga Skallagrímssonar tillige med Egils större kvad.* Copenhagen.

Larsson, M.G., 1997: *Från stormannagård till bondby: En studie av mellansvensk bebyggelseutveckling från äldre järnålder till medeltid*, Acta Archeologica Lundensia. Series in 8° 26. Stockholm.

Odelman, E. et al. (trans) 1986: *Boken om Ansgar. Rimbert: Ansgars liv*, Skrifter utg. av Samfundet Pro fide et christianismo 10. Stockholm.

Robberstad, K., 1937: *Gulatingslovi*, Norrøne bokverk 33. Oslo.

Sjöholm, E., 1988: *Sveriges medeltidslagar: Europeisk rättstradition i politisk omvandling*, Rättshistoriskt bibliotek 41. Stockholm.

Vikstrand, P., 2001: *Gudarnas platser: Förkristna sakrala ortnamn í Mälarlandskapen*, Acta Academiae Regiae Gustavi Adolphi 77, Studier till en svensk ortnamnsatlas 17. Uppsala.

Tynwald Hill and the 'things' of power

TIMOTHY DARVILL

Within archaeology, political and institutionalized power is most often explored by reference to objects that are believed to have conveyed status and position. From the fine limestone macehead attached to a bone-inlaid wooden haft of the mid-second millennium BC buried with a tall male in the Bush Barrow, Wiltshire,[1] to the heavily ornamented whetstone sceptre in the richly furnished ship-burial at Sutton Hoo, Suffolk,[2] and eventually on to the Crown Jewels[3] and the Honours of Scotland,[4] these symbols of power are the tangible remains of authority. From at least the eleventh century AD onwards there are increasing levels of documentary records, often rather good in respect of the higher levels of power and authority, and these serve to connect not only the regalia of the rulers, but also, as Steane has shown, the royal and ecclesiastical palaces, courts, and assembly halls of the period.[5] For that strange detached part of prehistory in the British Isles partly separated from earlier times by the Roman interlude, and in many areas lasting well into the later first millennium AD, understanding the higher levels of Christopher Hawkes's rather memorable 'ladder of inference'[6] is considerably harder and requires an appeal to quite different sources.

One approach is to return to the archaeological evidence as the primary source and consider the physical contexts in which institutionalized power was exercised. Most of these appear to have been open-air meeting-places, generally known in Norse areas as 'things' and in Germanic areas as 'moots'. It is well-established that both of these structures (here seen both as physical and institutional) were variously involved in one or more of four key activities: communal assembly; the administration of justice; the debate and promulgation of laws; and the perpetuation of lordship through the reiteration of allegiance and, when necessary, king-making.[7] Recent excavations at such sites, for example the Secklow Hundred Mound investigated in 1977–8 as part of the development of Milton Keynes,[8] have served to refocus attention on the

1 Ashbee 1960, 76–8; Clarke et al. 1985, 107–15. 2 Bruce-Mitford 1972, 22–5; Simpson 1979. 3 Butler 1982. 4 Burnett and Tabraham 1993. 5 Steane 1993. 6 Hawkes 1954, 161–2. 7 Gomme 1880. 8 Adkins and Petchey 1984.

existence of these places and have highlighted their potential, but in general fail to situate them within wider social and political structures.

In this paper I would like to develop a broader perspective, geographically and socially, focusing on north-western Europe. As a starting point, however, I will consider first the only ancient assembly-site in Europe that still functions as such: Tynwald Hill in the Isle of Man. Following a brief review of the archaeology and structure of this site, discussion will broaden out first to consider its relation to other assembly-places in the Isle of Man, and second to review a little of its broader context in the Norse world of the late first and second millennia AD.

TYNWALD HILL, ISLE OF MAN

Tynwald Hill (*Cronk Keeill Eoin* in Manx; Fig. 10.1) lies at St John's in the parish of German, Sheading of Glenfaba (NGR SC 278818), towards the northern end of the central valley running across the island between Douglas and Peel.[9] Its situation is an impressive one, being set on a broad plateau above the confluence of two branches of the river Neb, overlooked by high hills. A more powerful geographical context would be hard to find on the island. It is also a position that is easily accessible from all other parts of the island.

The earliest documentary record of the site is in the *Chronicon Manniae et Insularum* and relates to the year AD 1228/9.[10] Records of the ceremonies themselves show that the parliament of the island (known as the Tynwald) has met regularly on the hill as an open-air assembly since at least AD 1417,[11] a tradition that still continues on Tynwald Day, 5 July, every year.[12] The place-name of the site potentially takes its history back still further, for it is clearly a Norse word – *þingvǫllr* – and is conventionally translated as the 'parliament field'.[13] This accords with the general historical evidence which records that in the early medieval period the Isle of Man was firmly within the Norse world, and between 1098 and 1266 was part of the Manx Kingdom of the Isles which lay under the rule of Norway.[14] However, there is a strong tradition, and some archaeological evidence too, that Tynwald Hill has pre-Norse origins which serve to link it with rather wider debates about the nature of the Norse colonization of the area, the extent to which existing political systems were perpetuated or replaced, and whether the distinctive pattern of landholdings and administrative units were Norse introductions or pre-existing arrangements.[15]

---

9 The Isle of Man is a small island, just 50 km by 20 km, situated in the Irish Sea between England, Wales, Scotland, and Ireland at a latitude of about 54° north. 10 Harrison 1871, 9; Broderick 1996, f 44r. 11 Clucas 1925a, 160. 12 Harrison 1871; Clucas 1925b. 13 Keen 1925–9, 416. 14 Megaw and Megaw 1950. 15 Megaw 1978; Moore 1999.

Figure 10.1 Tynwald Hill, St John's, Isle of Man (photograph: T. Darvill).

Looking at the Tynwald site in recent times there are four main elements (fig. 10.2). First, the assembly hill itself: 25m in diameter at the base, rising to a height of 3.6m. It has a stepped profile with four levels or tiers to it. The main route up the hill is on the east side, although there is now a second, modern set of steps on the south side. Second, about 190m to the east of the hill, is St John's Chapel. The present building was constructed in 1849, replacing an earlier chapel constructed in 1706, itself a replacement for a still earlier structure. Third, is the enclosure that contains the hill and the church. In its present form this is a dumb-bell shaped embanked structure, rather regular and neat, constructed as an earthwork in the early nineteenth century and later modified with the addition of the wall in the mid-nineteenth century. Fourth, is the fair-field that surrounds the whole complex. It provides the arena within which the ceremonies take place, and like the other components of the complex has evolved and changed over recent years; additions during the twentieth century include the Manx War Memorial and the Millennium Stone.

Clearly, much of what can be seen today is relatively modern, most of it dating from the mid-nineteenth century onwards. In June 1993, as part of ongoing researches on the island, Bournemouth University was commissioned by Manx National Heritage to carry out an archaeological survey of the Tynwald site and its surroundings with the aim of assessing the nature and

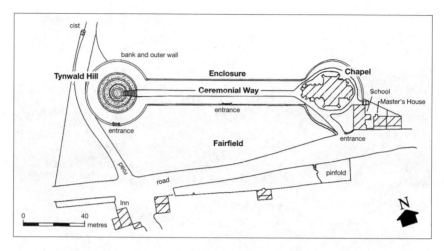

Figure 10.2 Plan of the Tynwald site at St John's, Isle of Man, in the mid nineteenth century.

extent of earlier remains. The work was carried out between 1993 and 1996 and involved topographic, geophysical, and geochemical surveys; an examination of early prints and photographs; and a review of the literature generated by travellers and antiquarians who visited the Island from the mid-seventeenth century onwards.[16] No excavation or interventional archaeology was involved, nor was there much emphasis on the nature of the Tynwald ceremonies as they have been well covered by Harrison and others.[17]

As a result of the survey, five broad phases to the development of the site and its surroundings can be suggested, although the three earliest should be regarded as provisional until tested through excavation.

The first phase is putatively prehistoric in date, perhaps the second millennium BC. There is certainly a Bronze Age round barrow with a central stone-built cist (*Follagh-y-Vannin*) to the north of Tynwald Hill, still partly visible in the side of the road. Tynwald Hill itself is often considered to be a prehistoric burial mound and one possibility is that it is a late Neolithic developed passage grave; certainly its situation, shape, and size is appropriate.[18] There was probably some kind of enclosure around these mounds and short

---

16 Darvill in prep.   17 Harrison 1871; Clucas 1925b; Craine 1957.   18 It is interesting in this regard that Tynwald Hill is almost exactly the same diameter and height as the developed passage grave at Quanterness, Orkney. Moreover, excavations at Quanterness have revealed that the construction of the cairn involved a series of two or three revetment walls within the core of the cairn which may well have given it a stepped profile with four terraces including the top (see Renfrew 1979, figure 32).

lengths of possible ditch were found through geophysical survey. Captain Grose made the earliest known plan in 1774,[19] and this shows the circular mound and chapel within an oblong enclosure defined by a bank and ditch. He shows four entrances each marked by stone portals. The north side of the enclosure is straight; the south side changes alignment east of Tynwald Hill suggesting that perhaps more than one phase is represented before it was remodelled at the end of the eighteenth century. There is no suggestion that the site was an assembly-place at this early time, although attention may be drawn to its similarity with the later prehistoric enclosures or *viereckschanze* found in central and northern Europe, which Matthew Murray has argued may have been associated with feasting and communal meetings.[20]

The second identifiable phase of the site probably belongs to the later first millennium AD (fig. 10.3). The mound and barrow are still there, as too perhaps the enclosure, but to the east there is now a burial ground from which a tenth-century cross-slab has been recovered, perhaps a keeil or small chapel, and there is some suggestion from geophysical surveys of a burial mound. Perhaps the most important aspect, however, is the more general setting of the site. Taking a wider view, it is clearly part of a very extensive group of cemeteries and barrows, and stands to the west of a double-ditched enclosure built on the edge of a marsh near another associated cemetery and a small pond or spring (fig. 10.4). Excavations at Purt y Candas by Peter Gelling in the mid-1970s established the presence of occupation between the sixth and eighth centuries AD, with finds suggesting a fairly high-status site.[21] Environmental evidence shows that woodland clearance was taking place in this part of the central valley between AD 560 and 1280 and thus provides support for an expansion of activity.[22] There are also obvious similarities between the arrangement of structures around Tynwald and the so-called royal centres such as Navan and Tara in Ireland where high-status settlements within ringforts and ceremonial sites cluster together.[23] It is quite possible that the site had become a meeting-place, and here there are possible parallels with the tiered structure, barrows, and halls at Yeavering in northern England.[24]

In the third phase, broadly the period AD 900 through to 1700, the site becomes more of what it is today. This is when it acquires its Norse name, and by this time it was certainly an open-air meeting-place comparable to many others around Europe. It may, however, have developed in relative isolation, as

---

19 Reproduced in Harrison 1871, opposite p.21. Of just slightly later date are two watercolours of the site by John (Warwick) Smith in 1795 (Megaw 1958). **20** Murray 1995. **21** Webster and Cherry 1974; 1975; 1976; 1977. The site was not published at the time of Gelling's death and is currently (2000) the subject of a publication programme and limited re-excavation by the Centre for Manx Studies. **22** Innes 1995. **23** For a general discussion of these sites see Warner 1988 and Aitchison 1994. **24** Hope-Taylor 1977.

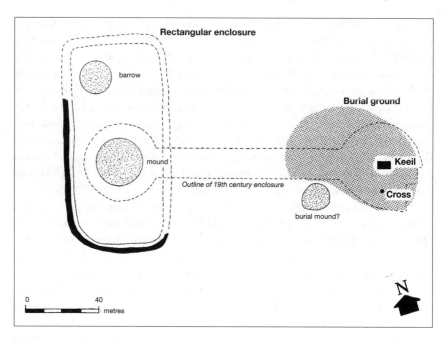

Figure 10.3 Provisional reconstruction of Tynwald in Phase 2, the later first millennium AD.

the focus of high-status settlement appears to have moved to Peel on the north-west coast of the island about 4km distant; Gelling recorded no evidence for continued occupation at Purt y Candas.[25] At Tynwald it can be suggested that a large rectangular enclosure was built around the hill and the chapel, and this is the enclosure recorded by Grose in the eighteenth century. It had four entrances. The mound is stepped from the time of the earliest illustrations in the seventeenth century, and from earlier written accounts of the ceremonies held at the site there is good reason to believe that its stepped profile is ancient. Before 1979, however, the steps were narrower and less level than they are today.[26] The tradition of using prehistoric burial mounds as assembly-sites, especially higher-order ones, is well known and relates to the metaphorical link between the ancestors and the deployment of power. Hilda Ellis notes that the practice of sitting on a burial mound is also a major theme of Old Norse literature.[27]

The fourth phase of the site is represented by an episode of tidying up in

25 Webster and Cherry 1974; 1975; 1976; 1977.   26 The steps were levelled and slightly widened by the addition of soil and turf in order to better accommodate the seating used at the Tynwald ceremonies.   27 Ellis 1943.

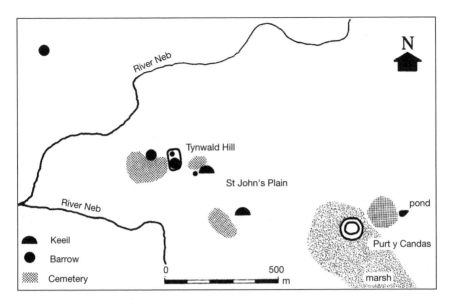

Figure 10.4 The St John's area, Isle of Man, in the later first millennium AD.

the years around 1795. Correspondence between Deemster Lace and the Governor of the island exists regarding the levelling of earthworks on the fair-field and the construction of new roads.[28] A more modest dumb-bell shaped earthwork enclosure was constructed around the Hill and the Chapel with a ceremonial way between. The political context is important here, for in 1765 the Lordship of Man returned to the British crown and for a short period no Tynwald ceremonies were held. Late eighteenth-century visitors consistently remarked on the decayed condition of the site. Refurbishment was thus very much in the context of re-establishing the Tynwald ceremonies. In a sense it is very fortunate that Francis Grose saw and recorded the site before these changes had taken effect.

The fifth phase is the creation of what we see today, the mid-nineteenth-century remodelling: the rebuilding of the church, the stone walling added to the enclosure boundaries, and the development of the site as a symbol of Manx nationhood.

Throughout the last three of these putative phases, Tynwald Hill has been more than something to stand on. It embodies and represents many other ideas and traditions, some of which relate to the exercise of power and authority, and the representation of social order. The use of the hill itself has changed little

28 Manx National Heritage Library X/66–20 and X/66–33.

since the earliest detailed account which relates to the ceremony of 1417. Three main elements to the event are clear enough: swearing allegiance (and in earlier times king-making), the declaration of new laws, and the administration of justice.

Social order is also physically represented in the arrangement of people on the hill. The top of the mound is occupied by the Lord of Man, the Lord bishop, and nowadays the president of Tynwald. The elected representatives of the national government, that is the members of the House of Keys, occupy the second tier down. The bailiff, clergy, registrar, and others concerned with regional and national administration, law and order, occupy the third tier. The captains of the parishes, who are locally elected representatives, occupy the lowest tier. Beyond the edge of the hill itself are the rest of the population. Originally, we know from archaeological evidence outlined above, these people would have been contained within an enclosure which bounded the assembly-site. We also know that those attending Tynwald came from all over the island, and would at other times have attended more local meetings and assemblies.

TYNWALD AND ASSEMBLY-PLACES ON THE ISLE OF MAN

The Tynwald at St John's is not the only assembly-place known on the island. In exploring the position and arrangement of these other sites, place-names and archaeological evidence come together to provide the broad picture. Since Man is an island there are strict geographical limits on the edges of the potential units that can be defined and this fact makes analysis and investigation easier.

Place-name evidence from the island has been well studied over many decades by a number of eminent authorities, although there are naturally areas of disagreement over the interpretation and meaning of certain names.[29] The place-names relating to assemblies of various kinds are not especially controversial, although they do not seem to have been looked at as a group before. Extracting the assembly names from published sources and setting these alongside historical references to the holding of courts and assemblies suggests the presence of six assembly-places (fig. 10.5A). Most are represented by a single place-name, but occasionally there are clusters of related names. Of the six, two include Norse elements. Tynwald, German, which combines two elements – *þing* and *vǫllr* – translatable as the 'parliament field', is discussed above.[30]

Normode, on the boundary of Braddan and Balwin, is the name of a small

---

29 Keen 1925–9; Marstrander 1932; Marstrander 1934; Gelling 1970; Gelling 1971. 30 See also Marstrander 1932, 216.

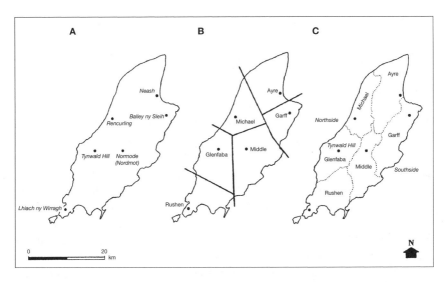

Figure 10.5 Assembly-sites in the Isle of Man. A. Position of recorded sites and place-name clusters. B. Thiessen polygons. C. Sheading boundaries.

estate comprising just two fields and may be read as *Norðmót* which again combines two elements – *Norð* + *mót* – and can be translated as the 'northern meeting'.[31] A cluster of other place-names in the vicinity perhaps serves to emphasize the former importance of this now-vanished site. Nearby is Keeill Abban, now St Luke's, which stood on the estate of Algayre, Braddan, which Keen derives from the Irish root *ealg* (nobility/justice) and the locative suffix *-ar*, to mean 'the place of justice'. He also notes a Tynwald Court here in about 1429 and local traditions that there is an ancient tynwald hill on the estate. The place-name Naish has also been recorded nearby in Braddan, which Keen links to the Irish *Nás* meaning a gathering or assembly.[32]

The remaining sites have place-names derived exclusively from Irish roots, and may thus be considered indigenous or non-Norse in origin. In the far south of the island is *Lhiach ny Wirragh*, Rushen, closely associated with the Neolithic tomb at Mull Hill. Keen takes *Lhiach* to be derived from the Irish *leac* meaning a 'pillar stone', while *Wirragh* he gives as the genitive plural of the Irish *forrach* 'a meeting or assembly'. The name *Ennaugh* also occurs nearby and may be associated with the Irish *an aenach* meaning a fair or gathering place.[33] *Balley ny Sleih*, Maughold, Keen translates as 'farm of the hosts or gathering' from the Irish *baile na sluaigheadh*.[34] Neash, Bride, translates as for the same place-name already mentioned in Braddan – 'assembly'.[35]

31 Keen 1925–9, 620.   32 Ibid., 175, 191 and 620; Kermode 1930, 61; Michell 1994, 99–108. 33 Keen 1925–9, 44.   34 Ibid., 280.   35 Ibid., 569.

Finally, there are historical records of assemblies at or near *Cronk Urleigh* (Reneuling), Michael, but no obvious place-names to go with them.[36]

At first sight these recognisable assembly-sites are widely scattered across the island, but their distribution and spatial relationships are significant and can be explored in a number of ways. One approach is to use Thiessen Polygons as a way of reconstructing, hypothetically at least, the territories that they might have served. The principles underlying the technique are well established and provide a simple geometric means of subdividing space such that any point within the defined territory is closer to the centre of the polygon than to any other centre.[37] The results are shown in figure 10.5B and represent a fairly convincing sub-division of the available space into similar-sized units.

In this case, however, a good deal is known about the boundaries of early medieval political units on the Isle of Man and these can be compared with the theoretical model. Known as 'sheadings' there were six major units on the island, the origins of which are obscure although widely considered to be pre-Norse.[38] The name sheading has been interpreted as meaning 'a sixth part'.[39] In medieval times the six sheadings were arranged into two groups – north side and south side – separated by a range of hills running through the centre of the island. When mapped out side by side, the sheading boundaries and hypothetical boundaries of the territories served by the assembly-sites correspond rather well (fig. 10.5C).[40]

Not all of the six assembly-sites are, in physical terms, the same. Four of them seem to be just places in the countryside, known because of the presence of some distinctive natural or man-made feature, mainly hills, although in the case of *Lhiach ny Wirragh*, in Rushen sheading, perhaps connected with the Neolithic passage grave at Mull Hill.

Two sites, the two associated with Norse names, are more complicated. Quarrying in the nineteenth century destroyed the site in Middle Sheading, although a stone structure at or near the original site probably perpetuates something of its form as a simple enclosure, perhaps originally a platform or mound. The second site, Tynwald Hill, has a large mound and a long history as already discussed.

Taking these Manx assembly-sites as a whole it is possible to suggest a model involving three organizational levels along the lines suggested for Orkney and Shetland by Hibbert back in the early nineteenth century:[41] local,

---

36 Ibid., 446 and 438; but Marstrander 1934, 323–4 suggests a possible derivation of *Cronk Urleigh* linked to the Irish *úrlainn* meaning open space or court.   37 Haggett 1965, 247–8; Hodder and Orton 1976, 58–60.   38 Megaw 1978, 284; Reilly 1988. See also Moore 1999 who suggests some divisions may be older still.   39 This is well argued by Megaw 1978, 284–5, who rejects earlier suggestions that the term meant 'ship-division'.   40 Indeed, Megaw 1978, 284 suggested that the sheadings may be regarded as six court-districts within his model of early Manx landholdings.   41 Hibbert 1831.

regional, and national. Thus at the lowest level each sheading had its assembly-place which, in medieval times at least was also a court. These sites were rather unelaborated and may not have been geographically fixed. Their pre-Norse names strongly suggest that the system of which they were part was already in place by the eleventh century AD, and probably a lot earlier. One assembly-site in each of the two regions of the island, north side and south side, seems to have been more elaborate than the others around about. These perhaps served as local and regional assemblies, in rather the same way that in England the Shire moots stood in superior relation to the Hundred moots. In the Isle of Man as a whole, one assembly-site, Tynwald at St John's, is markedly larger and more elaborate than all the others. Historical sources suggest that it had a wider range of high order functions too, including law-giving and the appointment of new lords and kings.[42] We have then, preserved on Man, not only the best surviving, and still functioning, example of an open-air assembly-site in north-west Europe, but also relics of its context and origins.

TYNWALD AND ITS BROADER CONTEXT

The arrangement of assembly-sites on the Isle of Man is only part of the picture. For much of the later first and early second millennia AD the island was part of a series of larger social and political units that embraced the coastlands of the Irish Sea Basin, the Western Seaways, and indeed lands beyond. E.G. Bowen has shown the extent of such connections through the distribution of churches dedicated to Celtic saints,[43] and Alcock has suggested that from this period an Irish Sea cultural province can be recognized.[44] Moreover, as previously noted, by the twelfth century the Isle of Man is firmly established within the Kingdom of the Isles.[45]

In this connection it is important to recognize that it is not only the Isle of Man that sees the early development of open-air assembly-places. Parts of eastern Ireland, Cumbria, and southwest Scotland also lay within this broad cultural province. On present evidence, only north Wales lacks comparable sites, probably because the area fell under a rather different kind of administrative system based around the royal court (*llys*) of the kind excavated at Rhosyr, Anglesey,[46] and the *gorsedd*.

42 Harrison 1871. Michell 1994, 102–12, argues that the Tynwald at Keeill Abban/Nordmot should be regarded as the highest Tynwald on the Island and that the St John's sites was subordinate to it. However, no substantial evidence is offered to support this view.   43 Bowen 1970, 22–4.   44 Alcock 1970.   45 Megaw and Megaw 1950; Megaw 1978.   46 Longley 1996. Note, however, that Megaw 1978, 284, draws attention to the similarities between the commote (*cwmwd*, neighbourhood) as a 'court-district' and the Manx sheading, noting that on Anglesey, as

Taking the known assembly-sites around the Irish Sea, there is one rather
conspicuous feature found at several of them: the presence of stepped mounds
(fig. 10.6). Tynwald Hill is the best known, but other equally impressive structures can be traced. The Thingmount, Little Langdale, Cumbria, clearly has
four terraces on the 2m high rather quadrilateral mound, 32m by 29m.[47] The
example at College Green in Dublin is depicted as being stepped on illustrations made before its destruction in 1685.[48] In southwestern Scotland the
Lincluden Mote in Dumfries and Galloway may be another stepped
example,[49] as too Doomster Hill, Govan, Glasgow.[50]

Slightly further afield there is the rather curious stepped mound at Maiden's
Bower, Topcliffe, North Yorkshire.[51] Although certainly part of a motte and
bailey castle, its position on the interfluve of the river Swale and the Cod Beck
and its uneasy relationship with the attached bailey suggests that it might be an
earlier structure utilized as the core for a later motte. Equally, the appearance of
the mound may owe something to the landscaping works for the nearby Cock
Lodge, manor house of the earls of Northumberland and one of the seats of the
Percy family. However, the presence of carved stone crosses with distinctively
Manx influence in Topcliffe church and elsewhere in the area[52] must raise the
possibility of other explanations worthy of further investigation.

Taken together, these stepped mounds may suggest another dimension to
the development of a distinctive Irish Sea cultural province, and one that can
be traced through material culture into the domain of power relations and
political institutions. It is part of a much broader set of traditions based around
the operation of the Thing within the Norse world extending northwards and
eastwards of the areas discussed so far.[53]

To the south of what may simplistically be characterized as the Norse lands
similar systems are represented by the moots of the Germanic territories. Here
too, the rather visible early medieval sites and institutions may perhaps be
traced back to later prehistoric times. Indeed, for these regions open-air assemblies can be glimpsed in the writings of the Roman author Tacitus when, in AD
96, he describes the geography and traditions of Germania, noting that:

> On matters of minor importance only the chiefs debate, on major affairs
> the whole community; but, even where the commons have the decision,
> the case is carefully considered in advance by the chiefs. Except in case
> of accident or emergency they assemble on fixed days, when the moon is
> either crescent or nearing her full orb.[54]

on Man, there were six units grouped together into larger primary divisions (two on Man and
three on Anglesey).   **47** Quartermaine and Krupa 1994.   **48** Anon 1882.   **49** Coles 1893, 118.
50 Driscoll 1997 and pers. comm., and see Brotchie 1913–18.   **51** Mitchell 1886.   **52** Elgee
and Elgee 1933, 216.   **53** For example Hibbert 1831; Gomme 1880; Crawford 1987, 206–10;
Björnsson 1994.   **54** Mattingly 1948, 109–10.

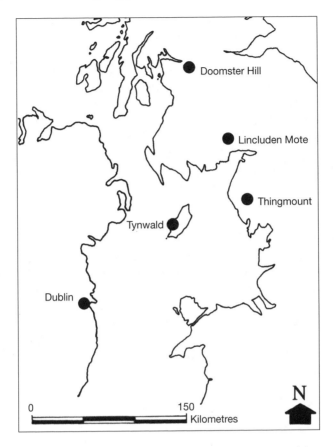

Figure 10.6 Map of the Irish Sea region showing the position of recorded stepped Things

CONCLUSION

Open-air assemblies have long been recognized as an integral element of Norse and Germanic political systems, which in a few cases have survived in various forms down to recent times. The only example remaining at the end of the twentieth century AD was the Tynwald Hill in the Isle of Man, which is also one of the earliest documented examples. Investigations here and at other proposed open-air assembly-sites in the Isle of Man suggest pre-Norse roots that connect back into the social order and political organization of the later first millennium BC. Among the high-level sites there are similarities in the arrangement of activities and the kinds of structures represented that can be traced westwards to the royal centres of Ireland and eastwards to the palaces of northern England. The use of stepped mounds at a number of thing-sites around the Irish Sea basin hints at a degree of shared tradition that deserves further exploration. There might be connections here with the presence of stepped mounds among the later Neolithic passage graves of the region. It is clear from studies of the Tynwald Hill that archaeology has a major role to play in the future study of open-air meeting-places. Further investigation of these places will involve casting aside some of the traditional period-based and regionally-based subdivisions that tend to strait-jacket the discipline, focusing instead on issues of power relations and political organization through long time periods and across broad areas.

ACKNOWLEDGMENTS

This paper is based on the results of a series of research programmes on the Isle of Man and elsewhere. Special thanks go to Wendy Horn for interesting me in the problems of the Tynwald site and to Stephen Harrison, Andrew Johnson, and Andrew Foxon of Manx National Heritage for their help and support for work at the site. Nicola King, Liz MaCrimmon, and Louise Pearson assisted with sorting out figures and references in Bournemouth. Thanks also to Phil Claris of the National Trust for making available information about the Thing-mount in Little Langdale, and Steve Driscoll for information about Govan.

REFERENCES

Adkins, R.A, and Petchey, M.R., 1984: 'Secklow hundred mound and other meeting place mounds in England', *Archaeological Journal* **141**, 243–51.
Aitchison, N.B., 1994: *Armagh and the royal centres in early medieval Ireland*. Woodbridge.
Alcock, L., 1970: 'Was there an Irish Sea culture-province in the Dark Ages?', in D. Moore (ed.), *The Irish Sea province in archaeology and history*. Cardiff. 55–65.
Anon., 1882: 'The Scandinavian "thing" in Dublin', *The Antiquary* **6**, 110–12.
Ashbee, P., 1960: *The Bronze Age round barrow in Britain*. London.
Björnsson, B.Th., 1994: *Þingvellir staðir og leiðir*, Mál og menning. Reykjavik.
Bowen, E.G., 1970: 'Britain and the British seas', in D. Moore (ed.), *The Irish Sea province in archaeology and history*. Cardiff. 13–28.
Broderick, G., 1996: *Chronicles of the kings of Man and the Isles*. Douglas.
Brotchie, T.C.F., 1913–18: 'The Moot Hill, Holy Well and Kirk of Govan', *Transactions of the Old Glasgow Club* **3**, 376–79.
Bruce-Mitford, R., 1972: *The Sutton Hoo ship-burial: a handbook* (2nd edn.). London.
Burnett, C.J. and Tabraham, C.J., 1993: *The Honours of Scotland*. Edinburgh.
Butler, T., 1982: *The Crown Jewels and coronation ceremony*. London.
Clarke, D.V., Cowie, T.G. and Foxon, A., 1985: *Symbols of power at the time of Stonehenge*. Edinburgh.

Clucas, G.F., 1925a.: 'Tynwald in ancient days', *Proceedings of the Isle of Man Natural History and Antiquarian Society* **2**, 160–3.

Clucas, G.F., 1925b: *Tynwald*. Douglas. Privately printed.

Coles, F.R., 1893: 'The motes, forts and doons in the east and west divisions of the stewartry of Kirkcudbright', *Proceedings of the Society of Antiquaries of Scotland* **27**, 92–182.

Craine, D., 1957: *Tynwald*. Douglas.

Crawford, B.E., 1987: *Scandinavian Scotland*. Leicester.

Darvill, T., *in prep*: *Tynwald Hill and St John's Plain, German, Isle of Man: an archaeological survey*, Bournemouth University School of Conservation Sciences Occasional Paper. Oxford.

Driscoll, S., 1997: 'The kingdom of Strathclyde's final chapter', *British Archaeology* **27**, 6.

Elgee, F., and Elgee H.W., 1933: *The archaeology of Yorkshire*. London.

Ellis, H.R., 1943: *The road to Hel*. Cambridge.

Gelling, M., 1970: 'The place-names of the Isle of Man', *Journal of the Manx Museum* **7** (no. 86), 130–9.

Gelling, M., 1971: 'The place-names of the Isle of Man', *Journal of the Manx Museum* **7** (no. 87), 168–75.

Gomme, G.L., 1880: *Primitive folk-moots*. London.

Haggett, P., 1965: *Locational analysis in human geography*. London.

Harrison, W., 1871: *Records of the Tynwald and St John's Chapels in the Isle of Man*, Manx Society 19. Douglas.

Hawkes, C.F.C., 1954: 'Archaeological theory and method: some suggestions from the old world', *American Anthropologist* **56**, 155–68.

Hibbert, S., 1831: 'Memoir on the tings of Orkney and Shetland', *Archaeologia Scotica* **3**, 103–210.

Hodder, I. and Orton, C., 1976: *Spatial analysis in archaeology*. Cambridge.

Hope-Taylor, B., 1977: *Yeavering: an Anglo-British centre of early Northumbria*, Department of the Environment Archaeological Report 7. London.

Innes, J.B., 1995: *The Dhoo Valley, Isle of Man: a palaeo-environmental assessment*, Centre for Manx Studies Research Report 2. Douglas.

Keen, J.J., 1925–9: *The place-names of the Isle of Man with their origins and history* (6 vols.). Douglas.

Kermode, P.M.C., 1930: *List of Manx antiquities*. Douglas.

Longley, D., 1996: 'Rhosyr', *Current Archaeology* **13** (no.150), 204–8.

Marstrander, C.J.S., 1932: 'Det Norske Landnåm på Man', *Norsk Tidsskrift for Sprogvidenskap* **6**, 40–386.

Marstrander, C.J.S., 1934: 'Remarks on the place-names of the Isle of Man', *Norsk Tidsskrift for Sprogvidenskap* **7**, 287–334.

Mattingly, H., 1948: *Tacitus on Britain and Germany: a new translation*. Harmondsworth.

Megaw, B.R.S., 1958: 'The Warwick Smith watercolours of 1795', *Journal of the Manx Museum* **6**, 45–8.

Megaw, B.R.S., 1978: 'Norsemen and native in the Kingdom of the Isles: a reassessment of the Manx evidence', in P.J. Davey (ed.), *Man and environment in the Isle of Man*, B.A.R. British Series 54. Oxford. 265–314.

Megaw, B.R.S. and Megaw E.M., 1950: 'The Norse heritage in the Isle of Man', in C. Fox and B. Dickins (eds), *The early cultures of north-west Europe*. Cambridge. 141–69.

Michell, J., 1994: *At the centre of the world*. London.

Mitchell, C., 1886: 'The maiden's bower', *Yorkshire Archaeological and Topographical Journal* 9, 241–50.

Moore, R.H., 1999: 'The Manx multiple estate: evidence for undertones on the Manx land-System?', in P.J. Davey (ed.), *Recent archaeological research on the Isle of Man*, B.A.R. British Series 278. Oxford. 171–82.

Murray, M., 1995: 'Viereckschanzen and feasting: socio-political ritual in Iron-Age central Europe', *Journal of European Archaeology* 3(2), 125–52.

Quatermaine, J. and Krupa, M., 1994: *Thingmount, Little Langdale, Cumbria. Archaeological survey*, Lancaster University Archaeological Unit for the National Trust. [Limited circulation printed report]. Lancaster.

Reilly, P., 1988: *Computer analysis of an archaeological landscape: medieval land divisions in the Isle of Man*, B.A.R. British Series 190. Oxford.

Renfrew, C., 1979: *Investigations in Orkney*, Reports of the Research Committee of the Society of Antiquaries of London 38. London.

Simpson, J., 1979: 'The King's Whetstone', *Antiquity* 53, 96–101.

Steane, J., 1993: *The archaeology of the medieval English monarchy*. London.

Warner, R.B., 1988: 'The archaeology of early historic Irish kingship', in S.T. Driscoll and M. R. Nieke (eds), *Power and politics in early medieval Britain and Ireland*. Edinburgh. 47–68.

Webster, L.E. and Cherry, J., 1974: 'Medieval Britain in 1973', *Medieval Archaeology* 18, 186.

Webster, L.E. and Cherry, J., 1975: 'Medieval Britain in 1974', *Medieval Archaeology* 19, 230–1.

Webster, L.E. and Cherry, J., 1976: 'Medieval Britain in 1975', *Medieval Archaeology* 20, 174.

Webster, L.E. and Cherry, J., 1977: 'Medieval Britain in 1976', *Medieval Archaeology* 21, 216.

The early Frankish *mallus*: its nature, participants and practices

P.S. BARNWELL

The focus of this paper differs from that of the others in this volume in as much as it primarily concerns matters of procedure rather than of site, and derives its evidence exclusively from written rather than archaeological sources. A recurring theme in both this and earlier contributions to the subject is the exploration of the relationship between local judicial assemblies – specifically the Frankish *mallus* of the sixth and seventh centuries – and the higher-level courts of the *comes* (count) and of the king. The early *mallus* has not attracted a great deal of scholarly attention in its own right, most work having focussed on the officials who were involved with it, particularly the *comes* or *grafio* (which are synonymous) and the *centenarius* and *thunginus* (the synonymity of which is probable, though less certain).[1] The reasons for this lie in the historiography of the subject, in which there are three broad strands. The first is what has been termed the 'old' Germanist school,[2] exemplified by such great scholars of the nineteenth century as Waitz and Brunner.[3] Adherents of this view saw the origins of the *mallus* as lying in the 'democratic' Germanic assembly, and its officials as being popularly elected; only later, with the rise of kingship, were such popular officials replaced with those appointed by the new royal administration. The second interpretation is that of 'new' Germanists, and is especially associated with the mid-twentieth-century scholar, Dannenbauer. According to this understanding, Germanic society had always been hierarchical, rather than 'democratic', and the functionaries associated with the *mallus* were successors of members of the old Germanic aristocracy, rather than popular officials.[4] There has for long, however, been a third, anti-Germanist, school, the prime nineteenth-century exponent of which was the versatile Fustel de Coulanges:[5] for him, the

---

1 See, for example, Zöllner 1970, 143, and Grahn-Hoek 1976, 283–5. 2 The following classification draws heavily upon Murray 1988, 59–65. 3 Waitz 1953–5, 1, 338–70, and 2 part ii, 135–242; Brunner 1887, 1928, 2, esp. 217–41 and 289–312. 4 Especially Dannenbauer 1942–9, 155–219. 5 Fustel de Coulanges 1930, esp. 220–38, 304–31 and 350–89; Fustel de Coulanges

mallus was not an assembly at all, but simply a legal court; there never was anything 'popular' about it, and its officials were successors of Roman provincial governors and lesser administrators. The last point has been more recently explored in two significant papers by A.C. Murray,[6] who demonstrates that both the *comes/grafio* and the *centenarius* and *thunginus* were indeed of Roman ancestry, but does not seek to address the question of the *mallus* as such.

The concentration on officials, while providing valuable insights into aspects of early-medieval society and the influences which shaped it, has not greatly advanced understanding of the *mallus* itself, and it is, therefore, to the *mallus* as an institution that the present contribution is primarily addressed. The discussion is centred around four questions relating to the types of business conducted at the *mallus*; the ways in which relevant business was brought before it; who participated in it; and, lastly, what we know of the procedures of the *mallus*. The answers to the first questions will be largely derived from the law codes (namely, the sixth-century recension of Lex Salica, the later sixth-century additions to it, and the early seventh-century Lex Ribuaria), which are almost the only documents to refer to the *mallus* as such. Later sections of the discussion will be increasingly influenced by the evidence supplied by other sources, particularly the earliest collections of specimen documents (formularies, associated with cities), in an attempt to cast light on the character of the *mallus* and its place in the judicial system of the Franks in the first half of the Merovingian period. Although the contemporary evidential base is very narrow, it is not here supplemented by later sources since, despite the fact that the *mallus* long outlived the Merovingian dynasty, it was reformed by Charlemagne and continued to evolve thereafter, with the result that it is not always possible to be certain of the antiquity of the arrangements reflected in later documents and texts.[7]

THE BUSINESS OF THE 'MALLUS'

Most of the evidence which can be used to illuminate the kind of business which could be brought before the *mallus* derives from the *Pactus legis Salicae*, issued late in the reign of Clovis (d. 511).[8] Although the text never recorded all Salic law,[9] it contains enough to show that the *mallus* was competent in a variety of cases. The subjects of the clauses which explicitly mention the

---

1923, esp. 372–499. **6** Murray 1986 and 1988, both of which contain extensive references to, and critiques of, the earlier literature on the subject, supplementing the very brief references given above at nn. 3–5. **7** For the Carolingian reforms, see Ganshof 1968, 8, 49, 52 and 76–80. **8** Wormald 1977, 108. **9** Wood 1994, 109–10.

mallus range from all kinds of theft,[10] the reclamation of stolen property,[11] arson and at least certain instances of homicide,[12] to the ability of men to move to a new settlement,[13] the upholding of agreements,[14] the transfer of property (including the renunciation of kin and inheritance),[15] and the betrothal of widows.[16] Other legal texts of the sixth and early seventh century confirm the overall variety and add to the detail.[17] It is also implicit that many of the other types of case to which the law codes refer would have come before the *mallus*.

Partial though the list is, it reveals that the *mallus* provided a forum both for what today are regarded as criminal matters and for those of a civil nature. Many cases, of each type, involved disputes, and were presented to the *mallus* for judgment and sentence; but the *mallus* could also act as a place in which various transactions were witnessed and recorded. Hence, for example, Chapter 46 of the *Pactus legis Salicae*, which concerns the donation of property, describes a ritual by which transfer was signified and which, by virtue of being conducted in public, helped to ensure the legitimacy of the transaction, as well as providing witnesses in the event of subsequent dispute. The provisions (Chapter 60) for the renunciation of kin are of a similar nature, as are those for the betrothal of a widow (Chapter 44). Activity of this kind perhaps suggests that the *mallus* could also be used as a forum for the making of public announcements, but that is uncertain since, on account of the largely legal nature of the sources, there is no positive evidence for such a function.

THE INITIATION OF BUSINESS

The mechanisms by which business was brought before the *mallus* varied according to the nature of the case. In matters which did not relate to a dispute, but simply required witnesses, the parties concerned approached the local official (the *centenarius* or *thunginus*) so that a *mallus* might be convened.[18] This suggests that *malli* were not held regularly, but other evidence implies that they were: a man wishing to renounce his inheritance was to present himself at a *mallus*,[19] suggesting that he knew when and where to appear, and a defendant found guilty of homicide but unable to pay the necessary composition was to be presented at four such gatherings in order that his kin or friends could save him from enslavement.[20] It is therefore possible that there were regular meetings, but that they could be supplemented by others if business was

---

10 *Pactus legis Salicae*, 39, 40. 11 Ibid., 47, cf. 33, 39. 12 Ibid., 16, 35, cf. 57. 13 Ibid., 14, 45. 14 Ibid., 50, 56. 15 Ibid., 46, 60. 16 Ibid., 44. 17 E.g. *Pactus Childeberti I et Chlotharii I*, 2; *Edictus Chilperici*, 8, 10; *Decretio Childeberti II*, 6; *Lex Ribuaria*, 32, 37.1, 75.1–2. 18 *Pactus legis Salicae*, 44.1, 46.1. 19 *Pactus legis Salicae*, 60. 20 Ibid., 18.

pressing, as seems to be envisaged both by the eighth-century Bavarian Laws as well as by Carolingian and later evidence.[21]

In cases involving disputes, the plaintiff summoned the defendant to a *mallus*. For example, a man who escaped from a house which had been subjected to an arson attack was to issue a summons against the arsonist,[22] while someone who objected to a new settler in his locality was to summon the migrant.[23] Procedures of this kind only related to freemen: if a slave or other dependent committed a crime such as homicide, it was for his master to present him to the court, presumably often in response to a summons, though he could 'summon' himself ('se obmallare') if he wished pre-emptively to demonstrate his innocence.[24] Penalties for non-compliance with a summons were severe, the seriousness with which such contempt was treated perhaps being indicated by the fact that it is very the first topic to be addressed in our text of the *Pactus legis Salicae*.[25]

There are, however, indications that the *mallus* was not the first forum in which an attempt might be made to resolve a case. According to one of the sixth-century additions to the Salic Law, the Edict issued by King Chilperic *c.*575, anyone with a complaint which could be referred to a *mallus* was first to inform his neighbours and then to take an oath before the local judicial leaders, the *rachimburgi* (see below). It seems that many cases may have stopped at that point, for the law provides that only those in which doubt existed (or, presumably, were contested) should be referred to the *mallus* itself for resolution.[26]

PARTICIPANTS

This leads to the third question posed at the outset, relating to those who participated in the *mallus*. The *centenarius* and/or *thunginus* have already been seen to have been responsible for convening the *mallus* to witness transactions, and there is some evidence, though it is very slight, to suggest that they were responsible for presiding over it, for the man who wished to renounce his kin performed the necessary ritual in the *mallus* in the presence of one of those two office holders;[27] and there were at least some circumstances in which one such

---

21 *Lex Bawiariorum*, 11.14; cf. the eighth-century (Lantfridian) recension of the *Lex Alamannorum*, 36.1, where meetings were to be held every two weeks in normal times, or weekly in more troubled days. On the difficulties of interpreting precisely what these texts mean, see Wood 1998, 234–5, and, for discussion of later evidence (and citation of literature) relating to assemblies which were routine and those which were specially convened, see Schmidt-Wiegand 1984, col. 217. 22 *Pactus legis Salicae*, 16.1. 23 Ibid., 48.1–2. 24 Ibid., 35.8; cf. *Pactus Childeberti I et Chlotharii I*, 5. 25 *Pactus legis Salicae*, 1; cf. 49 and *Lex Ribuaria*, 36, 51; cf., also, a number of provisions in the early formularies, such as *Formulae Andecauenses*, 12–14, 16, 53. 26 *Edictus Chilperici*, 10. 27 *Pactus legis Salicae*, 60.

official was responsible for summoning parties to appear.[28] That does not mean
that men of these kinds were judges, since there is other evidence to suggest
that the *centenarius* was a local military official with what we might consider to
be police duties such as the pursuit of criminals,[29] and it may be more accurate
to think of his role in the *mallus* as administrative rather than judicial.
Judgment was, rather, the preserve of men known as *rachimburgi*. The first
element of the word is of uncertain etymology, but may encapsulate the idea
of judgment,[30] while the second part indicates that such men were in some way
the guarantors of the proceedings.[31] In the city-based documents exemplified
in the formularies, the place of *rachimburgi* is taken by *boni homines*, the precise
origins of whom are a matter of debate.[32] It is clear from the law codes that the
rachimburgi not only had power to determine which cases should reach the
mallus, but, once a case had been referred there, seven of their number on any
one occasion had to be prepared to 'speak the law' when requested to do so, on
pain of a substantial fine.[33] They were not merely mouthpieces: they had
powers to judge, to assess the amount of compensation payable in certain cases,
and to gather evidence (by means including the administration of ordeal) and
enforce payment of composition.[34] How the seven *rachimburgi* who acted on a
particular occasion were selected is unclear, though that not all (free) members
of the local community could act as *rachimburgi* is suggested by the way in
which a would-be plaintiff was to inform his neighbours of his case, and was
only subsequently to involve the *rachimburgi* in witnessing his oath. Freemen
in general could also presumably act as witnesses and/or oath-helpers, particularly since some procedures involved large numbers of them (often twelve),[35]
and it is perhaps unlikely that men who acted as *rachimburgi* on a given
occasion could also be witnesses in the matter under consideration. There is
also evidence to suggest that all freemen were in some sense part of a local
mallus, for a clause in Lex Ribuaria provides that a plaintiff could bring his
case either at the king's court or at the place where he was *(g)amallus*[36] – a
word of slightly unclear meaning, signifying something like 'a member of a
mallus' or 'able to be judged'. This, together with the function of the *mallus* as
a place where transactions were witnessed suggests that it was something other

---

28 Ibid., 50. **29** The most significant texts for police duties are the *Pactus Childeberti I and
Chlotharii I*, 9, 16, 17, and the *Decretio Childeberti II*, 9, 11, 12; for detailed discussion, see
Murray 1988. **30** Gothic *ragin* means judgment, decree or opinion. **31** Kaspers 1948–50,
318; Wood 1998, 227 (comment by D. Green). **32** The best short account of *boni homines* is
Dilcher 1971; but for a comprehensive review of the evidence, see Nehlsen-von Stryk 1981.
33 *Pactus legis Salicae*, 57; *Lex Ribuaria*, 56. **34** *Pactus legis Salicae*, 56, 57; *Edictus Chilperici*,
8. **35** E.g. *Pactus legis Salicae*, 39.2, 47, 56.2, 58; *Pactus Childeberti I et Chlotharii I*, 2; *Lex
Ribuaria*, 69.1 (as many as seventy oath-helpers); *Formulae Andecauenses*, 50; *Formulae
Turonenses*, 30. The list is far from comprehensive. **36** *Lex Ribuaria*, 37.1; cf. *Pactus legis
Salicae*, 47.2.

than a court, and that it can at least loosely be characterized as an assembly, particularly since the name of one of its officials – the *thunginus* – is etymologically related to 'thing' (assembly).

The concentration of previous historians on the officials connected with the *mallus* has led to a great deal of debate concerning the relationship of the gathering to royal administration, and, in particular, to the relationship between the *rachimburgi* and the *comes/grafio*. The law codes suggest that, once a dispute was referred to the *mallus* by the *rachimburgi*, it was for the latter to propose a resolution, obtaining the truth by confession or administering oaths and ordeal if required. Only if the procedure ran into insurmountable difficulties, usually if one of the parties to a case repeatedly failed to obey a summons, or persistently refused to accept a decision, did the *comes/grafio* become involved, in order to enforce compliance. This point is of sufficient importance to merit exposition of examples from a variety of sources. According to the early seventh-century *Lex Ribuaria*, three *rachimburgi* were to witness failure to obey a summons, and were to take an oath at the *harahus* or sanctuary (see below).[37] This procedure could be repeated until the summoned party had defaulted seven times, but, on the seventh occasion, the oath was taken by seven *rachimburgi*, and, for the first time, mention is made of the *comes/grafio* (here described as 'iudex fiscalis'), who was to go to the defaulter's house and seize goods to the value both of the disputed property and of fines for non-attendance. That the *comes/grafio* was not involved, or even present, at any earlier stage seems clear from a late sixth-century provision concerning a slave accused of theft, whose master failed to produce him at court on several occasions; when time ran out, the *comes/grafio* could intervene in a way similar to that described above, but only if summoned by the *rachimburgi*.[38] This is equally explicit in the early sixth-century recension of the Salic Law, which states that there should be no more than three men described as 'sagibarones' at a *mallus*; if they made a final decision in a case, it could not then be referred to the *comes/grafio*. Precisely who the *sagibarones* were is obscure, as is their relationship to the *rachimburgi*, but it is clear that cases were expected to be resolved at the *mallus* without involving the *comes/grafio*.[39]

Some of the material contained in the early formularies seems to point in a similar direction, since specimens of documents marking the ends of cases refer to only the *boni homines* as witnessing transactions[40] or providing security against renewed action.[41] Other documents in these collections, however, do

---

37 *Lex Ribuaria*, 36; cf. *Formulae Andecauenses*, 53. 38 *Edictus Chilperici*, 8. 39 *Pactus legis Salicae*, 54.5; for further instances of the *comes/graphio* being called in at a late stage, see, for example, *Pactus legis Salicae*, 45, 50, 56.6a. 40 E.g. *Formulae Turonenses*, 2, 3, 12, 14, 17, 18, 20, 24. 41 E.g. *Formulae Andecauenses*, 5, 39, 43, 44.

refer to activity on the part of royal agents, usually seeming to indicate the *comites* of the cities with which the formularies were associated.[42] It is possible that procedures in the cities involved *comites*, who were based there, more often than those in the predominantly rural areas with which the law codes seem primarily concerned; but it is equally likely that the volume of business would have precluded their participation in mundane cases, particularly since the administration of justice was only one of many functions fulfilled by such officials.[43] However, since the documents generally record the end of a case or set of proceedings, it is not clear at what stage the *comites* had become involved in the cases they describe, and the contrast with the laws, which set out the processes (rather than the conclusions) of justice, may be at least partly due to the different character of the documents.

A partial solution to the apparent differences of emphasis between the laws and the formulae may flow from consideration of a rare account of procedure in a narrative source, Gregory of Tours' *Ten Books of Histories*.[44] The episode centres around a protracted dispute between Sichar and Austregesil and their supporters, during the course of which several people lost their lives. The earliest recorded episode in the dispute occurred in a village in the territory of Tours, and involved the murder of a priest's servant, following which the two main protagonists became increasingly lawless and violent. Despite the gravity of the initial offence, and the fact that further loss of life rapidly ensued, the first attempt to solve the problem was made by a citizen tribunal ('a iudicio ciuium') rather than by the *comes* of Tours. When that failed the bishop (Gregory himself) and the *comes* called the parties together to negotiate a resolution, but with no better success. At that point, Sichar made (abortive) preparations to appeal to the king, but it seems that the final concord, although ultimately made by the *comes*, who specifically summoned the parties to the city ('ad ciuitatem'), was again brokered in private.

It appears from this account that the citizens' attempt to resolve the issue took place at what the laws would term a *mallus*, and that the intervention of the bishop and *comes* was what Patrick Geary has described as 'extra-judicial':[45] that is, it sought to broker a 'pact' rather than invoking the full weight of the legal system with its attendant formality, costs and uncertainties. Such arrangements had long been familiar in the Roman world where, to take but two examples, no less a man than the great aristocrat Sidonius Apollinaris had, in mid-fifth-century Gaul, negotiated an unofficial settlement in a case

---

42 E.g. *Formulae Andecauenses*, 12–14, 16 (all concerning default), 28, 50; *Formulae Turonenses*, 30, 31, 39, 41. 43 For the sixth century, see Barnwell 1992, 108–11; the seventh century is discussed in Barnwell 1997, 43–6. 44 Gregory of Tours, *Decem libri historiarum*, vii.47; for another, more insignificant, instance of a *comes* brokering a composition-based end to a case see Gregory of Tours, *Liber uitae patrum*, viii. 9. 45 Geary 1995; cf. Barnwell 2000, 18–19.

involving household servants, explicitly in order to avoid criminal proceed-ings,[46] and where, in the late 520s or the 530s, a dispute in the Egyptian village of Aphrodito was resolved by arbitration in the very courthouse where it would have been tried had formal resort been made to law.[47]

If this reading of the case of Sichar and Austregesil is correct, it may be possible to refine understanding of the relationship between the evidence of the law codes and that of the formularies. The procedures outlined in the law codes may relate very largely to 'extra-judicial' means of conflict resolution, in which leading local men sought to deal with matters without involving the representatives of royal government. The advantage of this was that at least simple conflicts could be resolved locally, speedily and cheaply. This does not mean that the procedures were unrecognized, unsystematic or lacked official sanction; in fact, the compilation of written law codes may in part represent an attempt to regulate local *malli* and to integrate them into the central, or royal, system of legal administration and control by regulating procedure and prescribing penalties.[48] Some of the formulae may concern similar kinds of procedure, but others certainly involved the *comes* – though it is unclear whether any or all of the latter relate to unofficial activity (of the sort illus-trated in the case of Sichar and Austregesil) or to the type of full legal procedure which would have been required if 'extra-judicial' procedures failed, or if a plaintiff took immediate recourse to judicial means. Beyond that, recourse could also be had to the king, as Sichar intended after the failure of the initial attempt at arbitration by the *comes* and bishop, or if one of the parties to the dispute failed to abide by local decisions.[49] According to the seventh-century *Lex Ribuaria*, it was also possible to invoke royal justice by going to a place, marked by a column or pole (*staffolus*), at which the king's court was known to meet.[50] The precise significance of this last procedure is unclear, since the *staffolus* may have marked a place where the king himself held court when travelling through the kingdom, and/or a place where the *comes*, the king's regional agent, held his official court, in which case the plain-tiff might simply have been seeking to use full legal procedures instead of 'extra-judicial' ones, and may not have been attempting to involve the king himself. Whatever the solution to that question, the original, though increas-ingly blurred, distinction between judicial and non-judicial procedures may help to explain the pattern, noted by Fustel de Coulanges, that *rachimburgi* and

---

46 Sidonius Apollinaris, *Epistolae*, v.19; for another case involving him, see ibid. vi.4, on which see Stevens 1933, 118–19, and Harries 1994, 211–13. **47** The text which records the case is split between *Papyrus Michigan inventory 6922* and *Papyri Vaticani Aphroditi 10*, and published with a translation in Gagos and van Minnen 1994; the Introduction to that volume contains a wealth of material on 'extra-judicial' agreements. **48** cf. Barnwell 2000, 26–9. **49** *Pactus legis Salicae*, 56. **50** *Lex Ribuaria*, 37.1, 69.5, 78.

boni homines seem to have resolved cases by proposing composition – a classic feature of pacts – whereas the *comes* could not only intervene to assist in 'extra-judicial' resolutions to conflicts, but could also administer punishments such as the seizure of property, imprisonment or execution, which were character-istic of full legal action.[51]

PRACTICES AND RITUALS

Before penalties were decided, however, evidence and proofs had to be obtained. By far the most common method of proof encountered in both the laws and the formulae is oath-taking, either by one of the parties alone, or by one of the parties with oath-helpers, or by witnesses.[52] The sixth-century laws do not indicate where the oath should be administered, but *Lex Ribuaria* several times mentions that it should be at the *harahus*, or sanctuary[53] – though it is not stated whether the latter was in the local settlement or was associated with a particular place at which the *mallus* met. Although the word *harahus* has pagan origins,[54] it may have become a non-specific term for a sacred place, since the contexts in which it occurs in the law codes are identical to those in which the formulae mention the main church (*basilica*) of the city to which they relate.[55] Another method of proof, this time not apparent in the formulae, is ordeal, the most common varieties being by boiling water and by lot, sometimes used when sufficient oath-helpers could not be found, or the accused was not free;[56] there is also reference to torturing (beating) the unfree.[57]

Once proof had been obtained and sentence passed, exaction of the penalty could sometimes, as noted earlier, come to involve the intervention of the *comes/grafio* acting in concert with *rachimburgi*, who assessed the damages. The payment of the composition or other penalty presumably normally occurred at the *mallus* (perhaps supported by peripatetic moneyers,[58] though their presence could also indicate the holding of fairs or markets to coincide

51 Fustel de Coulanges 1923, 485–90; for instances of *comites* condemning a man to be hanged, see Gregory of Tours, *Decem libri historiarum*, vi.8, with idem, *Liber in gloria confessorum*, 99, and *Vita Amandi*, 14. For their power of imprisonment see Gregory of Tours, *Libri I-IV de uirtutibus sancti Martini episcopi*, iv.16, 39.   52 E.g. *Pactus legis Salicae*, 14.2, 14.3, 16.5, 42.5, 46.4–6, 47.2, 49.4; *Pactus Childeberti I et Chlotharii I*, 2; *Edictus Chilperici*, 6; *Decretio Childeberti II*, 12; *Lex Ribuaria*, 34a, 36, 69.1, 75.1–2, 80; *Formulae Andecauenses*, 19, 28, 29, 50; *Formulae Turonenses*, 30, 31, 39, 40; Gregory of Tours, *Decem libri historiarum*, v.5, 49, vii.23, ix.22; idem, *Liber in gloria martyrum*, 33: this list is not intended to be comprehensive. For the importance of oath-taking, see Wood 1986.   53 *Lex Ribuaria*, 34a, 36.2–3, 75.1–2, 80.   54 Wood 1998, 227 (comment by D. Green).   55 *Formulae Andecauenses*, 13, 14, 16, 28, 50; *Formulae Turonenses*, 39 cf. 40.   56 E.g. *Pactus legis Salicae*, 14.2–3, 16.5, 53, 56; *Pactus Childeberti I et Chlotharii I*, 4, 5, 8, 10, 11; *Edictus Chilperici*, 8.   57 Notably *Pactus legis Salicae*, 40.   58 Halsall 1995, 196.

with *malli*). In cases of default, however, a visit to the defendant's house could ensue. If, for example, a lord whose slave was accused of theft persistently refused to co-operate with the local authorities for twenty-one weeks, the defendant went to the next *mallus* carrying a stick (*festuca*), after which the *comes/grafio* went to the lord's house with the seven *rachimburgi* of that *mallus* to take sufficient property to cover damages and fines.[59] Procedure also moved to a defendant's house in the case of a man found guilty of homicide who was unable to pay the necessary composition: he was to go to his house, presumably in company with at least some of the *rachimburgi*, collect dust from each of its four corners, stand on the threshold looking inwards and throw the dust over his shoulders on to his nearest relative, who then assumed responsibility for the debt; the guilty man then symbolically abandoned his property by jumping over the fence, barefoot and shirtless, with a stick in his hand.[60]

A stick, or *festuca*, formed an important prop in other types of case as well. A defendant sent to the ordeal because he could not produce witnesses, and who also lacked the means to give surety (bail), seized a stick in his left hand and passed it to his right hand as a symbol of compliance with the ruling of the court.[61] In a different kind of case, a man who wished to renounce his kin was to attend the *mallus*, break a stick of alder wood above his head and throw the pieces in four different directions;[62] and an elaborate ritual for the transfer of property involved the donor throwing a stick into the lap of the beneficiary.[63] Although most of the ritual acts described in the laws refer to the use of a stick, there is at least one different example, which concerns a man who wished to marry a widow: both the man and the woman were to go to a *mallus*, the man taking a shield (a symbol of protection?), three solidi (evidence of means to support a wife?) and a penny; three men appraised the purity of the solidi and the marriage was permitted if they were satisfied of it.[64]

CONCLUSION

There may at first appear to be little direct relationship between the early Frankish *mallus* and the assemblies discussed elsewhere in this volume. That impression may be heightened by the emphasis of this chapter on procedures and practices rather than on places, and on written forms of evidence rather than on physical remains. Notwithstanding that difference in focus, several features of the *mallus* suggest that it belonged to the same family as the assemblies examined by other contributors. It has, for example, already been noted that one of the main officials of the *mallus* was the *thunginus*, a word etymo-

---

59 *Edictus Chilperici*, 8.   **60** *Pactus legis Salicae*, 58.   **61** *Edictus Chilperici*, 7.   **62** *Pactus legis Salicae*, 60.   **63** Ibid., 46.   **64** Ibid., 44.

logically related to *thing* and therefore to the concept of an 'assembly'. Similarly, the religious sanctuaries associated with assemblies elsewhere, particularly those in Scandinavia, are echoed in the *harahus* mentioned in the Frankish legal texts, while the *staffolus* (pole or column) at which the king's court was held may find a parallel in the timber pole set in the ground behind the platform at the focal point of the 'theatre' at the Northumbrian royal site of Yeavering in England.[65] Here, then, are enough hints that the *mallus* was an institution with parallels elsewhere in the world of north-west Europe, a view which derives support from the kinds of ritual which were associated with the *mallus*: for Sir Samuel Dill, a scholar of the first half of the twentieth century, it was, indeed, 'clear that in these picturesque symbolic usages we are carried back to remote ages in regions beyond the Rhine'.[66]

The formularies, by contrast, seem to depict practices with origins in the late Roman world. Several individual formulae refer to Roman law,[67] suggesting a judicial system very different from that of the *mallus* and its rituals. This is emphasized by the fact that the procedures envisaged by the formulae involved the extensive use of written instruments, while the evidence relating to the *mallus* does not, there being only one reference to a document in the *Pactus legis Salicae*.[68]

Rituals and documents were not, however, mutually exclusive. There are, for example formulae for documents recording the taking of oaths as means of proof, and others relate to procedures for defaulters which are similar to those of the laws (above). The king's own court produced and used many documents,[69] two of which reveal that rituals involving a stick formed part of its procedures.[70] Further, such features cannot simply be dismissed as signs of 'Germanism', for impeccably Roman legal sources contain hints of similar usages. Theodosius II, the great fifth-century systematizer of Roman law, allowed that wills could either be written or made by an oral procedure involving witnesses,[71] while, the works of one of the famous Roman jurists, Gaius, reveal a ritual involving the use of a stick for claiming property, in a way which may be echoed in the Frankish laws discussed earlier.[72]

In relation to the evidence supplied by the Frankish sources, the *boni homines* of the formulae discharged functions very similar to those fulfilled by the *rachimburgi* of the laws, while some of the formulae refer to a *basilica* in contexts in which *Lex Ribuaria* mentions the *harahus*. A relationship between

---

65 Hope-Taylor 1977, 119–21, 161.   66 Dill 1926, 53.   67 Explicit in *Formulae Andecauenses*, 40, 46, 54, 58; *Formulae Aruernenses*, 1, 3; *Formulae Turonenses*, 15, 20, 22, 24, 25, 29, 32. 68 *Pactus legis Salicae*, 14.4, which indicates that a man might have a document from the king giving him permission to change his abode.   69 There is a convenient discussion of the evidence in Wood 1990.   70 Fouracre 1986, 33–34, 41, citing, in particular, two royal documents, *Chartae Latinae Antiquiores*, nos. 573 and 576.   71 *Nouellae Theodosiani II*, 16.1. 72 Gaius, *Institutiones*, iv.16.

the *mallus* and the kind of tribunal in which *boni homines* participated is perhaps also indicated by the fact that two specimen documents use the verb 'mallare' to describe the pleading of cases at tribunals. Conversely, the fact that the laws express penalties in monetary terms suggests at least some Roman influence on their procedures – a point brought into sharp focus by the use of coins in the ritual whereby a man gained the right to marry a widow, one of the most 'picturesque symbolic usages' in the *Pactus legis Salicae*.

Factors such as these suggest that there is no sharp dividing line between the institutions and procedures revealed by the formulae and the laws. The difference between the two sets of documents may, rather, stem from the fact that the formulae relate to procedures in the cities, where Roman and literary traditions were relatively strong, while the laws seem to have been addressed more to rural communities where such traditions were weaker. A degree of unity and cohesion in the system is also indicated by the apparent ease with which the case of Sichar and Austregesil was able to move between the countryside and the town, between the involvement of the 'cives', of royal and ecclesiastical officials, and (potentially) of the king's court. The distinction between urban and rural procedures was not, however, caused by the Frankish invasion of Gaul: in the sixth-century Roman east, Justinian, even while promoting the use of written law, explicitly recognized that there were (predominantly rural) places where there were no literate men and where various forms of 'custom' should be used, safeguarded by the provision of a sufficient number of witnesses rather than by documents.[73] That 'custom', which may have varied from one region of the Empire to another, was, by its nature, not written down, so that its details remain extremely shadowy even in areas better documented than late-Roman Gaul. This renders it almost impossible to distinguish between the customs and local institutions of the 'Germanic' world and those of the north-western provinces of the Empire. It also opens a question as to whether, no matter what the roots (which may have varied) of individual procedures, assemblies of the character of the *mallus* could have existed in parts of the Roman world, and as to whether they were ultimately of Germanic, Roman or wider Indo-European origin.

ABBREVIATIONS

MGH   *Monumenta Germaniae Historica*
SRM   *Scriptores Rerum Merovingicarum*

---

73 *Codex Iustinianus*, vi.23.3 (*a*. 534); see Barnwell 2000, 15.

PRIMARY SOURCES

Chartae Latinae Antiquiores, ed. H. Atsma and J. Vezin, vol. 14. Zurich. 1982.

Codex Iustinianus, ed. P. Krüger. Berlin. 1900.

Decretio Childeberti II, ed. A. Boretius, *MGH, Leges*, Section II part i. Hanover. 1883.

Edictus Chilperici, ed. A. Boretius, *MGH, Leges*, Section II part i. Hanover. 1883.

Formulae Andecauenses, ed. K. Zeumer, *MGH, Leges*, Section V. Hanover. 1886.

Formulae Aruernenses, ed. K. Zeumer, *MGH, Leges*, Section V. Hanover. 1886.

Formulae Turonenses, ed. K. Zeumer, *MGH, Leges*, Section V. Hanover. 1886.

Gaius, *Institutiones*, in S. Riccobono, J. Bauer, C. Ferrini, J. Furliani and A. Arangio-Ruiz (eds), *Fontes iuris Romani anteiustiniani, 2: Auctores, Liber Syro-Romanus, Negotia*. Florence.1940.

Gregory of Tours, *Decem libri historiarum*, ed. B. Krusch and W. Levison, *MGH, SRM*, 1 part i. Hanover. 1937–51.

Gregory of Tours, *Liber in gloria confessorum*, ed. B. Krusch, *MGH, SRM*, 1. Hanover. 1885.

Gregory of Tours, *Liber in gloria martyrum*, ed. B. Krusch, *MGH, SRM*, 1. Hanover. 1885.

Gregory of Tours, *Liber uitae patrum*, ed. B. Krusch, *MGH, SRM*, 1. Hanover. 1885.

Gregory of Tours, *Libri I–IV de uirtutibus sancti Martini episcopi*, ed. B. Krusch, *MGH, SRM*, 1. Hanover. 1885.

Lex Alamannorum, ed. K.A. Eckhardt, *MGH, Leges*, Section I, 5 part i. Hanover. 1966.

Lex Bawiariorum, ed. E. von Schwind, *MGH, Leges*, Section I, 5 part ii. Hanover. 1926.

Lex Ribuaria, ed. F. Beyerle and R. Buchner, *MGH, Leges*, Section I, 3 part ii. Hanover. 1952.

Nouellae Theodosiani II, ed. P.M. Meyer, *Leges nouellae ad theodosianum pertinentes*. Berlin. 1905

Pactus Childeberti I et Chlotharii I, ed. A. Boretius, *MGH, Leges*, Section II part 1. Hanover.1883.

Pactus legis Salicae, ed. K. A. Eckhardt, *MGH, Leges*, Section I, 4 part i. Hanover. 1964.

Sidonius Apollinaris, *Epistolae*, ed. A. Loyen. 2 vols. Paris. 1970.

Vita Amandi, ed. B. Krusch, *MGH, SRM*, 5. Hanover. 1910.

SECONDARY LITERATURE

Barnwell, P.S., 1992: *Emperor, prefects and kings: the Roman west 395–565*. London.

Barnwell, P.S., 1997: *Kings, courtiers and imperium: the Barbarian west 565–725*. London.

Barnwell, P.S., 2000: 'Emperors, jurists and kings: law and custom in the late-Roman and early-medieval west', *Past & Present* **168**, 6–29.

Brunner, H., 1887, 1928: *Deutsches Rechtsgeschichte* (2 vols.: **1**, 1887; **2**, 2nd edn, 1928.) Berlin.

Dannenbauer, H., 1942–9: 'Hundertschaft, Centena und Huntari', *Historisches Jahrbuch* **62–9**, 155–219.

Dilcher, G., 1971: '*Boni homines*', in G. Erler, G. Kaufmann, and R. Schmidt-Wiegand (eds), *Handwörterbuch zur deutschen Rechtsgeschichte* (5 vols.). Berlin. 1, cols 491–2.

Dill, S., 1926: *Roman society in Gaul in the Merovingian age*. London.

Fouracre, P., 1986: '"Placita" and the settlement of disputes in later Merovingian Francia', in W. Davies and P. Fouracre (eds), *The settlement of disputes in early medieval Europe*. Cambridge. 123–43.

Fustel de Coulanges, N.D., 1923: *Recherches sur quelques problèmes d'histoire* (4th edn.). Paris.

Fustel de Coulanges, N.D., 1930: *Histoire des institutions politiques de l'ancienne France, 3: la monarchie franque* (6th edn.). Paris.

Gagos, T., and van Minnen, P., 1994: *Settling a dispute: toward a legal anthropology of late antique Egypt*. Ann Arbor.

Ganshof, F.L., 1968: *Frankish institutions under Charlemagne*. New York.

Geary, P.J., 1995: 'Extra-judicial means of conflict resolution', in *La giustizia nell'alto medioevo* (secolo V–VIII), Settimane de studio del centro italiano di studi sull'alto medioevo 42 (2 vols.). Spoleto. 1, 569–601.

Grahn-Hoek, H., 1976: *Die fränkische Oberschicht im 6. Jahrhundert: Studien zu ihrer rechtlichen und politischen Stellung*. Sigmaringen.

Halsall, G., 1995: *Settlement and society: the Merovingian region of Metz*. Cambridge.

Harries, J., 1994: *Sidonius Apollinaris and the fall of Rome*. Oxford.

Hope-Taylor, B., 1977: *Yeavering: an Anglo-British centre of early Northumbria*. London.

Kaspers, W., 1948–50: 'Wort- und Namenstudien zur Lex Salica', *Zeitschrift für deutsche Altertum und deutsche Literatur* 82, 291–335.

Murray, A.C., 1986: 'The position of the graphio in the constitutional history of Merovingian Gaul', *Speculum* 6, 787–805.

Murray, A.C., 1988: 'From Roman to Frankish Gaul: "centenarii" and "centenae" in the administration of the Frankish Kingdom', *Traditio* 44, 59–100.

Nehlsen-von Stryk, K., 1981: *Die boni homines des frühen Mittelalters unter besonderer Berücksichtigung der fränkischen Quellen*. Berlin.

Schmidt-Wiegand, R., 1984: '*Mallus, mallum*', in G. Erler, G. Kaufmann, and R. Schmidt-Wiegand (eds), *Handwörterbuch zur deutschen Rechtsgeschichte* (5 vols.). Berlin, 1971–. 3, cols 217–18.

Stevens, C.E., 1933: *Sidonius Apollinaris and his age*. Oxford.

Waitz, G., 1953–5: *Deutsches Verfassugsgeschichte* (8 vols.). Graz.

Wood, I.N., 1986: 'Disputes in late fifth- and sixth-century Gaul: some problems', in W. Davies and P. Fouracre (eds), *The settlement of disputes in early medieval Europe*. Cambridge. 7–22.

Wood, I.N., 1990: 'Administration, laws and culture in Merovingian Gaul', in R. McKitterick (ed.), *The uses of literacy in early medieval Europe*. Cambridge. 63–81.

Wood, I.N., 1994: *The Merovingian kingdoms, 450–751*. Harlow.

Wood, I.N., 1998: 'Jural relations among the Franks and Alamanni', in I.N. Wood (ed.), *Franks and Alamanni in the Merovingian period: an ethnographic perspective*. Woodbridge. 213–37.

Wormald, P., 1977: 'Lex scripta and verbum regis', in P.H. Sawyer and I.N. Wood (eds), *Early medieval kingship*. Leeds. 105–38.

Zöllner, E., 1970: *Geschichte der Franken bis zur Mitte der 6. Jahrhunderts*. Munich.

Index